Gisela Kaplan (PhD, PhD, hon.DSc) is a field biologist and Emeritus Professor of Animal Behaviour at the University of New England, Armidale, New South Wales and also serves as Honorary Professor at the Queensland Brain Institute. She has published 23 books so far, authored more than 250 research articles and has conducted ground-breaking research into vocal learning, communication and cognition in birds and other vertebrates. Her books include award-winning and bestselling titles such as *Australian Magpie* (2019), *Tawny Frogmouth* (2018), *Bird Minds* (2015) and *Famous Australian Birds* (2004). For the past two decades, she has also raised and rehabilitated injured native birds. Her vast experience with native birds in their natural environment is only surpassed by her passion for all things to do with native birds.

GISELA KAPLAN

BIRD BONDS

Sex, mate-choice and cognition in Australian native birds

Pan Macmillan Australia

First published 2019 in Macmillan by Pan Macmillan Australia Pty Ltd

1 Market Street, Sydney, New South Wales, Australia, 2000

Cataloguing-in-Publication entry is available
from the National Library of Australia
http://catalogue.nla.gov.au

Typeset in 11/15 pt Minion by Midland Typesetters, Australia

Printed by McPherson's Printing Group

The paper in this book is FSC® certified.
FSC® promotes environmentally responsible, socially beneficial and economically viable management of the world's forests.

To Lesley Joy Rogers,
a giant in Australian science and the
quiet, incorruptible scientific conscience
behind all my writings

Contents

Preface

At no time in history have we talked and written about birds as much as in the last two decades. While dismissible as a fad, there may be deeper reasons for birds' rise to eminence in the research literature, in magazines and books.

With some degree of caution, one can perhaps make the global observation that humans have always focused on stories that relate to their own self-understanding. As we are the only species left in the genus of hominids, there is an almost nervous awareness that we are on our own. While, at some level, some people take great comfort in believing that humans are the evolutionary pinnacle of the natural world, there is now a wealth of evidence that so many of the characteristics once thought to be unique to humans – and seemingly to confirm the human status as the most advanced life form – had antecedents in non-human species. Some species have qualities very similar to our own and, in some aspects, even surpass human abilities. For decades, great apes, especially chimpanzees, were enthusiastically promoted in documentaries and magazine articles premised on the information that chimpanzee DNA was 98 per cent identical to human DNA.

One suspected that much of the interest in great apes, even when not stated, was really an interest in human behaviour, as clearly shown in studies on communication and language. Years of research have been spent identifying the intelligence of great apes and any possible antecedents of language. This is still a vibrant research field and has revealed many important biological and evolutionary facts. However, the biological facts were often distorted and led to new mythologies, all hinging on the roughly 98 per cent of DNA similarity.

Biology does not work this way, as evidenced by the mapping of the mouse genome. This was published in 2002 in *Nature* and it showed, to the shock and disappointment of many, that mice share about 99 per cent of their DNA with humans. Hence, mere similarity of DNA is hardly good evidence for physical similarities and shared capabilities.

In recent years, researchers have started looking more at basic patterns in the evolution of vertebrates and this has led to broad-scale examination of brain power, especially the perceptual apparatus. Some researchers now believe that a basic cognitive 'software' may be common to all animals and humans (Vallortigara et al. 2010).

Birds have a very important role to play in this new perspective. One of the highly innovative areas in bird evolution is vocal learning in songbirds and parrots and its associated aspects of brain structure. And then there is the question of cognition (how well do animals do cognitively, and does it go by brain size) and even social organisation. Are there advantages and disadvantages?

This book is based on the hypothesis that, in birds that evolved in Australia, sophisticated measures were developed to choose the right partner. There are biological, physiological, cognitive and emotional variables combined to assure long-lasting bonds, entire devotion to each other and to their offspring's safety and long lives as a product of cooperative sharing behaviour, in which differences are set aside to a large degree. For years we have been told that sexual selection may be as simple as an extra bright feather or a more complex song, and that males have to display these specific qualities and females then choose the best.

First, as others noted many years ago, colours, sounds or even smells are not inherent properties of the object, but the product of the brain of the animal perceiving the object. Second, the facets of what is perceived has traditionally been confined to sights and sounds. We now know that a sense of smell may have been underestimated, and this alone is a complex business. We may also have underestimated emotional states, let alone more advanced mechanisms involving planning and decision-making in mate-choice, and even more sophisticated cognitive processes.

Australian land birds make an excellent test case as to whether such an approach will provide us with a deeper understanding of how mate-choice in long-bonded pairs actually works.

Some of these questions will be raised in this book. The very impetus for writing this book is the excitement and suspicion that the examples seen in birds may resonate with certain patterns of behaviour in humans. Birds and humans may have some common social rules and similarities in how much and for how long they can learn and live. This connection is possible despite the enormous evolutionary distance between humans and birds.

There are some advantages and capabilities that we, as humans, value particularly highly and, not surprisingly, these are the topics that have fired the imagination. Among them are vocal learning, life expectancy and intelligence. In Australia, we are particularly privileged to find countless species in which these social and biological factors, and their possible co-dependence or inter-relationship, can be discovered in birds.

This book explores the fundamental life-history events of sex roles and sexuality, reproduction, bonding and separation, and parenting options. Is there evolutionary evidence that Australian avian species have evolved in ways that increase life expectancy and the survival of offspring? Why does Australia have so many long-lived and cooperative species? What does it take to make intelligent choices and lead to the best outcomes?

When thinking about life expectancy in the context of cognition, and the kind of social organisation the most intelligent species choose, one comes across some exciting evidence that there are basic principles of core relationships which may lead to outcomes that are superior to others. In Australia, we have a unique opportunity to contribute to theories of avian evolution because this is where modern songbirds and parrots first evolved. Charles Darwin has provided us with a universal law of natural selection and a secondary principle of sexual selection. The latter is one of the important topics in evolutionary biology. In the present realisation that so many of Australia's native birds are declining in numbers, it is an urgent task to learn as much as possible about their behaviour and also establish what the ancestral lines of birds produced as innovation, particularly for the safe raising of offspring.

In discussing animal behaviour generally and bird behaviour specifically, we have for far too long concentrated on competition and male attributes. This book will produce evidence that many Australian birds have achieved outstanding success by the clever use and practice of cooperation and by securing the trust of a partner, often lifelong. It will also be argued that the cooperative model has further consequences, something we have long known and described as social intelligence. The reproductive strategies they use and how sex differences play out cooperatively are worth knowing because, it seems, these may be the lynchpin to a long life, a large brain and healthy, long-lived offspring.

Gisela Kaplan

1

The gift of Gondwana

Patrick White, one of Australia's foremost novelists, once described modern Australia as huddled on the edge of the continent, always at risk of dropping into the ocean, pretending to be a modern society while people's hearts are filled with fear of the land that lies beyond. White tried to imagine what the land might do to the human spirit, threatening its understanding of reality and giving rise to hallucinations, self-doubt and a sense of humbling insignificance, in stark contrast to a nervously sea-hugging urban society. Robyn Davidson wanted to explore her own sense of being and belonging by tracking westwards through 2700 kilometres of the Australian outback, with just camels to help her (her book is now also a film of the same name, *Tracks*).

Both Patrick White and Robyn Davidson described the need to find some inner strength and that the land, far from the European notion of 'nothingness' and 'emptiness', had its own beauty and majesty, sometimes confronting, sometimes alluring, sometimes awe-inspiring.

And there is the national anthem stating that we are 'young and free'. I cannot help but feel that this is the least inclusive, least representative way one can speak about Australians and Australia. It evokes a sense of alienation by explicit denial of this especially ancient land and its first inhabitants, an ongoing testament to one of the oldest living human cultures. Australia has it all, because to this day, there is a continuity of life dating back 1000 million years and more. Few people, beyond palaeontology experts, the mining industry and petroleum companies, know that Australia provides access to prehistoric and evolutionary processes. It is a living laboratory.

There are many places in Australia where one can literally touch the beginnings of time of the continent, as I was privileged to do when sitting at a waterhole at the Finke River. The Finke River runs through the Amadeus Basin, not too far south-west of Alice Springs. People call Uluru the heart of Australia but perhaps it is the Amadeus Basin, silently persisting in rocks known to be somewhere between 500–1000 million years old, an age altogether incomprehensible to our very brief human lives and very recent evolution.

Only recently 22 new species of tribolites and agnostids were identified in the Amadeus Basin, dated to be from the Cambrian period 543–490 million years ago (Smith et al. 2016). Maps and data are no preparation for the emotional turmoil that the knowledge can engender when one is actually at such a place. These days, tourists swarm over a small section of the Finke River, jump over boulders and briefly look at the ancient cabbage palm trees, *Livistona mariae*, a species separated from its nearest relatives by more than a thousand kilometres and seemingly out of place in this eerie desert wilderness. When I sat there, looking into the clear water, full of life, suddenly all the voices of people had faded and the place itself was pulling me into a different reality.

Then, right in front of me, I saw a small bird hopping from rock to rock and going about its daily business of finding food. It was a thick-billed grasswren, *Amytornis modestus*, perhaps a little too far north of its natural range. The bird was concentrating so completely on its foraging expedition, it barely acknowledged my presence. I thought how extraordinary it was that this little bird (just 15 cm in all and a few

Fig. 1.1 The elusive thick-billed grasswren of Central Australia. The colour of this grasswren is the same reddish ochre as the soil, and were it not for the flag of an upright tail, typical of all wrens, it would blend totally into the environment. These grasswrens are opportunistic breeders but cooperative when they breed. They feed on insects.

grams of weight) could survive in this area. The heat was oppressive but quite common, 42°C in the shade (of which there was rather too little) and the air was dry and still. Australian magpies, *Gymnorhina tibicen*, stop foraging at around 27°C and start panting when the thermometer goes over 32°C (Edwards et al. 2015).

The magpie is a large bird and has problems even at relatively lower temperatures. According to the scaling rules in metabolism, the smaller the organism, the larger the surface area in relation to body size, hence the metabolism is higher in smaller birds than in larger ones. High metabolism, as in hummingbirds, requires an ongoing supply of food to meet the bird's energy demands. Thus, being as little as this grasswren was would seem to make it especially vulnerable to the relentless heat, but it was not. A puzzle, as there are so many about so many Australian birds.

The gift of birds

Australia offers two gifts to the world. The one already noted is its ancient history, the other, its birds. They are an important gift.

For the last fourteen years I have been inspired by the research results, published in 2001 and 2004 by Barker and co-workers, that led scientists worldwide to accept that Australia was the cradle of all modern songbirds and of many other avian species. Australia – once East Gondwana – is the one and only place on earth, it seems, where certain bird lineages survived the mass extinction of life some 65–66 million years ago, a destructive event so large, most vertebrates around the globe vanished.

Today, we have a fascination with dinosaurs as a symbol of that lost world, of which we find remnants everywhere on earth, including and increasingly in Australia (new dinosaur species are still being discovered inland). But it is a lost world in many ways. We still have the crocodiles, monitor lizards and Komodo dragons as reminders of what happened when one asteroid (or several) crashed near the Gulf of Mexico and darkened the skies for long enough to kill plant life and the animals dependent on it. When the sun appeared again, most forests and plants had died or been burnt. Life had perished almost everywhere, except for patches in East Gondwana where some plants and lineages of birds survived.

In 2018, a fascinating study by Daniel J Field and colleagues covering Europe, North America and New Zealand showed that forests in these localities simply collapsed and, they argued, all perching birds vanished. Fossilised remains of birds with longer, sturdier legs suggested to them that largely only ground birds must have survived. In Australia, these included the ancestors of ducks and chickens, brush turkeys, emus and southern cassowaries. It appears, however, that the precondition for the survival of some Gondwanan lineages was the survival of some forests.

Australia was a Noah's Ark for birds and other vertebrates. The large group of modern extant songbirds, cockatoos and others so far identified, are now known to have evolved in Australia (Edwards and Boles 2002; Barker et al. 2004). For anyone studying evolution, this changed everything. Up to 2004, it was still widely believed by many that birds evolved in the northern hemisphere and Australia somehow had eventually acquired some of the northern-hemisphere species. So deeply engrained was this belief in western, northern-hemisphere societies (which also had the economic power and conducted most of the avian research) that the first white generations in Australia kept introducing species (plants and animals) from the northern hemisphere in order to 'improve' local Australian flora and fauna, with disastrous long-term effects. Melbourne and Sydney had very active acclimatisation societies. From foxes, rabbits and carps, to blackberries and the prickly pear, the range of introductions was far-reaching and dizzying in the harm they were to do. In introduced bird releases alone, we know that several introductions were made in Victoria between 1863 and 1872 (mentioned in *The Emu*, vol. 5, 1906, p. 116). These included starlings, sparrows, goldfinches, nightingales, greenfinches, Indian turtle doves, skylarks, Indian mynas, possibly blackbirds and others, especially gamebirds. Some of them did not establish themselves but the Indian or common myna, *Acridotheres tristis*, did, and increased its range over the years. This one species alone has certainly done substantial damage in its competition with tree-hole nesting and roosting native species (parrots and gliders). Mynas have been known to evict and even kill residents. Particularly affected are rosellas and red-rumped parrots (Pell and Tidemann 1997a, b) and the endangered superb parrot (Tidemann 2005). The folly went so far that the 1880 annual report of the NSW Zoological Society contained a submission for a bill to protect the introduced birds (Hindwood, 1948) and mynas were apparently listed as a protected species for a while. Today, mynas are listed among the top 100 worst invasive species (Mittelmeier, IUCN 2000).

It was the largest ever deliberate transfer of living species and, coupled with extensive clearings that have accelerated today, the Australian continent was subjected to the most violent rape ever recorded and a rape and destruction of country that has no equal anywhere in the world – and all in the space of a mere two hundred years. In the same period, more than 70 per cent of Australia's rainforests disappeared and in the last few years, clearing of scrubland and forests has exceeded the acreage cut down in the Amazon Basin (Australian State of the Environment, 2016). The land has been ravaged over and over again, to the immense detriment of wildlife in this country. We pay a very high price for these events today with extinctions, desertification, salination of the soil, ever-extending droughts, more intense heat and related issues.

Before 2004, when Australian researchers had anything to say on bird behaviour which was different from prevalent models, they were dismissed either by not citing the texts (a problem that occasionally still exists to some extent) or by somehow arguing around issues as exceptions and oddities. Since 2004, however, Australian species have become central to evolutionary studies of the vast majority of land birds, particularly parrots, cockatoos and songbirds, many of which have ancient roots.

The emphasis has shifted from assuming that birds eventually colonised Australia to realising that birds were at home in Australia and left the Australo-Papuan shores to colonise other islands and continents. That is, the stream of birds went in the opposite direction from that once thought – instead of being immigrants to Australia, they were emigrants from Australia. It is now a matter of identifying the traffic out of Australia and of establishing the dispersal dates of modern birds. In 2003, Ericson and colleagues suggested that such dispersals of modern songbirds out of Australia may have happened 30–40 million years ago and that northern continents such as North America probably only received its first bird migrants some 3–4 million years ago. A more recent study suggests a much later dispersal, and not across continents but, as Moyle and colleagues reported in *Nature* in 2016, by island hopping after the uplifting of Wallacea, and the lowering of sea levels as a result of several Ice Ages. Borneo, Sumatra, Java and Bali were not islands then but part of the south-east Asian landmass called Sunda, and Australia's plate extended well beyond its current shape to the north, linking the entire top end with Papua New Guinea to form the landmass called Sahul. Wallacea is the group of islands in between Sunda and Sahul (Fig. 1.2).

The biogeographic analyses of Moyle et al. (2016) indicate that all dispersal out of the Australian region via Asia began later than had been suggested. They argued that such dispersals to Asia started in the early Miocene, about 24 million years ago, followed by several lineages of corvids around 23 million years ago and then again followed by another set of passerine dispersals around 16 million years ago. They demonstrated that the rapid colonisation of new continents fits the timeframe of Australia colliding with proto-Sulawesi in the early Miocene, and these specific events, not just the lowering

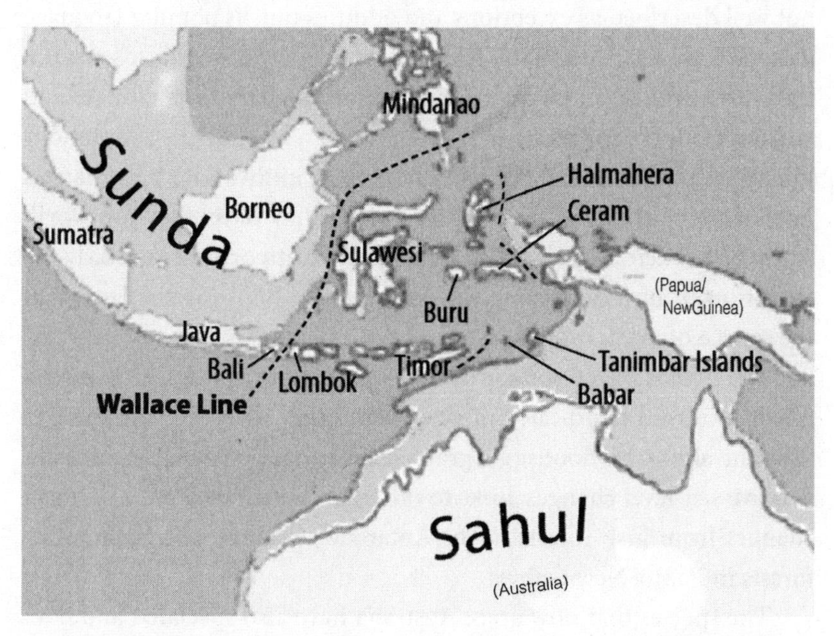

Fig. 1.2 Sunda, Sahul and Wallacea. Wallace discovered that mammals from west of the deep channel between Bali and Lombok did not occur to the east of that channel. The dotted line on the left is referred to as the Wallace line. The area between Sunda and Sahul is called Wallacea as a biogeographic concept – east of the Wallace line and ending as marked per dotted line in the east. Lombok, Timor, Ceram, Halmahera and Sulawesi belong to Wallacea. ('Creative Commons Sunda, Sahul and Wallacea' by Maxmilian Dörrbecker (Chumwa), licensed under CC BY-SA 3.0 / Adapted from original by Altaileopard.)

of sea levels, created new islands in Wallacea, providing land-bridges and making island hopping easy enough for birds to get from Sahul to Sunda.

These new findings about radiation to Asia, Africa, Eurasia and beyond raise probably as many new questions as have been answered. No doubt many more theories will be developed, getting us closer to the complex patterns of radiation and dispersal. The matter is complicated by the fact that birds are capable of long non-stop flights across oceans, as we know well from modern migratory birds, be they shore or land birds.

Australian land birds, especially songbirds and parrots, are thus not well described as exceptions and oddities but, as popular language use will have it, they are 'the real deal' and all other songbirds around the world are later speciations, encountering changes in climate and environmental conditions over millions of years. These adaptations might have included behavioural short-cuts, innovations and changes necessary for survival but whatever merit they have, they are worth studying in their own right. We now have the opportunity to study the evolution of bird behaviour within Australia, knowing that we sit at the source of avian evolution.

The evolution of songbirds and other avian species in Australia is not a second-hand tale but one interwoven with the vast changes brought about by floods, geographic position, geological upheavals, massive sea-level changes, links to other lands and substantial climate changes from lush forests in the Antarctic to (then) temperate rainforests in Papua New Guinea.

The species that now grace Australia have also speciated and have adapted to a drying out of the continent that began at the latest around 20 million years ago. Tropical birds, especially neotropical birds (central and South American) have always had a special place in the bird literature and so has Oceania, which conjures up an image of the tropics and of island nations and that has implications for any discussion on birds. Australia, by contrast, has relatively few areas that are truly tropical (such as Cairns to the tip of Cape York). Most of Australia's landmass falls largely into arid and temperate zones and while Australia can be called an island because the country is surrounded by water, it is also a continent almost the size of Europe.

Thus, Australian birds have their own evolutionary history which then becomes part of the evolution of all modern songbirds, parrots and others species worldwide. This was already pointed out by Scott Edwards and Walter Boles in 2002 in 'Out of Gondwana', as a remarkable development both symbolising the survival of avian species in general as well as a set of actual events of birds thriving and speciating within Australia and their radiation.

In fact, Australia as a modern and very recent political entity has the burden, the privilege and the evidence that it is a very ancient continent. In 2014, a bird's footprint was found in Dinosaur Cove in Victoria, estimated to be 115 million years old. We know they were here in the Cretaceous period (145–65 million years ago) and their descendants are still with us today (Cracraft 2001; Barker et al. 2004; Wright et al. 2008).

Unfortunately, birds have left few fossils because their hollow bones disintegrate much more rapidly than the solid bones of dinosaurs and large mammals, but DNA investigations can help trace birds back and we now know that there are many ancestral lineages. Today, depending which species are added in or excluded from the total, Australia has nearly 900 bird species (Dolby and Clarke 2014).

Climate and life histories

The metabolic rates of animals are directly linked to climate and slower metabolism tends to prolong life (Wikelski et al. 2003). It is known that avian species generally live longer in the tropics than at high latitudes but it is important to remember that the power of this climatic explanation for longevity does not sit well in Australia. Australia's coastal bands and tablelands have largely temperate climates, where humans and many avian species especially thrive, and even in such climate zones birds live considerably longer than their high-altitude cousins in Europe and North America.

The southern hemisphere, the tropics north of Australia and around the Himalayas are the bird-rich areas of the world and the northern hemisphere is the relatively bird-poor area, often holding just a third or even a quarter of the species of their southern counterparts (Fig. 1.5). 'Bird-rich' here means both the absolute number of birds and species diversity.

Many of the species in the tropics and regions south of the Himalayas have barely been studied beyond the most basic field-guide information, making it still very risky to make global pronouncements about 'what birds do'.

The equator does not divide habitats evenly to north and south (Fig. 1.3) as the 'Oriental' or Indian subcontinent shows. However, high latitudes (temperate and cold climates with short summers) are avian habitats almost exclusively found in the northern hemisphere.

All bird-rich continents (largely southern hemisphere) are determined by climate zones that have little to no snow (except at altitude) and, in large parts, have lower temperature variation (Ahumada 2001). It has long been known, as a paper by Fry in the 1980s showed, that species around the equator and in low latitudes live longer, tend to have better survival rates and have a much-extended breeding season. It has also been found that there are life strategies such as cooperative breeding (Brown 1969, Cockburn 1996) and permanent pair bonding that are clustered in species of low latitude (Boland 1998). Moreover, many of these factors are related to the climate, allowing species to occupy a territory or home-range throughout the year. In addition, longevity is correlated with pair bonding or cooperative group living. Although some writers have dismissed this as inconclusive for Australian passerines (Cockburn 1996, Poiani and Pagel 1997), it remains a tantalising correlation that shall be explored further later (see Chapter 8).

That aside, songbirds belong to the immensely successful group of animals that have spread to every corner of the world, more than

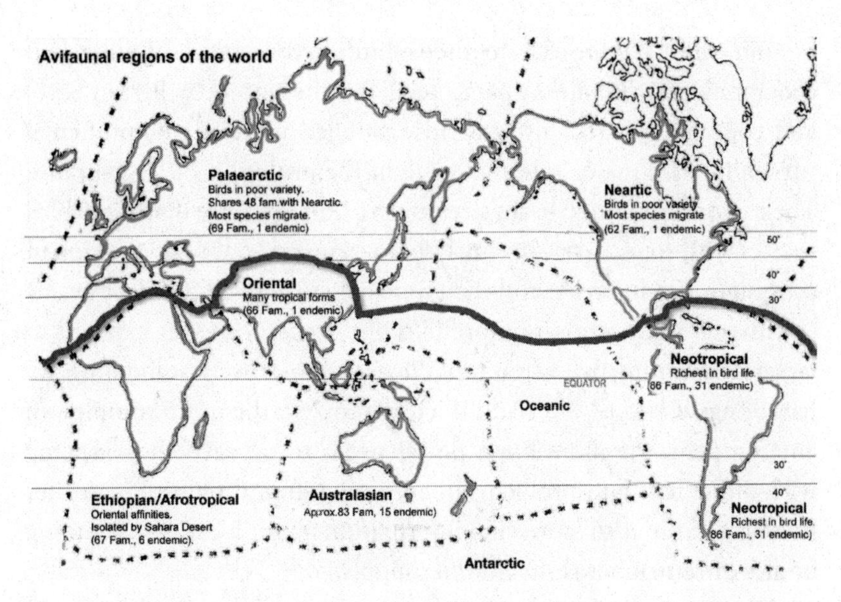

Fig. 1.3 Distribution of birds in the world and the general ornithological designation of bird-rich and bird-poor areas in the world. Biogeographic regions were identified by the English ornithologist Philip L Sclater (1829–1913) and German botanist H. G. Adolf Engler (1844–1930). Originally, six regions were identified: Palaearctic (Europe and Asia), Nearctic (North America), Neotropical (Mexico, Central and South America), Ethiopian (Africa), Indian (South East Asia, Indonesia) and Australian (Australia and New Guinea). Currently, eight are recognised since the addition of Oceania (Polynesia, Fiji and Micronesia) and Antarctica. Note that the Palaearctic and Nearctic regions are bird-poor areas including all of North America, Europe, Asia, Russia and China. The bird-rich areas are below the Tropic of Cancer and largely below the equator to the south. These include Africa, Australia and South America and, above the equator, semi-tropical or tropical areas of Central America and the Indian subcontinent, relatively sharply separated (solid line) from the bird-poor areas. Yet most studies on birds have been conducted on species from bird-poor areas. See also sahultime.monash.edu.au for additional information.

10,000 species in all (the official International Ornithology Union/ IOC site list, Gill and Donsker 2017), and people all around the world are enjoying the benefit of their presence, be it because the birds deal with pests, pollinate flowers and trees, disperse the seeds of fruit trees, or just because people enjoy the music they make, the colours they sport or even the companionship they offer.

But why is it important to discuss birds in the context of Australian geography and climate? A paper published in *Nature* by Ferran Sayol and colleagues (2016) drew a close parallel between environmental variability as a major selective force in the evolution of large brains. Their paper combined brain size information for more than 1200 bird species with remote-sensing analyses to estimate temporal variation in ecosystem productivity, and they were able to show that larger brains (relative to body size) are more likely to occur in species exposed to larger environmental variation. What this means is something we have long suspected but had difficulty proving: the more complex an environment, the more brain power needs to be devoted to dealing with difficulties and problems of survival. Often it requires a greater memory in order to store vital information about location of fruiting bodies or remember shifts in water supply.

Cockatoos were originally forest species and have lived in forests on this continent for an almost unimaginable period of time (some suggest a mid-Cretaceous origin of 95 million years (Wright et al. 2008) and throughout their long existence they have had to cope with tremendous variations in the Australian environment. The gradual drying out of the continent was certainly a challenge for many species, but the cockatoos are still here. The Australian climate is fickle in what it bestows – droughts and heat, storms and devastating fires and floods. Changing food and water sources constantly shift the goalposts. Data so far collected of brain sizes of Australian songbirds and parrots suggests that the mean brain size adjusted for body size is particularly large (Franklin et al. 2014).

While intensive farming with vast stretches of introduced but desirable items such as fruits, nuts, maize and seeds has often sustained and even increased numbers of inland birds, especially cockatoo populations, these vast spaces still represent deserts for perching birds. There are often no trees or shrubs as far as the eye can see and there are no laws that insist that some large-scale farms leave tree corridors or tree islands for the birds (as well as for livestock), in which they can rest, shelter and roost. Irrigation may be in pipes, and in small water puddles, the water heats up to such an extent that birds cannot partake of it.

Especially in the past decade, the devastating heatwaves and droughts of the inland have forced flocks of cockatoos of several species to flee to better lands closer to the coast, at least during prolonged droughts. Some of the most ancient species of cockatoos and parrots are now endangered as a result of climatic conditions and severe shortages of suitable nesting places and food sources. I suspect that poaching is an ongoing problem as well because of the high prices each individual cockatoo can fetch overseas. In addition, in some pockets they were even declared as pests, allowing them to be shot. Given their ancient claim to this country, they should be celebrated. Birds such as the palm cockatoo, *Probosciger aterrimus*, sulphur-crested cockatoo,

Fig. 1.4 Corellas are very smart and are among the most playful of all psittacine species, with a repertoire of play behaviour possibly unmatched by a single other species. Their behaviour is similar to that of three- to five-year-old children. The area around the eyes is light blue and around the beak there are hints of a light pink. The bird is otherwise white. Shown here is a little corella, *Cacatua sanguinea*.

Cacatua galerita, the galah, *Cacatua roseicapilla*, and the various corellas rank not just among the oldest but among the most intelligent birds to have evolved worldwide.

We may well ask why such ancient birds are equipped with such large brains? Even a small parakeet, such as the budgerigar, *Melopsittacus undulatus*, has a very large brain compared to its body size, well above the mean correlation of brain/body of songbirds. And we may also ask why cockatoos are so long-lived. Sulphur-crested cockatoos may live to 100 years, palm cockatoos 90 years, galahs and pink cockatoos to 85 years and all others can live to at least 50 years of age, as far as we can ascertain. These are just some of their unusual qualities but there are many more worth exploring, such as their ability to engage in vocal learning (imitating other species and humans) as only humans and some cetaceans can. Our nearest relatives, the chimpanzees, cannot learn to vocalise speech sounds, but birds, like humans, were given a voice presumably to communicate over long distances or in environments with many obstructions. We can only imagine what life was like for birds in Gondwana some 100, 50 or 20 million years ago. However, unlike the dinosaurs, we sometimes do not need to reconstruct the life-cycle of birds when we have avian species still among us today that carry that very long past of their ancestry into their present-day lives.

Period of care of offspring in Australian birds

Another notable feature of southern-hemisphere bird life is related to breeding and reproduction. Breeding periods are generally much longer in low latitudes compared to high latitudes. The extended breeding calendar is matched by the extended length of parental care for a brood. This means that, generally, birds in low latitudes have more flexibility when they breed and offspring are given more time to develop and learn post-fledging, still under parental guidance, than birds in high latitudes. In fact, Russel and colleagues (2004) actually compared length of parental care post-fledging in 126 species of the northern hemisphere versus 220 species of the southern hemisphere (Australian based). Their figures are very convincing (Fig. 1.5) in the sense that they support the notion that the reproductive system of many native Australian avian species is based on both pair commitment and long-term commitment to raising young. Sixty per cent of Australian land birds receive more than 50 days of post-fledging care as opposed to 18 per cent of birds from high latitudes. Barely any Australian songbirds have to be independent two weeks after fledging while over 43 per cent of high-latitude birds stop getting any parental support two to three weeks after fledging. In Australian magpies, post-fledging feeding continues for three months and the youngsters continue to beg for food, sometimes with success, for a further month, but then any begging is seriously discouraged or even punished and the juveniles are encouraged to find their own food while still being supervised in their natal territory.

Apart from care in terms of feeding, there is also the issue of how long the youngsters stay within their natal group. Just staying with the

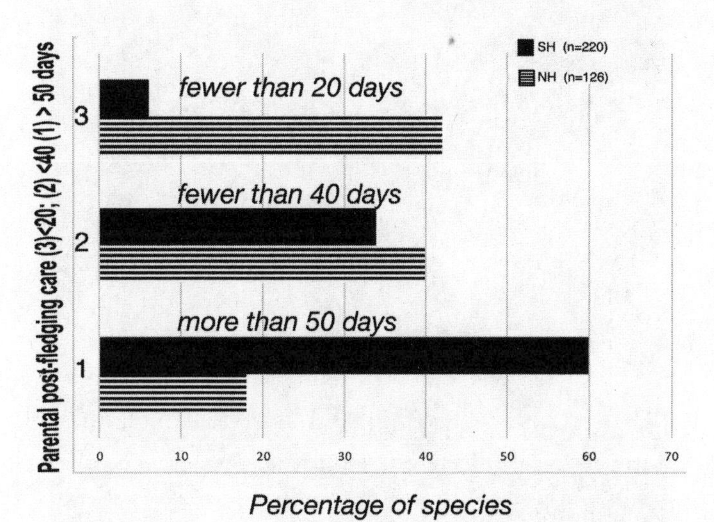

Fig. 1.5 Post-fledging parental care (based on Russell et al. 2004). Black (SH): Southern Hemisphere birds; Striped (NH): Northern Hemisphere birds. 1: longest period of parental care, 2: medium, 3: shortest period of post-fledging parental care.

parents improves the odds of survival. In the Canberra region, some juvenile magpies remained for three to four years within the territory before they dispersed and results indicated that this ensured an almost 100 per cent survival rate (Veltman and Carrick 1990), reducing to 40 per cent when departing within the first seven months post-fledging.

Survival rates are not directly correlated with larger brains. Experience, exposure to new situations and circumstances alone can help in survival.

Indeed, many Australian land birds may get protection and support for much longer than three months post-fledging and they may not just benefit from parental care but from that of helpers at the nest. Australia has the highest concentration of cooperative avian species of any country and it is not entirely clear whether cooperative behaviour evolved gradually or was an ancient model that was gradually abandoned and replaced by bi-parental care. Apostlebirds, *Struthidea cinereal*, as shown in Figure 1.6, certainly provide substantial help and

Fig. 1.6 Apostlebird nestlings have the advantage of being fed by several members of the group (photo courtesy of Robyn Burgess).

protection for their offspring and, like many other Australian species, enjoy such protection and learning well beyond the time they have fledged and can feed themselves.

No-parent to one-parent model of extant land birds of ancient lineages

The very first and possibly oldest model of how extant Australian land birds organised reproduction is provided by the malleefowl, brush turkey, emu and the southern cassowary, the handful of birds that do not form adult bonds and do not feed offspring. They have their place here as symbols of an ancient world and how things might have been different when dinosaurs were roaming Australia, and to support the notion that birdlife in Australia has found many ways to survive.

Chickens before domestication, *Gallus gallus*, and the great flightless emu, *Dromaius novaehollandiae*, belong to two distantly related orders of birds in the carinate and ratite subclasses that diverged at least 80 million years ago, deep in the Cretaceous. Their evolutions on different continents (ostriches in Africa, tinamou and rhea in South America, kiwi and moa in New Zealand and the emu and cassowary in Australia) have been a puzzle for a long time until a largely South Australian team in collaboration with New Zealand (Mitchel et al. 2014) suggested that dispersal across vastly different regions was most probably achieved because these species were not always flightless or as large as some of them are today. Indeed, early ratite evolution appears to have been dominated by flighted dispersal and parallel evolution, with flightlessness evolving a minimum of six times, and gigantism a minimum of five times. This is a powerful reminder that evolution is a dynamic process and certain characteristics are dropped or developed over time, and can appear and disappear as circumstances permit or require. The kiwi, *Apteryx australis*, and the tinamou (47 species in the family of Tinamidae) are relatively small while the only species now remaining that are flightless and large are the rhea, the ostrich, the emu and the cassowary.

Still, they all have in common that they lay their eggs (a single egg in the case of the kiwi) on the ground. Their incubation periods of 62 days for malleefowl, *Leipoa ocellate*, and 49 days for brush turkeys, *Alectura lathami*, and around 56 days for emus are the longest incubation periods among all birds. The eggs are extraordinarily large and thick-shelled; in Australia and New Zealand these are at the upper limit of eggs that can be produced by a bird. Presumably such thick eggshells offered some protection from dinosaurian thieves.

The size of the egg in a way determines the social role parents can play in the upbringing of the hatchlings, a point made very obvious in Australia's malleefowl and brush turkeys.

In malleefowl and brush turkeys, the only parental involvement is by the male during incubation and prior to hatching. He digs the mound and continues to adjust it to remain at the best incubation temperature but when the hatchlings emerge, they are on their own. There is no parental involvement from thereon. These hatchlings are among the most independent of any birds.

Male emus, like all other ratites except ostriches, assume sole responsibility for incubation. It is amusing and irritating that in all documentaries I have seen on emu behaviour, the tone of the commentary suddenly seems to become almost moralistic and unsympathetic when it comes to stating the fact that females 'walk away' and the (poor) males do the incubating and raising of the young on their own. Despite the role reversal, in their way of reproducing, there is absolutely no choice. When the female has laid her large and thick-shelled eggs, she is physically so depleted she would die if she had to incubate as well. The male, on the other hand, before his incubation stint spends time putting on substantial amounts of weight, on which he relies when sitting on and guarding the eggs. He sits for nearly two months, in a torpid state apparently, without feeding once, while the female spends the next months just regaining weight and substantially replenishing the nutrients she had to deposit in each egg. For both parties, male and female, the nutritional requirements and the energetic needs are such that both female (post-laying) and male (post-hatching) are very nearly at the end of endurance and near death. Biologically, it is a risky strategy and it is little wonder that the offspring have to be on their feet and able to get their own meals right from the start. At least they have the male's protection and guidance to, and at, waterholes.

There is a physical cost for the parents and a developmental cost for the offspring. In terms of body and brain weight ratios, the emu ranks well below the mean among Australian birds. Nutritionally, the brain is the most expensive part of an organism and the most time-consuming to develop. In emus, the little energy that inland open grassland foods provide goes into the body. There is not much left nutritionally to 'feed' the brain. Indeed, most developmental processes have to be complete at time of hatching. The species offers its young protection from predation (more parental care than brush turkeys) but does not feed the offspring (Coddington and Cockburn 1995). As a species, they are not even very supportive of each other – many young get abused and even killed by juvenile emus, and nobody seems to know why. Still, the surviving emus may live up to twenty years in the wild and longer in captivity.

Southern cassowaries may live even longer. Their reproductive model is very similar to that of emus, although female cassowaries are clearly dominant and even wear the more colourful ornaments during breeding time. As with emus, the male incubates the eggs and while the hatchlings are fully able to stand, run and feed themselves, and are camouflaged well in their lovely striped downy feathers, they would make an easy meal for predators. In their current remaining domain in the northern tropical coastal forests of Queensland, cassowary offspring, at least for the first year of life, have the added problem of dogs and wild pigs. They may get their adult plumage as late as 18 months and are sexually mature at about three and a half years (females) and often a year earlier in males. It is a shame that close behavioural studies have usually only been available in documentaries. It appears, though, that both emus and cassowary males actively wait for their offspring when they have fallen behind, will defend their offspring against predators as best they can and, in cassowaries, males have taken great care to show their offspring how to de-flesh some large fruits or they may even do it for the fledglings while they watch closely. There are moments when one can speak of 'parenting'.

It is noticeable that these forms of reproduction still take the parent a considerable time before the youngsters go their own way.

Other birds with ancient Australian lineages and no- or single-parent systems include at least one cuckoo. Most cuckoos parasitise other nests and make no personal investments in their offspring. Australia has thirteen species of cuckoo and the only Australian one, to my knowledge, that raises its own offspring is the pheasant coucal, *Centropus phasianinus* (Fig. 1.7).

The remaining cuckoos allow their offspring to be raised by species with bi-parental care. The pheasant coucal is a large, shy bush bird that tends to scuttle along the forest floor although they have not lost the ability to fly. They are ground-nesters and the male usually builds the nest and is the main provider for the offspring (Maurer 2006; Maurer et al. 2011). Pheasant coucals are also an ancient lineage and the only

Fig. 1.7 Pheasant coucal – the only Australian cuckoo raising its own offspring and, in a role reversal, it is the male that does the nest-building, raising and feeding.

survivor of a large radiation in the Pleistocene (2.5 million years ago – 11,700 years ago; Shute et al. 2016).

There are only two other groups of Australian land birds, also of ancient lineage, which have attracted worldwide attention and research. These are the lyrebirds and the bowerbirds. Their offspring also grow up with just one parent. Lyrebirds occupy only a relatively small stretch of the east coast of Australia and live in areas of remaining dry sclerophyll and wet forests. Rainforest (whether temperate or subtropical) is its main habitat. There are two species. The superb lyrebird, *Menura novaehollandiae*, has a wide but patchy distribution extending from near Melbourne to the rainforest hinterland of Brisbane. The Albert lyrebird, *Menura alberti*, is now found only in very small patches of rainforest south-west of Brisbane, at the northern border of New South Wales.

The birds have retreated to the relatively few intact forests on the eastern seaboard, such as Sherwood Forest in Victoria and Barrington Tops, Dorrigo or the New England National Park, all in New South Wales. The latter is part of the small isolated remnants of the Gondwana Rainforest System and, in such places, lyrebirds may still be abundant, especially in areas where Antarctic beech trees are found at altitudes over 600 metres (Lowman 1992).

There is a patch in the cool-temperate forest of the New England National Park that consists entirely of these ancient Antarctic beech trees; it is a rare, single-species stand. The forest has an eerie silence and there is a stillness and strangeness about it – vast root systems are visible and moss grows on them. There is no understorey at all, just these trees and lots of leaf litter on the ground. It seems lifeless until one stops and looks over the strange, gnarled forest floor and notices fleetingly quite a number of lyrebirds scuttling about, scratching the forest floor with powerful swiping motions. They turn over the knee-deep leaf litter with ease and with an almost obsessive preoccupation. At those moments, one somehow begins to sense that the birds and the trees belong to an entirely different era and were adapted to each other.

In this beech forest environment, a displaying male lyrebird would be visible from some distance, having no shortage of suitable display areas. The forest also produces an undeniable echo and when a displaying lyrebird male begins to sing during his mating display, the sound is enhanced and bounces back between the trees. The forest becomes a singing forest – by its structure and by having forced out any understorey via its extensive and surface-protruding root system, making it seem almost an active participant in the effect of the song. Interestingly, lyrebird males in particular, after a fire has burned off the undergrowth, leave their own territorial patches and often congregate in such bare understorey areas for a period of about two weeks (Doty et al. 2015). It is not quite clear whether the food supply or the forest cleared of understorey act as attractants. Both are possible.

Male lyrebirds are polygamous and promiscuous and they fertilise several females in a season (Lill 1979; Schodde and Mason, 1999). They take no share in nest building, incubation or in rearing the young (Lill 1986) but it appears that the young males later take their father as tutor for song-learning. In Powys' seven-year study of lyrebirds, there was structural, locational and temporal constancy of territorial song from one generation to the next (Powys 1995).

Surely, the male lyrebird's display song is one of the most dramatic and among the loudest and most beautiful songs anywhere, and all that vocal panache is accompanied by dance and rattling of feathers, a separate 'lyre' that adorns only the male. The lyrebird's gala performance and aria-like delivery of impressive segments of mimicry of other birds, beautifully put together, often sounds better than the original vocalisations of other birds, delivered with confidence and considerable amplitude (Dalziell and Magrath 2012). The offspring of lyrebirds are, however, vulnerable. They have to hide as best they can in the elaborate nest that the female alone constructs, usually a metre or so off the ground, sometimes wedging lots of material between deep forks of trees, stuffing the space from bottom to nest floor with rough material, but, inside, the female furnishes the nest with soft materials and even constructs a roof. The helpless young remain in the nest and are fed solely by the female.

Bowerbirds, largely at home in Australia with some species also found in Papua New Guinea, also evolved without any male commitment to raising offspring. Remarkably, the mate-choice game in this ancient lineage did not lead to extraordinary musicianship as in lyrebirds but to males turning dancers, architects and artists to impress a female. The satin bowerbird, *Ptilonorgynchua violacens*, may build bowers often using elaborate decorations and also display using his vocalisation like percussion instruments.

Bowerbird males mate with several females in their area but do not participate in the building of the nest or in the provisioning of nestlings. These and similar cases of demonstrative male displays have been studied for many decades in a never-ending fascination with the choreography, plumage use, colour or virtuosity of song and the dramatic effects of male dance performance, swinging flight feathers and revealing colours that flash in dappled light.

The female usually gets little benefit from such a male other than his genes, since he takes no part in the upbringing of his offspring and, given this state of affairs, she might as well be choosy. Her offspring, usually just one or two, may be able to fly after about three weeks post-hatching, but depend on the female for feeding for several more months (Fig. 1.8).

The eggs of satin bowerbirds are well above average for their weight class, reminiscent of ancient origins. As they hatch and fledge asynchronously, there is also the age difference to consider when fledging. Since the nests tend to be of loose construction high up in a tree, asynchrony means that the first may be ready to fly while the second one may not be able to do so. In tawny frogmouths, *Podargus strigoides*, it is known that all offspring fledge at the same time and often this means that the youngest falls to the ground and is unable to fly up to a higher site and is at great risk of being captured by predators (Kaplan 2018b). Whether the last hatched satin bowerbird

Fig. 1.8 Satin bowerbird nestling, still sporting an impressive mane of downy feathers in its second week of life and, despite flight feathers erupting, looking nothing like an adult bowerbird.

is as much at risk at fledging time as tawny frogmouth youngsters are is not known.

These no- or one-parent models are sparse and, among Australian land birds, they are few and far between. One wonders whether these truly ancient lineages, of which some may have graced this continent for an inconceivable 90 million years or even longer, are still representative of the kind of nesting and parenting that may have been common in the Cretaceous period. Their co-habitation with dinosaurs may have constrained choices as well, or the model may have remained relatively unchanged for eons of time.

Ancient birds such as those examples featured above have no pair formation but they have certainly gained a reputation of unique and outstanding qualities as singers, performers or builders. Both bowerbirds and lyrebirds can mimic other species, including humans, but only the lyrebird (both species) (Kaplan 1999) has attained substantial virtuosity in this regard.

There is a general rule in nature – the higher the risk of being someone's next meal, the more abundant the numbers produced. To give two examples, the giant Pacific octopus lays clutches of around 100,000, and sea turtles lay 110 eggs in a nest and average between two to eight nests. The numbers are staggering but the numbers that survive to adulthood are even more telling. Of the 100,000 octopi, fewer than ten may become adults. In turtles, that ratio is almost as bad – generally it is thought that only one in 1000 turtles hatching will make it to breeding age.

It is noteworthy, therefore, that most Australian avian females of ancient lineage produce few offspring a year. If we take all land birds as a group, including the largest and smallest songbirds, attrition rates decline to 30–70 per cent per clutch per season. Yet the matter of quantity versus quality of eggs per clutch (or even several clutches) is a constant seesaw between environmental conditions, including climate and time factors (Badyaev and Ghalambor 2001). Large birds tend to nest just once per season while small birds, as Yom-Tov (1987) confirmed in his detailed study, have longer breeding seasons, breed more frequently and have larger clutches.

Modern birds evolved in East Gondwana and speciated here, and some of the lineages date back well into the Cretaceous. Hence, we can study their strategies and abilities and their evolution in their original location of origin. The birds are a gift indeed.

2

The gift of vocal learning

Vocal learning is of special importance. Humans depend on it and most human progress has been based on the elaborate ability of formulating sounds with specific meanings. Much of the human communication system is built on words and symbols, both in speech and in print. Mistakenly, it was thought that the ability to acquire specific sounds was unique to humans and that any form of vocal behaviour in songbirds was genetically pre-programmed and purely devised for and limited by its reproductive purpose.

Hence the discovery, less than 100 years ago, that birds were able to learn sounds was a major, even heart-stopping event. And here mimicry also played a special role. The realisation that mimicked sounds belonging to other birds or animals could not be part of a species' genetic template but had to be learned was a major game-changer. A good many other biological facts are associated with it. It forced a rethinking of the role of genes and the extent to which vocal behaviour is inherited or learned.

In order to learn, an organism also needs to remember, and 'memory' is something associated with intelligence or referred to as cognition. These are qualities that animals were not supposed to have according to the seventeenth-century French philosopher René Descartes (1596–1650), who formulated the idea that animals are just automatons guided by instinct and cannot think, and we therefore owe them no moral debt. His Latinised name, Renatus Cartesius, gave rise to a system of thought called Cartesianism, believing in rationality (and thus giving impetus to science as a new way of looking at the world) and the total separation of mind and body. The latter claim has had many critics (Damasio 2006). Cartesianism, in many respects, was superseded by Isaac Newton (1643–1727) but this was not so for Descartes' ideas about animals, which were still taught in schools as late as the 1960s. Neo-Cartesians are still around to this day.

It is highly regrettable that such fateful statements were influential well into the 20th century (and still in some quarters to this day). Aligned with this view was the idea that unthinking animals do not feel pain, a thought that led to cruelties beyond imagining, even in dog and primate experimentations. Descartes' was a very useful premise because it freed the abusers of any shackles of remorse or pity, let alone empathy and care.

One may well ask what changed perceptions about animals in recent times. There are probably many factors, but one is certainly the discovery of learning ability in birds. The mere fact that birds demonstrably learn their vocalisations suddenly challenged and wiped out many assumptions that Descartes had introduced.

Thus, in the 20th century, the study of birdsong began to take a very high priority position in science, not because of the quality of birdsong but because the information signalled that birds were apparently far better equipped for learning and cognitive tasks than previously imagined.

This may not sound all that inspiring but, looking around the animal world, vocal learning is indeed a gift. Apart from humans and songbirds, it is bestowed on only very few other species (parrots and some hummingbirds) and classes (cetaceans, elephants).

Of course, birds do not generally speak human language. Speech is peculiar to humans and is its own species-specific set of utterances. However, this is a very untidy, murky area and has been so for some time. For instance, definitional problems arose immediately when forms of communication and interaction in birds were framed with reference to human language (Kaplan 2009).

To say that birds do not have 'language' requires a logical somersault as silly as claiming that birds lack human culture. Of course they do, not as a 'lack' but as a realisation that they have their own species-specific forms of communication. For some, song belongs to music, for others the entire communication system belongs to language. Some writers such as Hockett (1959) insist that animals do not have language (i.e. a fully-fledged vocal communication system) and his view is counteracted by others. For instance, Cadková (2015) asked whether humans are the only animals endowed with language and what makes language a unique communication system, concluding that there is no need to distinguish human language from non-human communication since each is a communication system with some similar characteristics.

Fortunately, neuroscientists did not care much about such definitional problems but about brain organisation, and initially just wanted to know what structures and connections existed in the songbird brain. Ultimately, no theories or large-scale ideas about the natural world can convince unless they are anchored in biological evidence. I keenly remember a seminar in which a general discussion about an aesthetic sense in animals was documented by wonderful watercolour paintings by captive seals showing very nice compositions of yellows and reds mixed in with greens and blues. Some saw this as evidence that some species may well have an aesthetic sense. Then someone who had studied the perceptual apparatus of these specific seals very closely dryly pointed out, 'They don't have colour vision and can see only in the blue range.' A silence followed. Perhaps animals have an aesthetic sense, but the argument collapsed once the biological facts were made known.

For learning to occur, there need to be appropriate brain mechanisms and a perceptual apparatus that can perceive, generate, support and/or adapt to such requirements. It was already known from human studies that the brain was sufficiently flexible to change size allocation to various centres but it presupposed that such centres already existed. For instance, the hippocampus is responsible for spatial memory. Significantly, it was found that the hippocampus in London taxi drivers was much larger than in the average population. Thus, the need to remember places and how to get there was thought to have a direct effect on their brain (Maguire et al. 2000, 2006) and this has also been shown in homing pigeons (Cnotka et al. 2008).

When starting to investigate the brains of songbirds, neuroscientists ended up mapping out an entire song control system and thanks to this work, we now even know in most cases how impulses and information travel from one collection of cells (called nuclei) to another and how the system works. Painstaking work followed to find nuclei that could register song and somehow transfer the auditory information to be embedded in memory, and then to uncover the processes by which such memories can translate back into motor responses when the learned song is meant to be produced – work that has been both very labour-intensive over something like 50 years of research and illuminating in more ways than initially expected.

The question is, how much does the environment contribute to the development and maintenance of typical song (in terms of learning styles, tutor help, hetero-specific vocal environment) and how much is controlled by mechanisms in which the environment has only a relatively limited role (reviewed in detail by Margoliash, 2002)? Song production, song development and song maintenance have been examined in detail in neuroscience. We now know that the ability to sing required an entirely new layer of neural structures in the brain, no doubt contributing to its overall increase in size. The most important nuclei in the brain that are responsible for a fully developed song repertoire are the nuclei HV (high vocal centre), RA and Area X (Zeng et al. 2007). These have been mapped in detail (Fig. 2.1).

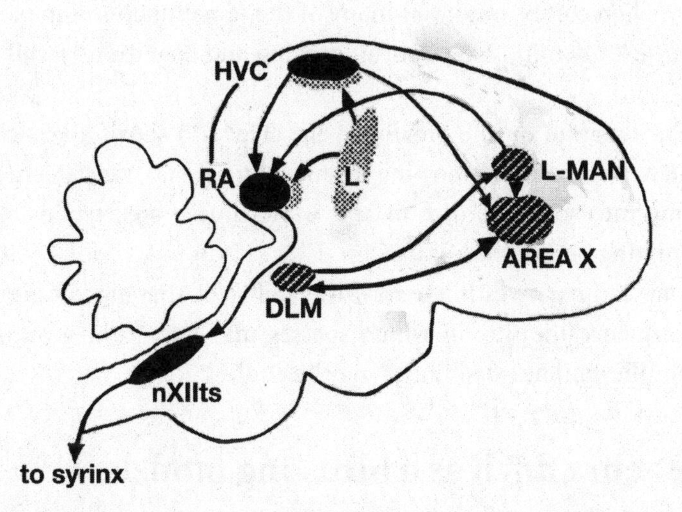

Fig. 2.1 Schematic presentation of the main song control pathways in the brain of songbirds. The song pathway (HVC to RA to n12ts to syrinx) includes brain areas specialised for learning and producing song. Lesions of these areas removes the ability to sing. The anterior song pathway HVC via Area X, DLM, LMAN, to RA, includes brain areas specialised for learning song (Bottjer et al. 1984; Scharff and Nottebohm, 1991). (HVC = High Vocal Centre; RA = the robust nucleus of the archistriatum; lMAN = lateral magnocellular nucleus of the anterior neostriatum; DLM = the medial nucleus of the dorsolateral thalamus, nXIIts = tracheosyringeal portion of the hypoglossal nucleus.) Arrows indicate the links to the sound-producing organ, the syrinx, and also to the spinal cord.

By comparison, emus, as all non-songbirds, lack a full song control system even though they can produce sounds, which they do solely via their air sacs. Their brains have generally remained relatively small partly because they do not require all this additional apparatus necessary for song.

Songbirds, parrots and hummingbirds are not closely related taxonomically (Sibley and Ahlquist, 1990). According to Gahr (2000), this suggests that vocal learning may have evolved independently among birds at least three times.

Remarkably, songbirds and humans have specialised vocal pathways not found in other animals. As we now know, the avian forebrain (now called the pallium) does not have the layered structure of the mammalian cortex, but it has many of the same functions, in particular those known to involve vocal learning and cognition (Jarvis et al. 2005).

The diagram on the previous page (Fig. 2.1) shows a vertical cut through the bird brain, showing the main nuclei that translate memory of song into song production and which nuclei are responsible for interpreting perceived sounds.

One can barely estimate how the ability of shaping vocalisations can influence the way in which species may live, form groups and communicate. The possibilities may be endless.

The zebra finch as a birdsong model

One of the grasswrens has already been introduced. There are eleven species altogether, largely belonging to the outback. Partly because of their location, their cryptic colouration and even their size, very few people have seen them, a state of affairs that a recent book by Andrew Black and Peter Gower (*Grasswrens: Australian Outback Identities*, 2017) has tried to address.

I would like to introduce another of the small natives: the zebra finch, *Taeniopygia guttata*, because of its importance for birdsong studies. The zebra finch is the only finch with a wide distribution across Australia. It is also comfortable in temperate climate zones. Due to pressure from human encroachments, it is now found more often inland. Spot a zebra finch in the outback and there is sure to be a permanent water source within a two-kilometre radius. It is one of eighteen native species of finches, not counting subspecies. Like the grasswrens, finches are small birds. A zebra finch may weigh just 12 g and be a mere 10 cm in length, much smaller than grasswrens which weigh about 20–22 g and are roughly about 15 cm long. The zebra finch male uses song in courtship to attract a female. Once the male has won a female, the pair will stay together for some seasons at least – some think they mate for life – and the male will defend the female. They will jointly feed their offspring.

Zebra finches are usually found in small flocks but they live in pairs when it is time to raise offspring (Zann 1996).

At first the zebra finch does not seem all that remarkable, especially not in the Australian context. Yet the zebra finch has become one of the major model species for the international neuroscientific study of birdsong (Griffith and Buchanan 2010). This may seem odd for several reasons.

One concerns the choice of finch. Of all Australian finches only one-third extend their range into temperate zones (the zebra finch being one of these six); the remainder are predominantly found in tropical or subtropical regions (Table 2.1).

Another concerns the choice of finch in terms of mating dynamics. Of all eighteen species, only six are sexually dimorphic, meaning that male and female have sex-specific differences in appearance such as different plumage patterns (there may also be size, eye colour or weight differences). The rest of the Australian finch species, twelve of them, are monomorphic, which means that there are no sex differences human observers have been able to identify. Being 'monomorphic' is more accurate than saying there are no sex differences because, as we have learned since (discussed in detail in Chapters 6 and 7), there may be sex differences the birds perceive but we do not (such as ultraviolet). Monomorphic tendencies in finches extend also to courtship behaviour. In 2015, Soma and Garamszegi showed that in quite a few Estrildid finches females also had song or dance. Their efforts of documenting the evolution of courtship displays revealed that in many Australian finches, females also performed courtship dances. These are the blue-faced parrot finch, chestnut-breasted, double-barred, Gouldian, long-tailed, painted, red-browed, star and zebra finches.

Yet the researchers chose the zebra finch that belongs to the few sexually dimorphic species of this genus (Table 2.1). Zebra finches are thus not terribly representative of finches in Australia.

In this sense, neuroscientists have chosen a model that fits many species in the northern hemisphere.

Common name	Latin name	Distribution in Australia	Status (wild)	Sex diffs.	Pet trade
1. Beautiful firetail	*Emblema bella* (was: *Stagonopleura bella*)	S.E. Australia	Rare	Mono	Rare
2. Black-throated finch	*Poephila cincta*	Coastal NSW/Qld	Highly endangered	Mono	✓
3. Blue-faced parrot finch	*Erythrura trichroa*	Cape York/Northern Islands/New Guinea	Rare	Mono	✓
4. Chestnut-breasted finch (also munia, or mannikin)	*Lonchura castaneothorax*	East coast (North Qld to Syd) and Top-end	Secure	Mono	✓
5. Crimson finch	*Neochmia phaeton*	Top end and New Guinea	Endangered	Dimorphic	✓
6. Diamond firetail	*Emblema guttata* (was: *Stagonopleura guttata*)	S. Qld to South Australia	Near threatened	Mono	✓
7. Double-barred finch	*Taeniopygia bichenovii* (or *Poephila bichenovii*)	Top, WA, Northern A., Qld to northern NSW	Secure	Mono	✓
8. Gouldian finch	*Chloebia gouldiae* or *Erythrura gouldiae*	Top-end (small pockets)	Endangered	Dimorphic	✓
9. Long-tailed (black heart) finch	*Poephila acuticauda*	Top-end	At risk	Mono	✓
10. Masked finch	*Poephila personata*	Across top of Australia	Rare	Mono	✓
11. Painted (firetail) finch	*Emblema pictum*	Dry inland, north/NW of Australia	Common	Dimorphic	✓
12. Pictorella (mannikin) finch	*Heteromunia pectoralis* (was: *Lonchura pectoralis*)	Dry, arid (species is nomadic)	Secure	Dimorphic	✓
13. Plum-headed finch	*Neochmia modesta* (was: *Aidemosyne modesta*)	Inland Qld, NSW	Relatively secure	Dimorphic	✓
14. Red-browed finch	*Neochmia temporalis* (was: *Aegintha temporalis*)	East coast of Australia, SA to North Qld	Common but declining	Mono	✓
15. Red-eared firetail finch	*Emblema oculata*	South-western Australia	Rare	Mono	✓
16. Star finch	*Neochmia ruficauda*	Top-end	Rare to locally near extinct	Dimorphic	✓
17. Yellow-rumped finch	*Lonchura flaviprymna*	Top Western + Northern Australia	Rare	Mono	✓
18. Zebra finch	*Taeniopygia guttata*	Across Australia, except Tasmania	Common but locally declining	Dimorphic	✓
Total:			Common/secure: 5 Mono: 12	Threatened: 13 Dimorphic: 6	100%

Table 2.1 Australian Finches (Mono: monomorphic; Dimorphic: sexually dimorphic; Pet trade: almost all species are readily available).

However, its habits do not suggest exceptional qualities, nor does its song. Zebra finches sound a little like weak rubber horns that one has to squeeze, and there is relatively minimal variation until one examines the finer details of song in sonograms. Zebra finches are loud and boisterous. The male's song consists of a few small beeps, leading up to a rhythmic song of varying complexity. The complete song of males is taught by an adult male tutor, usually the father (Roper and Zann 2006), and research has emphasised the father-teaching-son scenario but has largely omitted to study what happens to females. It is actually not true that female zebra finches are entirely without song, and they do have other vocal utterances. Moreover, the female too remembers the song of the father, which she can compare with that of any courting young male zebra finch's song (Shaughnessy et al. 2019). She also vocalises and, when bonding with a male, the vocalisations between the two begin to converge (Benichov et al. 2016) as occurs in budgerigars (Hile et al. 2000).

This small Australian zebra finch, although not gifted with the most appealing or complex song among songbirds, nevertheless has superstar status in bird research. There have been, in any one decade since the 1970s, at least 13,000 research articles written on the zebra finch, largely on the brain, hormonal levels, vocal learning and the apparatus required for achieving such learning. The number of papers published about zebra finch vocal learning to advance our knowledge in the song control system and memory is simply phenomenal.

The attraction of the zebra finch (Fig. 2.2) has been several-fold. On a pragmatic basis, they are small, resilient, cheap to keep and they reproduce readily in captivity. They are classified as part of the pet trade and lack the common protections of Australian native birds and therefore do not require much paperwork or special permission.

Theoretically, the zebra finch has thus proved a very useful model, largely because it also fitted so well with habits of high-latitude avian species.

The zebra finch model has led to descriptions of song and the brain being in the service of reproduction. Song is said to be a male

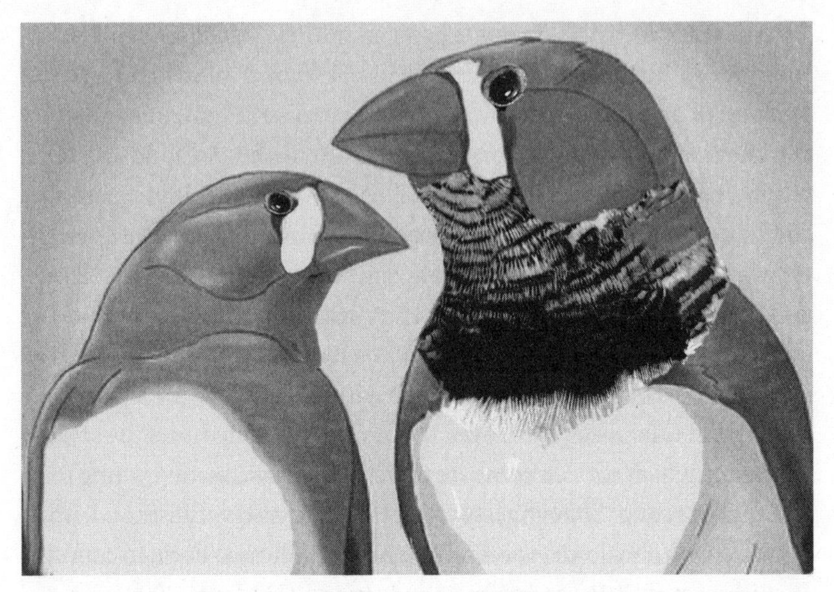

Fig. 2.2 Female and male zebra finch. A mature dominant male has a clearly visible, conspicuous black bib (on the right) and the patterned/striped feathers below the beak and around the neck, earning the species the name zebra finch. The beak is bright red.

reproductive behaviour and is sung in spring to attract a female. The latter gave rise to the expression of a 'seasonal brain'. A seasonal brain in this context refers to a (male) brain that is activated in spring to remember a song the bird had learned the previous year but not sung since. Since this is so every year, it is indeed a seasonal song circumscribed by the function it serves. Zebra finches, when learning song from a tutor, do so within a relatively small window of time (Slater et al. 1988). They then disperse and, sometime later, need to find a mate on the basis of what was learned. It is intriguing that a memory can be laid down one year and then miraculously, so it seemed, be recovered months later in a brain as small as that of a zebra finch. This has led to many fruitful studies on memory (Chew et al. 1996; Funabiki and Konishi 2003; Yanagihara and Yazaki-Sugiyama 2016).

Importantly, we have also learned that bird species, such as the zebra finch, have a sensitive period for acquiring song. Song learning goes through a memorisation phase (25–65 days) and a motor phase (ending about day 90) about the time the zebra finch male becomes sexually mature. At that point, song usually becomes crystallised, meaning that it does not change anymore and the learning phase is over and the song perfected, although it can be modified by early experience (Jones et al. 1996). The courtship song is then used, surprisingly intact without any further practice, in the next breeding season (Slater et al. 1988).

The question that has also been asked is how a female can tell whether the singer is a quality male and worth having? What has been studied in particular is to ascertain what the courtship signals are and what it takes for the female to accurately detect, perceive and interpret them. Male song, as we believed for a long time, may simply indicate 'I am available' and/or 'I am healthy' but it has been shown in countless studies since that courtship songs can also convey substantial information about the identity, state, or overall quality of the signaller.

Even if the female of a particular species is not well equipped to sing herself, or she may have just a small repertoire, she still needs to be an expert in song. How else would the female ever be able to arrive at an accurate interpretation of the song quality or the signals embedded in a specific song unless she had some way of assessing the message? In species that are vocally sexually dimorphic, this has been a question that has only been answered very recently. A study by Van Ruijssevelt and colleagues (2018) searched for neurobiological mechanisms (brain activity) that might contribute to a female's sexual decision-making and preferences based on auditory stimuli. They looked outside the traditionally studied auditory forebrain pathways to discover that one area of the female's forebrain (called the caudocentral nidopallium, or simply, NCC) was activated when females heard acoustically similar but categorically divergent stimuli. Their study is very exciting because it suggests that there is a firm biological basis for claiming that sexual selection by females is based on subtle discrimination of sounds. In order to make choices on song alone, it was reasonable for the researchers to assume that such an ability needs nuclei in the brain which can compute fine auditory differences. Indeed, having asked this question they actually found such a novel spot (node) in the female's avian song circuitry. We would now need to know whether the same ability and neural node (NCC) is activated in males at the time of their own performance or whether the females alone have the brain power of assessing the subtle cues in song. If it is the latter, males could not manipulate these underlying cues and their song would be an honest signal. If, however, they are able to compute these signals as well, their song might improve with more practice if females had turned them down.

Other variables may also be assessed, but these may be visual rather than auditory. Boag (1987) found that nutritional deprivation during development can never be overcome entirely. The adult bird will remain smaller throughout its life and this is certainly a noticeable feature if it is 'health' that the female will assess when she chooses a mate.

More importantly, it is claimed song is the main measure of a male's quality in female mate-choice as demonstrated in a paper by Nowicki and colleagues in 1998. They presented a developmental neurobiological profile of the zebra finch brain in the first 90 days of life. Significantly, it showed that the song control system is not yet fully developed when zebra finches fledge (around day 20). Indeed, several nuclei (such as HVC and RA) continue to increase in size until day 50, and Area X, which barely starts developing at the time of fledging, still increases in size at least until day 55 (see Fig. 2.1 on page 31). Equally important, but rarely raised with respect to song development, is the fact that these nuclei need to have connections to each other in order to be fully functional. However, like an Achilles heel of zebra finch song learning, these connections only begin to form and grow close to fledging and, if all goes well, then only fully develop in a period immediately post-fledging and prior to independent feeding. Before feeding independence (between days 20 and 35) is thus the main period when the connections to the song nuclei are being grown and finalised (called neurogenesis). That is, very important neural developments very precariously occur only during the riskiest and most stressful period of a zebra finch's life. When finding sufficient food is a problem, as it can be particularly at that time, brain development can be delayed or arrested and, presumably, can directly affect the connectivity of neurons in the song control system. Such stress intervention at a crucial growth stage may have repercussions for song performance and show up as qualitatively poorer or even deficient song later. Many fledging zebra finches actually do not even survive this early post-fledging period (Nowicki et al. 1998).

Brain plasticity and social interaction

Using the zebra finch model has been of tremendous value but, to some extent, has led to distorted ideas that findings related to male song acquisition and function can be generalised to apply principally to all songbirds. It became clear that the comfort of this model made it run the risk of being viewed, even if only implicitly, as if this model were universally true for all or most songbirds. This claim would certainly not be true. However, the basic architecture of the song control system of the zebra finch brain is indeed representative of songbirds. Discovering all the nuclei and their function was a major breakthrough. When our laboratory conducted an investigation into the brain of the Australian magpie, we were entirely guided by, and found confirmed, the 'map' that neuroscience had provided for the song control system and its various centres.

However, there is a second level of investigation, which circumscribes the song behaviour. Because males in some avian species sing seasonally and for reproduction, the literature at times went so far as to call 'song' a male reproductive behaviour, which, most definitely, would be an incorrect, or at least misleading, claim. At this level, the zebra finch certainly cannot stand in for all songbirds. The translation of brain function into reproductive behaviour is species-specific, and it depends entirely on which reproductive and mating system a species has as to whether a comparison with zebra finches is appropriate or even relevant.

There are species that sing all year round, others that sing new songs each season and yet others that do not use song for reproductive purposes but to defend a territory, and the role of the sexes in finding a suitable mate may be very different from one another in important ways. Moreover, even the supposedly simple 'reproductive behaviour' of some male breeding song, on closer inspection, may not be quite so simple after all. One particularly well-studied song is that of the European songbird the nightingale, *Luscinia megarhynchos*, which has recently revealed new facets of male song. The assumption had always been that male song had to be the best it could be and would signal health and readiness for mating. This new study headed by Conny Bartsch and colleagues (2015) has found that male nightingales apparently do a lot more than just advertise prowess. They discovered that the male's song contained elements used in the rearing of offspring and, it seems, by using these elements, the nightingale male more than hinted that he would be a good parent. The presence of these elements and the strength of such elements including many different 'buzz', 'whistle' and 'trill' songs, entailed a promise of future paternal effort and, apparently, these were the specific song elements that persuaded females to accept the male.

Among the number of songbird species in Australia, every conceivable model of song use is in place and that diversity is also of theoretical importance. Song can have many different functions and the wide range of strategies is particularly obvious in Australia. Some species use song specifically to attract a mate, either just to mate, with no male parenting commitment, as in lyrebirds, or to mate and pair up, as in zebra finches. Many species use song for territorial defence, such as the magpie lark, *Grallina cyanoleuca*. Others, even if they have specific calls for territorial defence, don't use song at all for purposes of either territorial defence or to attract a mate, such as the Australian magpie (Kaplan 2018a).

Plasticity refers not to the number of songs learned in a small window of time but to the ability to learn new sounds and vocal sequences later in life, and to incorporate these in novel situations. This is far removed from the courtship model with fixed song after a relatively short period of learning/plasticity.

Brain plasticity in vocal acquisitions in lifelong learners is a little more difficult to test experimentally because, ideally, this would require testing the same birds at different ages. Drawn-out timeframes are not always achievable in the laboratory or within timeframe settings of funding bodies (usually three-year periods, in which the entire project has to have finalised data). Voigt and colleagues showed that in cooperatively breeding white-browed sparrow weavers the transition from subordinate helper to dominant breeder male induces the production of a new type of song (Voigt et al. 2007). This new song can only be produced if the HVC nucleus is enlarged. Expressed differently, changing social cues alone can lead to physiological changes as dramatic as actually generating enlargement of the HVC necessary for producing the new song (Voigt et al. 2007). Such differentiation and plasticity in a bird brain would have been considered implausible just 50 years ago. If a single change in the dominance hierarchy can have such profound consequences on the brain within one lifetime of one bird, then other group pressures could conceivably have profound effects too, especially over long periods of time. Pozner et al. (2018) recently produced evidence that questioned the limits of neuronal plasticity even in species that had been identified as seasonal performers (in song or migration). They argued that 'fixed' song, especially seasonally expressed, misleadingly suggests neuronal inactivity. Instead they produced evidence that even in those cases the brain is equipped to remain substantially responsive to new or changed conditions and can recruit new neurons when conditions change (Pozner et al. 2018).

There are other specific contexts, such as inheriting someone's pet bird with one set of 'vocabulary' (literally mimicked human words) and transposing the bird to a new vocal and even sound environment. While it may take several years before the bird feels comfortable enough in its new surroundings, a parrot should eventually produce new sounds if its brain has this kind of plasticity to learn even through adulthood.

Most of these experiences remain anecdotal but offer a window into the learning capacity of a bird. We inherited a sulphur-crested cockatoo, *Cacatua galerita*, with serious health problems. It took five years before these were overcome and one day he simply said, 'hello' and that 'hello' marked the beginning of a new era in his communication with us. At the time of his arrival, he was 35 years old, 40 years of age when he started talking to us and now, at 50 (only half his lifespan), he has shown the capacity for absorbing new information and even learning new sounds from whistles to words. Cockatoos have among the largest brains among birds in actual size and, when adjusted for body weight, it is still one of the largest brains (in the top five in the world) of any bird (see Chapter 10). They are smart. Even this cockatoo, with a severely traumatic past, recovered well enough to learn new words, routines and habits at the age of 40 years and beyond (Fig. 2.3).

Every researcher studying cockatoos has been impressed by their cognitive and problem-solving skills. In Vienna, Alice Auersperg and her colleagues (2013a, b; 2017) for some years have studied the Goffin cockatoo, *Cacatua goffiniana*, a close relative of the sulphur-crested cockatoo and corella, and they keep discovering astonishing skills and problem-solving abilities in this species. In the wild, they are now confined to the Tanimbar Archipelago Islands of Indonesia (see Fig. 1.2 on page 7) and are near threatened.

Brain plasticity does not just refer to an ongoing ability in vocal learning but may also refer to other areas of brain activity, for instance, problem-solving. Problem-solving has usually been tested in individual birds to assess cognitive abilities. Another relatively recent set of

Fig. 2.3 Our sulphur-crested cockatoo, with erect crest, head-bobbing and vocalising, indicates that he is ready to play, and sparing no trick to alert us to this fact. The cockatoo is a substantial bird, ours weighing as much as 950 grams and 50 cm in size. The beak, as in all large cockatoos, is extremely powerful and capable of cracking a macadamia nut. The eye colour, a deep black/brown, is more typical of males but there are overlaps with female eye colours, usually being either lighter or having a tinge of red.

problem-solving experiments creates problems in such a way that they can only be solved cooperatively and/or may require sharing, as was tested in tufted capuchin monkeys (Hattori et al. 2005) and some other primates (Cronin et al. 2005). I was reminded of these primate experiments while in Vienna as a guest of the Konrad-Lorenz Institute. There, I also met two adult keas, *Nestor notabilis*, a New Zealand parrot that, in cognitive ability, can well compete with cockatoos, ravens, and the African grey parrot. This opportunity came about because guestrooms had a window that opened inwards directly into an aviary that housed keas. As far as I recall, keas were tested at that time for their technical and problem-solving abilities. The institute had been given a loan of an artificial fruit-box encased in strong and transparent plexiglass that required complicated sequences of locks and slides in order to gain access to a desirable food item (Whiten et al. 1996, Custance et al. 1999).

The significance of the experiment was that the same box had been used to test the abilities of chimpanzees to solve the problem of the locked box with a food award inside. The keas were slightly faster in solving the problem and retrieving the food than were the chimpanzees (Miyata et al. 2011).

The windows in the guestroom also had bars so I could safely leave that window to their aviary open. It took less than five minutes for the keas to come close and investigate. By the second morning, they whistled for me to come to the window. I had a pine cone to give them and delivered it through the bars. It was swiftly taken. I wondered whether the two keas would compete for the one pine cone (a second cone was also available, just in case) but they did not. They both took hold of it, facing each other, with a firm grip on the pine cone each with the left foot, and then shared the spoils, expertly removing the kernels. Towards the end of this small feeding bout, there was almost a fight when they relinquished the cone with their feet but hung on to it with their beaks until one of them used the left leg and stretched it, in a right angle to the body and foot extended towards the other, but not to strike. The second bird immediately relinquished the pine cone and gently put it in front of the first.

This interaction deeply impressed me, first for the peaceful sharing and second, because of the non-vocal gesture. The outstretched leg raised halfway and definitely pointing towards the belly of the other, but not touching it, seemed an almost human-like gesture to say 'stop', particularly since the one to whom it was directed did not come any closer thereafter and disengaged its beak from the food item at once. It seemed, from observation, that both birds received the same amount of seeds and enjoyed this snack also as a social occasion. The problem of having just one cone, instead of a cone each, did not result in a competitive squabble which, incidentally, could have resulted in a loss of seeds and less food for both of them.

My observations of this interaction tie in well with some experiments on cooperative behaviour in pairs of keas (Schwing et al. 2017). The gesture of the raised leg was particularly surprising, and it seemed more significant because of the response it received. Many years later, I conducted field experiments with Australian magpies and discovered that they were pointing at an object, a half-hidden bird of prey (Kaplan 2011), and I was suddenly reminded of these keas. Using a limb or part of the body to express an intention, and for that intention to be understood by another, is rightly regarded as a very rare cognitive ability, because it presupposes that one bird can 'read' the state of mind and intention of another, something that was always thought to be a uniquely human attribute. An intentional and symbolic act, such as pointing, requires cognitive, even abstract abilities of the highest order (called theory of mind). Keas, the only mountain parrot in the world, are exclusively at home in New Zealand but are now thought to also be of Gondwanan origin (Chambers et al. 2001, Wright et al. 2008).

These glimpses into their behaviour and interactions show not only brain plasticity and complex cognition but also suggest that these traits had evolved in social interactions, were designed to promote communication and, in some species, such interactions took on identifiable meaning within the social unit. Indeed, such initially anecdotal observations were probably responsible for the hypothesis of social intelligence in birds, a hypothesis that has been tested ever since Dunbar (1998) first proposed it, largely referring to primates and humans. The social intelligence hypothesis posits that complex cognition and enlarged 'executive brains' evolved in response to the challenges associated with social complexity. The hypothesis has since been tested and discussed in relation to birds (Shultz and Dunbar 2010).

It is not only the large cockatoos and parrots that have remarkable features. It has increasingly emerged that some clades of songbirds, entirely 'modern' in origin (post the extinction events of 65 million years ago) have cognitive capacities on par with those of cockatoos and great apes, and can demonstrate them in vocal, social and problem-solving contexts (Olkowicz et al. 2016). Songbirds also offer researchers the opportunity to study song under natural conditions and assess its complexity, meaning and the memory required. Repertoire size may not be an indication of 'intelligence' per se (thinking of the lyrebird, for instance) but a large repertoire may well be evidence of a substantial memory. For instance, if an adult bird moves to another area and then adopts some elements of neighbour songs that its own repertoire did not contain to that point, we have evidence of brain plasticity.

Learning as an adult presupposes that the individual bird is a lifelong learner. Why dwell on this lifelong learning? The idea of vocal plasticity throughout adult life is a special gift that humans and only some bird species possess but few other classes of animals. Humans can learn a new language even in very advanced years and every budgerigar owner knows that their pet can pick up new words at any time in its life.

Brain plasticity does not seem to be related to life expectancy but those that have both vocal learning plasticity and large brains are all very long-lived species compared to birds in their own weight class without large brains. More generally, longevity seems to be broadly related to environmental factors because in almost all Australian native birds and birds in the tropics, on whichever continent they are, life expectancies are far higher than in birds of high latitude, and such climatic factors are of considerable importance.

Female song

It is perhaps strange for the modern and more egalitarian-minded reader to comprehend that, for a long time, almost none of the research on birdsong included female song. No great attempt was made until recently to investigate female song and what the role of their song might be, and even when they do not sing, what the vocal communication might reveal (Langmore 1998). With the socially monogamous zebra finch, the pair incubates and raises its chicks jointly, but recently it was discovered that zebra finch pairs perform highly structured duets at the time of changeover of incubation duties and that duets change depending on delays of the partner to return to the nest. Boucaud and colleagues concluded in 2016 that zebra finch duets may function as 'vocal negotiation' over parental care. This goes well beyond earlier studies that generally identified duetting in other bird species either as a form of mate-guarding or as an expression of the quality of the pair bond, although it has now also been found that vocal duets can be used for deception (Ręk and Magrath 2017). Mahr and colleagues (2016) demonstrated this by studying the song of female common European blue tits, *Cyanistes caeruleus*, and showed that females use song not just in the context of choosing a partner or defending a territory but in the context of predators.

Among the Australian examples of duetting are the purple-crowned fairy-wren (Hall and Peters 2008; Boekel 2016), the chirruping wedge-bill, *Psophodes cristatus* (Austin et al. 2019), the Australian magpie (Brown and Farabaugh 1991), magpie larks, *Grallina cyanoleuca* (Hall and Magrath 2007, Ręk and Magrath 2016) and eastern whip-birds, *Psophodes olivaceus* (Rogers AC et al. 2006, 2007). What my own studies into Australian magpie song behaviour have shown clearly is that female vocal participation is not only equal to that of males, but the song repertoire of females tends to be slightly larger (Kaplan 2019). And, if I am not mistaken, female magpies are actually better mimics than males, with a wider variety of mimicked sounds. Still, the female's calls and song contributions have been rather understudied, cementing the view that female song was not important and relatively rare. Yet it has become very clear in the accumulated evidence of the last decades that vocal communication is vital for pair bonding and between bonded partners, and such vocal behaviour is also expressed in song. Indeed, convergence of partner behaviour is usually studied at the level of vocalisation (Luef et al. 2017).

Female song has begun to come under much closer scrutiny more recently. An extended study in 2014 by Odom and colleagues conducted a substantial survey and found that female song occurred in 32 out of 44 songbird families (a total of 229 species), while female song was absent in 19 families (94 species). Studies in the last five years or so have slowly unraveled the extent to which female song has been neglected or entirely ignored. Most people to this day think only the male superb lyrebird, *Menura novaehollandiae*, can sing and mimic. The female lyrebirds sing too and can mimic, perhaps not as spectacularly as males, but it means that a female lyrebird also has a song control system. Non-songbirds and females of some songbird species simply lack the HVC (one crucial vocal centre in the brain; see Fig. 2.1, page 31). We do not know to what extent or for what purpose her singing is designed and when the female might use her abilities although there are now some studies of territorial songbirds that have shown female–female vocal contests (Tobias et al. 2011).

Females of Australian species which have so far been identified as singers include the purple-crowned fairy-wren, *Malurus coronatus*, brown thornbills, *Acanthiza pusilla*, scarlet robins, *Petroica boodang*, grey butcherbirds, *Cracticus torquatus*; drongos, several fantails, many honeyeaters, pardalotes, whistlers and the corvids (Odom et al. 2014). This is quite a respectable list of female singers among native Australian species but we have next to nothing to link this to any findings in neuroscience or to assess levels of development (or presence of song nuclei and their connections) of the song control system, let alone any functional similarities or differences. We also do not know what functions their song might serve. We have very few studies of birdsong in Australian species that compare male to female song and even fewer that have investigated the neural preconditions for the production of song in species that have similar or different vocal abilities between the sexes, let alone their function.

Our laboratory examined the brains of female and male magpies in order to establish whether there were, in fact, sex differences at the level of brain organisation. We found none, other than a slight developmental difference (Deng et al. 2001). Females were fully developed in their song capacity earlier than males and, as my later research has shown, the song repertoire of females is slightly larger than that of males. Whatever typical songs waft through the bush and are heard in people's backyards, those of magpies and others can be sung by either a male or a female; both contribute to the melodious and beautiful sounds.

Importantly, Odom and colleagues have argued that song in females is ancestral. That may well mean that male and female songbirds once all had song. Given there can be no fossil evidence of song and behaviour, what if one speculated that when song began, both males and females sang and only thereafter, with changed circumstances, female song was made redundant in some cases? That is possible. It is worth remembering that all modern songbirds evolved in East Gondwana, now Australia, hence 'ancestral' refers to a long-standing history of songbird evolution on the Australian continent and carried to the rest of the world over many tens of thousands, even millions of years.

One of the reasons for female song loss may have been fostered by climatic circumstances. For example, the Ice Ages and especially their effect at high latitudes and the necessity for most animals to either find a way to hibernate or to migrate are each sufficient reason. Birds leaving Gondwana often found themselves in climate zones with sharp delineations of liveable and unliveable conditions. They would have been forced to speed up breeding preparations so substantially that, presumably, some shortcuts might have needed to be taken. Song certainly requires energy and it is not difficult to imagine that such energy could be more usefully and urgently employed in other and more vitally important functions (as survival is).

One may cite an interesting study by Sillet and Holmes (2002) of long-term adult survivorship in black-throated blue warblers, *Dendroica caerulescens*. Black-throated blue warblers breed in New Hampshire, USA and overwinter in Jamaica. It showed that far more males than females survived in New Hampshire but there were no differences in survival between the sexes in Jamaica. No doubt, sudden shortages of females in New Hampshire would increase the vigour with which males would sing to secure a mate while the female had plenty of choices. So, why should she sing? If song facilitates mate-choice and there is already a glut of males, she has no need for any negotiated social choice. In time, this may well lead to a gradual disappearance of female song. Although it is not known whether one can generalise this, there is some evidence for precise reasons why female song could be lost. Logue and Hall (2014) actually found that migratory behaviour is associated with loss of female song and duetting. Even more dramatic is the conclusion reached by Liker et al. (2013) in suggesting that an ongoing imbalance in the sex-ratio can lead to sex-role reversal (Liker et al. 2013). If females are spoilt for choice in mating partners, her need to sing may well be redundant.

In temperate zones, raising offspring that can migrate unaided in just two to four months from egg laying to setting out on the big journey to overwintering quarters is certainly living life in the fast lane and, no doubt, has substantial negative repercussions for learning and bonding, and perhaps even an impact on lifespan. In such tight timeframes for reproduction, it is easily conceivable that the entire mate-choice and mating rituals would have to be cut to an absolute minimum.

One could well imagine that, over time, song was pared back to shortcut communication and females would most likely need to conserve energy to produce eggs after long, exhausting flights. Of course, not all of this speculation is plucked out of thin air. A study by Price and colleagues (2009) found that female song in New World blackbirds, Icteridae, a family with both temperate and tropical representatives, was lost simply by changing from tropical to temperate breeding.

When male song is described as a reproductive behaviour, the reference is to the signals used in sexual selection, but such signal function may have nothing to do with overall repertoire. Males and females may still both sing despite a designated role for a specific courtship song (Price 2015). In some species in which song is important in mate-choice, good singers are chosen by females, but song is not neatly tied to song repertoire. As a paper by Byers and Kroodsma (2009) so eloquently pointed out, song repertoires have generally arisen not through selection for repertoire size per se, but rather as a by-product of social conditions that favoured the evolution of complex signalling systems. In other words, song repertoire may have little to do with a signal for sexual selection. If male and female both sing, one would more likely speak of social selection. This topic will be discussed in detail in Chapters 3 and 4. Suffice it to say there is plenty of evidence that some bird species have developed song into an art form, no more apparent than in the Australian magpie. Here, both males and females sing beautiful, elaborate songs at about the same rate, but the song is used neither in mate-choice nor in territorial defence.

In other species, it is not so much song but the development of vocal signals that can become as complex and meaningful as words are to humans. These are called referential signals because such calls may have very specific meaning and have become fixed or stereotyped calls that everybody, at least within the same species, understands (such as 'careful, eagle about'). Referential signals were first discovered in primates (Seyfarth et al.1980) but then began to be examined in birds as far apart in origin as chickens (Evans 1997) and ravens (Bugnyar et al. 2001). The usefulness of such calls can barely be disputed. It is a most efficient way of warning family members of danger and possibly even indicating what kind of danger it might be (terrestrial or aerial). It presupposes, however, that there is a sense of family or a group bond. In other words, some avian species have learned to communicate in complex ways, now well recognised in the relatively new research field of avian cognition. Our work on magpies has been able to confirm referential signalling in Australian magpies (Kaplan et al. 2009) and a recent study found that Torresian crows, *Corvus orru*, have more than 200 sounds, to the great surprise even of the researchers (McCaig et al. 2015), raising the question, so far unexplored, why they have so many different vocalisations and whether some of these might be referential.

Such vocal records take us away from sexual selection, because they tend to be aimed at social interactions and these, depending on social composition and pair bond, in some cases become very complex. There is a wealth of research opportunities for scientists to uncover what these communication systems are in Australian land birds (songbirds and parrots). The level of sophistication that may be involved in communicating has barely been explored apart from a handful of researchers whose work has clearly shown that vocal behaviour in Australian land birds is more sophisticated than ever thought.

Still, it is becoming clear that songs and calls of Australian birds may contain far more information than had been thought and complex vocalisations, simple or complex song included, have social functions. We already know that some Australian species among worldwide avian species vie for the position of having the largest brains – whether any of this has translated into or influenced vocal repertoire is not clear. From work on zebra finches, magpies, fairy-wrens and others, it appears that type and quality of social bonds have fostered a varied and complex level of communication. Vocal repertoire tends to evolve in specific ecological contexts and that too may determine how useful or necessary vocal expressions are.

High latitude and songbird studies

To clarify 'high latitude' and the distinction made between high and low latitude, Table 2.2 has been added here to show the range of latitudes both south and north of the equator for major cities of Australia and in the world, showing clearly that Australia's best efforts at high latitude in Melbourne and Tasmania are still just 40/42°. High latitudes refer to geographical locations with clear seasonal changes and cold winters with ice and snow. The higher the latitude (i.e. the lower the sun in winter), the colder it gets and the longer such cold conditions last – far north or south at very high latitude, ice conditions may last for seven months of the year. In Table 2.2, it can be clearly

Australian Mainland cities	Latitude	Longitude	Cities (Worldwide Comparison)	Latitude	Longitude
Darwin	12.4634 S	130.8456 E			
			Bangkok, SEA	13.7563 N	100.5018 E
Cairns	16.986 S	145.7781 E			
			Miami, NA	25.7617 N	80.1918 W
Brisbane	27.4698 S	153.0251 E	Durban, AF	29.8587 S	31.0218
Perth	31.9505 S	115.8605 E	Cairo, NAF	30.0444 N	31.2357
Sydney	33.8688 S	151.2093 E	Santiago, SA	33.4489 S	70.6692 W
			Los Angeles, NA	34.0522 N	118.2437 W
Adelaide	34.9285 S	138.6007 E	Buenos Aires, SA	34.6037 S	58.3816 W
			Tokyo, JAPAN	35.6895 N	139.6917 E
Auckland NZ	36.8485 S	174.7633 E	Gibralta, EU	36.1408 N	5.3536 W
Melbourne	37.8136 S	144.0631 E	Palermo, EU	38.1320 N	13.3356 E
			Beijing, CHINA	39.9042 N	116.4074 E
			New York, NA	40.7128 N	74.0060 W
			Istanbul, AM	41.0082 N	28.9784 E
			Rome, EU	41.9028 N	12.4964 E
Hobart	42.8821 S	147.3272 E			
Christchurch NZ	43.5321 S	172.6362 E	Toronto, NA	43.6532 N	79.3832 E
			Munich, EU	48.1351 N	11.5820 E
			Vienna, EU	48.2082 N	16.3738 E
			Paris, EU	48.8566 N	2.3522 E
			Vancouver, CA	49.2827 N	123.1207 W
			London, EU	51.5074 N	0.1278 W
			Amsterdam, EU	52.3702 N	4.8952 E
			Berlin, EU	52.5200 N	13.4050 E
Macquarie Island NZ	54.6208 S	158.855 E6	Ushuaia, SA	54.8019 S	68.3030 W
			Moscow, EU	55.7558 N	37.6173 E
			Edinburgh, EU	55.9533 N	3.1883 W
			Stromness, Orkneys, EU	58.9809 N	3.2965 W
			Helsinki, EU	60.1699 N	24.9384 E
			Anchorage, NA	61.2181 N–	21.8174 W
			Reykjavik, EU	64.1265 N–	149.9003 W

Table 2.2 Major cities: High and low latitudes – geographical overview.
Note that the coldest mainland city of Australia is at a latitude still well below that of most European, mainland Asian and North American cities. Low latitudes (whether in the southern or northern hemisphere) are between 0 (Equator) and 30° while reference to high latitude as a summary term in Europe refers to areas above 45°, although climate conditions in North America change nearer to 40°. NZ = New Zealand; SEA = South-East Asia; NA = North America; NAF = North Africa; AF = Africa; SA = South America; EU = Europe; AM = Asia Minor. Data are presented in chronological order of latitudes, regardless of hemisphere.

seen that mainland Australia is not located in any of the high latitude regions of 45–70°, hence the reference to high latitude is a shortcut and refers to the fact that countries such as Canada, the northern USA, and all European countries are located in high-latitude areas. The very southern and warmest climate tip of Europe, Gibraltar, is comparable to the most southern mainland, coldest climate city in Australia, Melbourne. Unless we cast our eye to the islands south and southeast, including Tasmania, Australian latitudes just do not compare with those at which most people and birds live in the northern hemisphere. It is in these high latitudes that birds have been studied more than anywhere else. While we may well think that Macquarie Island is a cold and windy place, it is at about the same latitude as Moscow, and the capital cities of Scandinavia are situated at even higher latitude and thus are colder with long winters. The USA ranges also into subtropical regions and the southern end of South America reaches well into the southern cold high latitudes. For studies of wildlife, these are variables of considerable importance. If one simply took high latitude results at face value and compared them to results in Australian bird studies, it would likely result in discordant or even misleading results.

While song and perching are common to all songbirds, their life histories are as different as can be. For instance, how long birds live seems to be partially dependent on climate or altitude and food sources.

The point is that the bulk of field studies conducted on songbird song has largely been conducted in high-latitude environments, where seasonality is a major influencing factor in bird behaviour and thus may raise different issues. Low-latitude birds tend to have extended breeding seasons, for example, live longer, and there is even a latitudinal bias in the diversification rates of passerines (greater in low latitudes; Cardillo 1999).

Of course, longitude also matters, particularly in a continent such as Australia. As a paper by Karubian (2013) about female ornaments in fairy-wrens pointed out, latitude cannot account for longitudinal and altitudinal variation. One look at east coast Australia shows how significantly environments can change within a few degrees of longitude difference. Take a lush subtropical coastal environment and move westwards across the Great Dividing Range, and the trees give way to open grasslands, even at the same latitude, offering profoundly different ecological conditions which may well affect song and breeding patterns.

Australian cockatoos, parrots and parakeets are not songbirds, of course, but it is important to note here that all of them tend to be vocally impressive both in the range of sounds they can produce and in their exceptional ability to mimic sounds from the environment. In captivity, they are past masters in mimicry of human speech, are lifelong learners and live to ages that often humans can barely rival.

What is remarkable about Australian birds is that the lifespan from the smallest to the largest songbird tends to be more often than not from two to four times longer than that of similar weight classes of birds in high latitudes. Long lifespan has thus not transferred generally to songbirds elsewhere in the world, at least not uniformly so. Why should this be so? It is puzzling. It is partly this question that has spurred me on to investigate further and ask about the life history of Australian land birds.

To return to the gift of songbirds and parrots that evolved and speciated in these low latitudes of the southern hemisphere: in this remarkable process, vocal learning and communication in birds also evolved. Who knows how exactly vocal learning proceeded and how it expanded, but contained in the vocal behaviour of Gondwanan songbirds may well be all the possible signal characteristics and functions that one finds generally in songbirds today.

Nowicky and Searcy (2014) outlined five different hypotheses on the selective benefits that they saw as leading to the evolution of vocal learning. One has to do with basic mate-choice ('you sound like me', leading to what is called assortative matings), called the local dialect hypothesis. Another concerns female mate-choice based on the ability of males to expand their repertoire and so be able to compete more effectively against other contenders (the sexual selection hypothesis). And then there is the social dimension of information sharing (the third hypothesis) and finally, as the pinnacle of vocal learning, the ability to recognise individuals by their vocal signature alone, leading to enhanced social interaction and complex systems of vocal communication (individual recognition hypothesis) that, furthermore, were attuned to their environment and ensured reliable transmission (environmental adaptation hypothesis).

Those processes, no doubt, have developed and endured because of the benefits they bestowed on a species. A more effective signalling is said to have increased the survival of individuals and of kin, ensured better mating success, and enhanced social interactions – altogether making vocal learning a very significant part both of mate-choice and of cognitive development in birds and in the few other groups of vocal learners, chief among them humans.

3

Mating systems and sexual selection

There is a view of nature, continuously promoted in documentaries, that it is ruthless, shameless, without rules and brutal. Nothing could be further from the truth. Nature is entirely rule-governed for plants and animals, even though climate and environmental conditions may impose occasional chaotic events. Elaborate protocols are in place even for fights and competitions among animals. A fight to the death may occur on a one-to-one basis, but such instances are rare, confined to equally matched males and largely to carnivores. Warfare, and the resulting chaos, killings and wanton destruction, is almost entirely reserved for humans, although intentional warfare has been discovered in chimpanzees too (Wrangham and Peterson 1996, Kaplan 2019b). Even in a very competitive species, such as the male capercaillie, *Tetrao urogallus*, a large black bird the size of a turkey, the largest in the family of grouse, fights between two males tend to be combative only to a certain point, then the two opponents part company, both still very much alive. Among birds, competing for a mate, at least in most Australian land birds, is rarely done by two males fighting, rather in some cases by males individually serenading the female.

This is a much gentler paradigm than we find in carnivores and many mammals, such as ungulates and kangaroos.

This and later chapters intend to turn around the argument about competitive routines as the basic motivation and driving force in evolution and in mate-choice. The plan is to slowly assemble enough evidence chapter by chapter to be able to make this very opposite argument: partnering in many Australian land birds is first and foremost a gentle, non-combative process and it may even be a cognitively and emotionally complex process.

Much of what has been written on mate-choice in birds is about species in which the female is the one doing the choosing and the male is the one advertising himself and displaying. This female mate-choice, as it is called, may lead to partnerships or may in fact result in sole parenting by the female. The international literature on female mate-choice is very substantial and has shown that specific vocal phrases, elements in dances or plumage displays, and sometimes just the degree of brightness of plumage, decides which males will be chosen by the female. Again, the impression is often given that this is the major model for sexual selection.

However, in many species it may not just be about the patches, colour, trills or song length displayed by the male but about gaining trust and, even more importantly, about compatibility and reliability, perhaps even about competence and confidence, especially in species that potentially bond for life. Who is to say that the evolution of birds in Australia has not been a continuous revision of an improved exercise in a system thriving on cooperation? Cooperation and stability may be the key for entire branches of birds, loosely grouped as the corvida and cockatoos. A surprising number of Australian birds have reaped the rewards of long and healthy lives and these outcomes are not always even related to reproduction.

Finally, to establish a context of mate-choice, it is also important to reinforce a point that is all too often overlooked, namely that not all birds have mates and not all reproduce. Indeed, one of the longest held myths about birds, and animals in general, is the belief that the life-cycle automatically includes reproduction. It does not. Indeed, a large number of individual birds never achieve reproductive status. They never mate, never have a brood of young to rear, never own a territory, and never defend a nest site. They are either not successful or die well before these processes could come into play or may well end up as itinerants and, in some cases, as sentinels or helpers but not as parents. In magpies, we know that there may be as few as 6–14 per cent of a given magpie population that actually breeds in any given year (Kaplan 2019a).

The minority of birds that are reproductive therefore raise a multitude of questions. Why do these ones breed at all and others do not, and what determines which ones succeed? What are, in fact, the processes by which breeders raise offspring that will again generate one or more breeders? What is different about individuals or pairs that not only successfully raise one brood, but a series of broods over a lifetime?

The male/female roles in finding a mate (mating systems)

The reproductive system and mate-choice systems are two different things. One model of reproduction, already mentioned, is 'anyone happening to come by will do' (the undifferentiated), or another 'anyone still standing is accepted' (pre-selected after intense competition). We have plenty of examples of the latter in mammals, as in seals, ungulates and kangaroos, for instance. Strong males fight each other and the ultimate winner can copulate with the entire female group. The females take little interest in the fights or who wins. At times, the challenges to the dominant males are so severe that, at the end of the rutting season, some male deer that have spent their time mating and fighting actually die from exhaustion, starvation and/or injuries. The females live together in loose aggregations while the males remain at the margin or roam on their own. In some cases, this maintains a matriarchy, as in elephants. They are often discussed under the rubric of fission–fusion societies, discussed at length in primates, elephants and bats as temporary associations with stable sub-groups and individuals splitting off such groups (Ramos-Fernández et al. 2014). In other mammals, from kangaroos to ungulates, from hippos to seals, one male rules over a group of females and is responsible for fertilising them all, as long as his status remains unchallenged. Only a very small percentage of avian species has a system of servicing most females in one area, but even in such cases, the males do not assume the role of male protector or consort.

But this is not what the topic mate-choice in birds is about. There are no beach masters among Australian birds, as there are in elephant seals. Mate-choice, as the word implies, involves choice; by the female, or by the male, or choice can be mutual.

The biology of mate-choice models is rather bewildering. Sexual selection, after natural selection, is central to evolution, as Darwin discovered. It is called sexual selection because either the male or the female does the choosing, although potential partners may have to meet some basic requirements and quality. The 'quality' usually includes health of a bird but, as West-Eberhard (2014) reminded us, 'health' is part of natural, not sexual selection. Male presentation of song, plumage, or dance are usually identified as the main criteria for a female's choice. I have always wondered whether these identifiers are adequate enough or even the most relevant ones in the dating agencies for birds.

Sexual dimorphism indicates that differences between male and female size or plumage are apparent and some have developed into exaggerated and significantly different attributes in order for males to stand out and secure a female. Since Darwin, sexual selection has been seen as a major driver in evolution. Darwin (1890, 1891) argued that mate-choice was the second most important variable for survival after other processes of natural selection had been taken into account. And since birds largely form partnerships, at the very least for the duration of raising offspring but often for the long haul, the way they get together and on what grounds is of enduring interest.

The territorial mate-choice system

The territorial system may include birds that do not form pair bonds and females raise offspring on their own, as in bowerbirds, or may lead to partial parenting as in polygynous species, or might include seasonal or long-term pair bonding. Despite substantial differences between territorial birds in mating systems, what territorial land birds and territorial songbirds have in common is that individual characteristics of male and female are less important than securing a territory that provides vital resources.

The concept of territoriality has generally been subdivided into six physical categories, ranging from wintering grounds, (non-breeding) all-purpose areas, to mere roosting sites. Colonially breeding birds usually maintain a nesting territory, a small area around the nest that is considered to belong to a breeding pair. Food source protection may often be the single most important reason for a home range or territory, as in hummingbirds and honeyeaters.

In a lekking system, a male will defend a display area called a lek. The lekking area is usually strictly defended and regarded as off-limits to other males, although some lekking birds tend to assemble in the same general area so that females can walk leisurely from one to another to assess the males' performances. Here males sing or strut and have display areas, be this on the ground, such as lyrebirds displaying on the forest floor, the bustard in open landscapes, on the water, such as musk duck males, *Biziura lobate*, splashing loudly while whistling and grunting (Fullagar and Carbonell 1986). Victoria's riflebirds, *Ptiloris victoriae*, display on branches making dazzling dance movements (Frith and Cooper 1996) or, on the plains, the less graceful Australian bustard, *Ardeotis australis*, displays feathers by expansion of the throat sac (called gular skin in birds) and fluffs himself up, which makes him look larger. These displays are certainly very demonstrative (Fig. 3.1).

In lek polygyny, males provide no parental care to their offspring and mating events are uniquely driven by the females' pursuit and

Fig. 3.1 The Australian (or Kori) bustard male during his lekking display will raise his feathers on the neck and the incredibly flexible gular skin stretches almost to the ground and can then be dangled from side to side. Left: normal feather position (photo G. Kaplan). Right: during a mating display performance (photo courtesy of malurus17, IBC1038996. Accessible at hbw.com/ibc/1038996).

choice. The lek mating system is widespread among vertebrates and found in fishes and mammals as well.

The two most often studied territorial systems are those that provide resources and room to raise offspring.

One type of territory is seasonally defined and thus short-term, established for breeding purposes and may have to be won or a different one found in each breeding season, as occurs in the superb fairy-wren, *Malurus cyaneus*. In northern latitudes, the relationship between mate-choice and territoriality has been studied quite extensively (often of the seasonal kind).

The other type of territoriality is gaining and defending an all-year-round territory and settling in it as a permanent residence in which all needs are provided, including the necessary resources to raise offspring, not just for a given year but possibly for a lifetime. In tropical and Australian regions, permanent territoriality is a pronounced feature.

Regardless as to whether a territory is seasonal or all-year-round, females in both systems tend not to choose males directly or by any of their physical attributes, but select a male that holds a territory to her liking. In North America marsh-wrens, *Cistothorus palustris*, for instance, an incoming female is prepared to share a male with another female as long as she can stay in the territory (Leonard and Picman 1988).

Thus, neither in seasonal or in year-round territorial birds may mate-choice be directly related to specific attributes explicable by appearance, song or plumage of the male. The female will first and foremost choose the territory. If she assesses that the plot is good and good food sources are on offer, she will settle there even if the male already has a mate. In the fiery-throated hummingbird, *Panterpe insignis*, of Costa Rica and Panama, the female will go where the nectar-producing flowers are that are to her liking. The female thus selects the territories on the basis of the best food source rather than the attractiveness of the male.

Many Australian honeyeaters are also strictly territorial in the protection of their food sources (Ford 1981). Two of the most vigorous defenders of such food sources are far apart in size but use the same defensive tactics and uncompromising attacks, such as the large red wattlebird, *Anthochaera carunculate*, and the very small brown honeyeaters, *Lichmera indistincta*. Noticeably, both species are monomorphic in plumage.

The best studied of the year-round Australian territorial birds are the Australian magpies, *Gymnorhina tibicen* (Kaplan 2019a), and the superb fairy-wren, *Malurus cyaneus* (Schodde 1982). Both species are or, in magpies, may be, cooperative breeders and defend year-round territories, at least in pairs but usually in groups varying between three to five individuals or even more. Both species are socially monogamous and sexually promiscuous as DNA research in either species has found (magpies: Hughes et al. 2003; superb fairy-wrens: Mulder 1997; Cockburn et al. 2016; Brouwer et al. 2017).

Yet magpies and wrens are as different as chalk and cheese in other and important ways. Apart from the obvious size differences (Fig. 3.2), their mating games are entirely different. In most of the wren species, the males change plumage spectacularly for the breeding season when, in superb fairy-wren males, the inconspicuous brown and buff plumage changes into bright blue areas around the head and at the nape of the neck. Even the tail feathers become a brighter blue. In addition, the males may even use ornaments to add to their courtship display. These may be flower petals (Rowley 1991) or, as I observed, small leaves, preferably bright yellow, that the males may carry in their beaks – whatever enhances the colour palette. The male's displays invite females to choose him for a mating even if she already has a partner. However, while sexual dimorphism is pronounced in wrens,

Fig. 3.2 Magpie on the left and a male superb fairy-wren in breeding plumage on the right. The crown on the head and the patch on the cheeks as well as the small strip on the nape of the neck are bright blue. The tail is upright, typical for all wren species, including the grasswren mentioned in Chapter 1.

there are also males that mate with their females before the seasonal change of plumage, and these males are almost indistinguishable from females.

By contrast, magpies have no elaborate courtship rituals. Indeed, they do not have any discernible ritual at all and in all the years I have studied them, I have only seen the arrival of one female in a male's territory once, followed by the briefest glance of the male at her before he resumed foraging. She could stay.

In the case of magpies, the female may arrive in a territory and the mate-choice may seem almost incidental (Kaplan 2019). Whether this holds true generally of magpies can still not be determined because such instances have rarely been observed. What can be said with certainty is that magpie males do not display. There is relatively little difference between males and females in their black and white plumage (in most eastern subspecies) and no changes occur in plumage colour or plumage patterns in the male or female at breeding times. In fact, when it comes to the mating event, the female has to draw attention to her readiness to mate by engaging in a full solicitation display. Such a display involves crouching on a wide branch and moving her tail in a figure of eight and, given that her tail is black and white, these fast movements can actually be seen as flashes of light (Kaplan 2019a). It is also known that magpies are long-lived, often form lifelong bonds and have been shown to have remarkable cognitive abilities.

Hence there is a substantial group of birds in which the female may not judge direct attributes of a future partner but instead the property and access to food sources he has secured. Of course, territory ownership in itself might be a strong indicator of male quality. It is not an easy task to keep it and may require experience, constant vigilance and determination to avoid losing such a resource.

Generally, in this entire group of territorial birds defending food sources and a larger territory, sex differences in song and/or plumage are not always highly developed or do not matter as much as the territorial conditions.

Or perhaps one should argue that in territorial birds, it may be futile to look for emotionality in the bonds. Here the well-functioning bonds that will work efficiently in the face of danger demand qualities that we would term reliance or integrity. A territorial group may be likened to team players and a good long-lasting bond is one that is experienced in collaboration, revealing a time-efficient and most effective manner in which relevant vocalisations, warning manoeuvres and relevant actions are carried out. This has been studied in detail in the Australian magpie lark, in some areas of Australia also known as the peewee or mudlark. Magpie larks are fiercely territorial and pairs duet, which

Fig. 3.3 The brown honeyeater, *Lichmera indistincta*, defends both its food source as well as its breeding territory. It occupies the same breeding territory each year and is a very feisty bird, despite its size. Like the tiny eastern spinebill, *Acanthorhynchus tenuirostris*, it also has a surprisingly powerful voice.

has led Hall and Magrath (2007) to conclude that such duets reveal the strength of the bond. In other words, the quality and consistency in cooperative behaviour become a lynchpin for survival, as Hall and Peters (2008) also found in duetting fairy-wrens, notwithstanding other possible functions of such vocal duetting (Dahlin and Benedict 2014).

One might at least note that in year-round territorial species, in which extra-pair matings seem to be particularly high (shown in magpies and in superb fairy-wrens), banking on good team efforts may well be enough for bonds to last but not enough to engender partial or full fidelity. One might propose a new hypothesis that emphasis on external factors, rather than individual personality factors, is offset by decreasing personal commitment to the partnership.

Sexual selection – female choice

In many songbirds, especially of high latitudes, finding a mate largely revolves around sexual selection by song and/or plumage displays. Such displays may either be reflected in male–male competitions in vying for females and/or, more often, in female choice of males with characteristics that research has established to be particularly important to the female.

There is plenty of evidence that a trill in a song or a colour patch in the plumage or a particular style of display may be deciding factors in a female's mate-choice. Male displays are often spectacular, as they certainly are in the birds of paradise in New Guinea or in their relative, Victoria's riflebird, *Ptiloris victoriae*.

These displays are certainly worthy of our attention, but they cannot give us an answer to the question about what mechanisms may be at work for pair bonds and long-term partnerships.

Bowerbirds are a family of birds (Ptilonorhynchidae) that also evolved without any commitment to raising offspring. Eight species occur only in Australia while ten species are endemic to New Guinea and two species occur in both nations. Remarkably, the mate-choice game in this ancient lineage leads to males turning dancers, architects and artists. As already mentioned, satin bowerbirds may build bowers, as do the other species of bowerbirds, often using elaborate decorations and using their voices like percussion instruments.

In the regent bowerbird, *Sericulus chrysocephalus*, I bore witness to a behaviour that, to my knowledge, has so far not been described in the literature, and differs from other bowerbirds in the emphasis of the male's advertisements. A paper on the bower activities had noted that the male does not actually stay near the bower but was found escorting a female to the bower from the direction of the canopy of a tree nearby or next to the bower, but did not discover the reason for the male's frequent absences from the bower (Lenz 1994). Nor could such absences be explained by observing the bower. As I discovered, there is a reason for the male leaving the bower unattended: the male's main drawcard to attract a female is actually a dance and a very unusual one at that. The display I witnessed took place on the vertical tree trunk, not on a branch nor near the bower. I watched the male running up and down a good part of the trunk at a height of at least 8 metres off the ground and with carefully placed little sideway steps. The bird was moving at an incredible speed and doing so up and down sideways (!) so that his body was at an almost right angle to the tree, his head firmly turned upwards towards the canopy. For seconds at a time, some branches partially obscured the bird, but it suddenly made sense why male regent bowerbirds have such stark contrasting black and bright yellow plumage. From a distance, the fast movements looked as if the wind or a passing cloud had suddenly allowed brief moments of bright sunshine into the forest. At other parts of the display, the bright yellow flashed during the quick up-and-down and willy wagtail–like tail movement, resulting in an action similar to a flashlight with pulsing on-off signals. Among birding friends, someone recalled seeing the flashing of yellow feathers in a near horizontal branch but had not given this any further thought. For the first time, it became clear how the male's striking plumage could be turned into a great visual asset

(Fig. 3.4). Against the background of a solid dark tree and heavily barked trunk, the yellow-black contrasting wings flicked slightly and looked spectacular. This could be seen from a good distance away – at least to 50 metres (my observational position was about 20 metres).

Only after this performance was over did he fly to the canopy, where a female was watching, and then he enticed her to follow him to his bower on the ground. Frankly, his bower was a disappointment to see: the decorations were sparse and the bower itself basic. Regent bowerbirds may occasionally decorate the bower with fruit

Fig. 3.4 Regent bowerbird. The light areas of the plumage on neck and wings are a bright, rich yellow. The rest of the body is black, the beak an orange-red and the eyes too are a bright yellow. This image was taken in northern New South Wales during the breeding season. The male is picking an unripe fruit from a wild tobacco tree (*Solanum mauritianum*), an introduced noxious plant: unripe fruit are highly toxic and can even kill pigs. However, this bird was not feeding on it but taking it back to the bower for decoration.

and other colourful objects, but because they tend to stay away from the bower for a good deal of time, objects may be stolen by competitors. It is also possible that the most remarkable attribute of regent bowerbirds, their ability to 'paint' the bower, has evolved because such decorations cannot be stolen. They may be among the few birds worldwide that use something akin to a paintbrush to decorate or paint their bower from the inside and such paints stay on (Kaplan 2015b).

Most bowerbirds are exceptional in some way. For great bowerbirds, *Chlamydera nuchalis* (Fig. 3.5), for instance, Kelley and Endler (2012) provided compelling evidence that bower design is anything but random, especially in key features. Their bower decorations involve optical illusions by using the size of pebbles, stones, perhaps some bones and some glass in specific ways. Males arrange the size of the pebbles in the order opposite to expected depth perception. Pebbles could be arranged willy-nilly without any attention given to the size of the pebbles, i.e. they were just decoration. Kelley and Endler showed, however, that these bowerbird males are very aware of both size of pebbles and visual perception of distance. Pebbles will generally appear smaller when further away unless manipulated in certain ways. The males place the smallest pebbles in front of the entrance of the bower and the largest pebbles at the end of the bower, creating a visual illusion, referred to as 'forced perspective'. The researchers tested this by rearranging pebbles and removing the effect of the illusion and found that, in each case, the bird not only spotted the changes made but at once proceeded to put the pebbles back into place for full effect of the visual illusion. It is 'forced' because visual expectations and experience would indicate that pebbles should appear smaller when further away. Clearly, as discussed elsewhere in some detail (Kaplan 2015b) each individual male actively maintains his design features. The task of the female is to assess which design is more surprising, effective or original and, one could argue, that it would take some cognitive ability in the female to identify the best design. The question is whether she is being tricked or whether the female has the cognitive ability to recognise and/or appreciate what the male was trying to achieve. But, as mentioned before, bowerbirds do not form pairs, hence female choice of best bower may only indirectly suggest that females choose the cleverest and most original (Day et al. 2005).

These and similar cases of demonstrative male displays have been studied for many decades in a never-ending fascination with the choreography, plumage use, colour or virtuosity of song and the dramatic effects of male dance performance, swinging flight feathers and revealing colours that flash in dappled light.

The female choice hypothesis argues that females will respond more to a male if he is brightly coloured, or builds the best bower,

Fig. 3.5 The great bowerbird, *Chlamydera nuchalis*, at home in the top end of Australia, builds one of the cognitively most interesting bowers by using forced perspective. It is, apart from the New Guinean golden bowerbird that builds huge edifices, actually also the largest of the bowers of all bowerbirds. It is nearly twice the length of bowers of other bowerbirds, presumably as it needs more length of passage in order to achieve a depth perspective and the effects that the male designed, and it is also thicker.

performs the best dance or sings the best song. This selection process, in turn, is said to have fostered greater and greater exaggeration of those features to which females seemed particularly attracted, be this the colour, a particular display performance or a song, magnifying specific features of sexual dimorphisms over time. Sometimes the males have such exaggerated features that they become a handicap, as in the case of the peacock's train (Zahavi and Zahavi, 1997).

Indeed, in some species males have evolved into doing incredible and clever things. And the question is what the females may need to know to make decisions about who is the appropriate ('the best') mating partner. There are two notable biases in sexual selection studies that still linger. One is the admiration for the beauty of a male (against the supposedly 'drab' female) and the other is the lack of investigation about the female's abilities to make choices that are meant to be incontrovertibly the best choices.

Let us just assume that the female chooses a male with the most beautiful song, even when she does not sing at all or only rarely or only at a reduced rate compared to the male. Is she really 'mute' and ignorant (Riebel 2003) and can she afford to be? What does this tell us about her? When one attends Eisteddfods and music auditions, the scene is set for the learning and budding musicians to be judged by a panel of adjudicators invariably consisting of established and experienced musicians within their field. Does one need to ask who knows more: the judges or the competitors? This seems an almost silly question but in the flurry of excitement of claims that avian males are more beautiful, more accomplished, bigger and better overall, the researchers literally forgot to ask (over decades) how the females could be judges unless they had some gifts and even special talents themselves. Research has well documented that females readily reject suitors and may search for a good while before they give consent to mate.

The displays so far described are male displays leaving the female to choose. However, there are also many mutual displays of prospective partners, in which both partners display in ritualised movements and dances, as will be discussed in more detail in the next chapter.

It is worth stressing here that these specific characteristics of males displaying and females choosing (but raising offspring alone) make up just three per cent of birds worldwide. It is these three per cent about which so much of the literature on mate-choice as a process of sexual selection has been based. Hence, it is extremely irritating to read as late as 2013 that, 'In most cases, males will be the larger, more colourful sex, and females will be the smaller, more drab sex' (Gammie 2013). This is patently wrong because such statements, though not unusual, suggest a majority of males, not three per cent, have special and noteworthy qualities that the females apparently 'lack'. Indeed, most texts on birds as late as the 1990s suggested or implied that avian males, in general, are more beautiful, more active, more accomplished (in song for instance), stronger or bigger and more aggressive than females, a view that was increasingly challenged (Van de Pitte 1998).

In recent years, some researchers have actually looked across the spectrum of songbirds (not a small undertaking since the category 'songbirds' has over 10,000 species in the IOC World List) and found, as was already discussed in Chapter 2, that in many species of songbirds, females also sing and often their retention of song from ancestral times may have functions that have barely been explored (Odom et al. 2014).

The claim that males are distinctly better and bigger 'in most cases' is a myth and is even more irrelevant with reference to Australian birds. This will be raised in different ways in the coming chapters, certainly when discussing plumage colours.

Identifying mating systems might help to put such assumptions into perspective. One is polyandry, the mating of one female with more than one male while each male will mate only with one female. This system is not accompanied by specific ornamentation or plumage colour statements of one sex or another. This system is found mostly in shore and waterbirds, as is the case in comb-crested jacanas, *Irediparra gallinacea*, also known as the lotus bird, at home in most wetlands across Australia. The male not only broods the eggs by himself, but also provides all post-hatching care. However, polyandry is a rare mating system and practised in less than one per cent of all bird species (and has seemed less attractive to study). Another system is called polygyny, a system in which the males will mate with several females, but without any guarantee that he will help at all in raising the offspring.

Female-only care arises in families where re-mating opportunities are apparently abundant for both sexes, whereas male-only care tends to arise in families where re-mating opportunities are rare for both sexes and particularly scarce for males. This in turn suggests that sex differences in re-mating opportunities are among the key ecological factors in determining male-only care and classical polyandry in birds.

These issues of one-parent care models have been described in so much detail here basically just to remove these from further debate. As mentioned before, the vast majority of birds have opted for bi-parental or even extended family care.

Sexual dimorphism

Having put these one-parent models aside, we can address the issue of pair-formation. Bonding may be for a season or longer, or even for a lifetime. Sexual dimorphism has been key in discussing mate-choice as a choice for females, an aspect of Darwin's theory of sexual selection that contemporaries found very objectionable.

In most Australian land birds, males and females are the same or nearly the same size. There are exceptions. Among most birds of prey (eagles, falcons, hawks, kites and owls) the female is larger and heavier than the male. In Australian wedge-tailed eagles, *Aquila audax*, which pair for life and tend to remain in the same territory, females may weigh nearly twice as much as males. Small adult males may weigh about 3 kg while the largest female that I have ever rehabilitated weighed in at just over 5.6 kg. The male would lose a fight with a female. Presumably, the size difference might be particularly pronounced in cases where males might be reluctant to return any quarry to the nest.

In the great frigate bird, *Fregata minor*, which frequents the coast of eastern and tropical Australia, females are also larger and heavier than males, and the male sports the highly visible red gular skin that is inflatable and used like a vocal instrument when females are trying to select a suitable mate (Fig. 3.6). There may be other reasons why size difference between the sexes, in this case the female, is large. Trefry and Diamond (2017) recently tested two possible hypotheses, one,

Fig. 3.6 Female great frigate bird, equipped with a massive beak and sharp tip. She is normally found on the nest (left image) with male (insert), the large, non-inflated gular skin fold under the beak clearly visible. This individual female had suffered a minor wing injury, was dehydrated and starving, and was treated back to health. Feeding this bird was an interesting exercise. The versatility of its neck was so great that approaching it from behind received the same powerful beak snap treatment as approaching from any other direction. Each response was at the speed of lightning. In the end, I used the tongs one can purchase for catching snakes, with a separate grip for opening and closing a metre away. The tongs look a little like a beak and the bird readily took the fish offerings from then on and fully recovered. It was released where it had been found.

the traditional perspective of intersexual competition, while the other concerned their method of hunting and stealing food from other birds (kleptoparasitism). They found no link between size dimorphism and intersexual competition but a very plausible link between the way frigate birds procure food (chasing other birds and snatching food mid-flight) and the males' smaller size. Frigate birds have to catch fish but have lost the ability to waterproof their feathers and would get seriously waterlogged and possibly even drown if they tried taking fish from below the surface of the ocean. Their adaptation to this contradiction has been to evolve hunting skills in the air and take from other fish-catching birds what they are mostly no longer able to get for themselves. As an aerial hunter, the frigate bird needs to acquire airspeed and it is of advantage for it to be of light weight. Even the wings of the male frigate are adapted, being narrower than those of the female for greater manoeuvrability, enabling the male to carry out sharp turns in the air. This is a clear example showing how alternative explanations make more sense than blanket assumptions about competition between males, or males and females. Competition between males does occur in this species but it is for nest sites and well before females arrive to inspect. The motivation to adapt here is clearly not solely related to sexual selection but to food acquisition.

Plumage colour and pattern differences are considered the other important markers of sexual selection but here there is a clear overlap with natural selection. Many researchers have found that levels of dichromatism are positively associated with breeding latitudes or other ecological factors (Price and Eaton 2014) as Alfred Wallace, Darwin's contemporary, argued in 1889. It is known that some species become more colourful the closer they get to the equator (Karubian 2013) and male/female differences in plumage evolution may also occur (Johnson et al. 2013).

When males are more colourful or differently patterned than females, noting that this actually applies only to a relatively small range of avian species in Australian native land birds, usually two conditions apply: the nest may have to be situated in relatively exposed terrain and the female alone incubates the eggs. Mostly, the two conditions function together. Obviously, it is of great advantage for the female to be camouflaged from predators by being small and/or inconspicuous. In species that manage to largely conceal their nest, male and female plumage cover is usually identical (independent of whether parenting is shared).

In nocturnal species, both male and female are usually equally feathered in grey, brown or buff tones, as seen in nightjars (including tawny frogmouths) and owls. Some patterning may be different (horizontal bars versus vertical strobes, for instance, between the juvenile and adult powerful owl).

There is another colour variation that has nothing to do with sexual dimorphism and this is exemplified in a number of species, such as in wedge-tailed eagles, little eagles, *Hieraaetus morphnoides*, or in shorebirds such as the eastern reef egret, *Ardea sacra*, that comes in two morphs, a grey and white form (Fig. 3.7). In most cases of different morphs, subspecies status has been assigned but those may interbreed.

Fig. 3.7 Eastern reef egrets freely form pairs regardless of morph. Male or female may be of grey or white morph. The image of this pair was taken on Heron Island.

In 1997, after decades of research on sexual dimorphism and mate-choice, Jennions and Petrie concluded that sexual-selection studies have paid far less attention to variation among females than to variation among males, and that there is still much to learn about how females choose males and why different females make different choices. Increasingly, it seems, one might also need to discuss mutual social choices and signals, even if oblique at times, that may provide valuable information about the prospective partner. Age as a factor has often been ignored (peak- versus low-performance years).

Social systems and flocking

Regardless of the primary mating system (polyandry, polygyny, social pair bonding, or sole parenting), very few birds go it alone. Some large shorebirds may, most hunters (birds of prey) and some of the flightless birds do, but most live in a group. The minimum size is two (dyads), and such dyads are the most common form of long-term social arrangements in birds. However, many of these paired birds may keep their offspring for some years. In addition, under certain circumstances, they may also join flocks, sometimes for gatherings and sometimes on a more regular or prolonged basis when the surrounding landscape may be unfamiliar (in overwintering cases), when predator numbers are high, or, routinely, when birds travel in the Australian outback.

In the outback, it is very rare to see just two birds flying along. The outback is a dangerous environment with a high number of aerial predators. In addition, there is the problem of searching for and finding waterholes, especially when known waterholes have dried up. This need to find water may temporarily make individual social units join with larger groups (Fig. 3.8). There is some evidence, at least in studies of homing pigeons, that more birds are more accurate in finding their goal than single birds (Hamilton 1967, Tamm 1980). In dire situations, such as droughts, flocks of corellas and of cockatoos may number in

Fig. 3.8 Corellas in a tree. Large gum trees are very valuable resources. Here, flocks can congregate, rest, interact and, where possible, avoid the heat. Such trees also offer protection from predators. Pairs usually roost next to each other. In many species, it leads to finding a mate and breeding at remote locations and such extraordinary events may then also offer opportunities for long-term bonding.

their thousands in a joint, often desperate attempt to survive. They will all willingly share a waterhole without competition and descend wherever there is the promise of a food source.

These large numbers are often mistaken as a sign that such species are plentiful, even a glut, but this is not true. Birds may fly hundreds, if not thousands, of kilometres and their convergence from all over the inland in flocks is a sign of urgency and even panic. Increasingly, the environment may exert an additional toll that even the combined intelligence and memory of better sites cannot counteract as a result of climate change. The inland may now have prolonged heatwaves in the high forties and even low fifties Centigrade and the effects of such temperatures may be death or exhaustion to a point where they can no longer reach coastal areas and more bearable weather.

A positive consequence of flocking is that the combined memory of large numbers of individuals may lead to the discovery and availability of water for drinking, feeding and breeding. Similar principles apply in herding mammals, such as wildebeest or elephants. In elephants, it is largely the memory and experience of the matriarch alone that guides the group to water (Poole 1997). In birds, it may be that a multitude of memories of different individuals may achieve the same

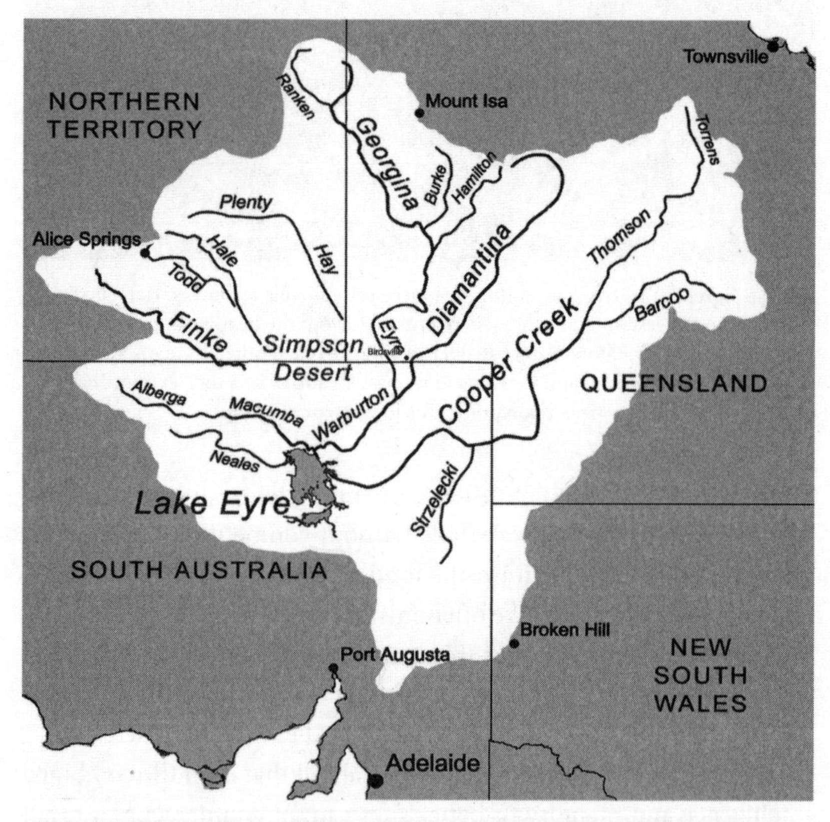

Fig. 3.9 The Lake Eyre Basin (light area) and its river system. The huge rivers of the Diamantina and Cooper from the east supply fresh water but in boom years, even the Hale, Plenty and Todd rivers from the Northern Territory may link up and so may the Neales and Macumba rivers flow into Lake Eyre. In boom years, the basin supports the breeding of around 80 species of waterbirds. ('Creative Commons Lake Eyre basin map' by Kmusser, licensed under CC BY-SA 3.0.)

outcome. These large groups may be loose aggregates but, at times, may provide rich opportunities for social interactions.

When the remote Lake Eyre fills with water (Fig. 3.9), usually no more often than once in 40–60 years, the water is supplied by a multitude of very slow-moving but large rivers. The rivers are freshwater but the lake bed is salt-encrusted and when filled, it has the same salinity as seawater. The rivers and the lake are also full of life.

However, such extreme boom and bust periods have been studied and explored in water-living organisms (plants, fishes, crustaceans alike) and mammals such as the sandy inland mouse, *Pseudomys hermannsburgensis*, and the spinifex hopping-mouse, *Notomys alexis* of the Simpson Desert (more on this later). While there are some extraordinary adaptations to such extremes, these are not the ecological context in which theories concerned with social interactions and bonding have arisen.

Complex environments are said to require larger brains, but in extremes such as those around desert environments, the only options may be to leave because circumstances are such that adaptations are impossible (temperature too high and no water sources). The only adaptation for animals may be to know when to leave before it is too late.

Social system theories

One may well ask whether 'group' can be defined in terms similar to the way we understand extended family and close neighbourhoods, or a lived sense of community. In human society, such terms are used to indicate social contexts in which all or most of the members feel a sense of belonging and freely communicate with each other, and even help each other.

Dunbar was perhaps thinking of such groups when he proposed a new theory, which came to be known as the social brain hypothesis. He argued that, in animals, the dynamics of closely tied individuals required increasing complexity of communication and thus might explain the evolution of greater cognitive abilities (Dunbar 1998). This hypothesis was at first formulated in the context of primate sociality. He suggested that some primates, and perhaps other orders and species, had developed large brains in order to survive and compete in complex social groups. According to Dunbar (1992) neocortex size in primates was strongly associated with group size. His is an attractive proposal but it is not always clear whether complexities are of the same kind and have the same evolutionary impact. Baboons of various species, as well as many other primate species, also have complex societies and their brains are nowhere near comparable to those of great apes. Further, orang-utans do not live in complex close-knit groups, but live on their own much of the time. Females rear their single offspring alone for extended periods (about five to seven years). The social context remains sparse and yet orangutans have impressed us with their extraordinary cognitive skills and abilities. Of the great apes, orang-utans are probably the most innovative tool users and they do very innovative things spontaneously, without requiring long training sessions as even some chimpanzees require (Kaplan and Rogers 2000).

Gisela Kaplan

A brush turkey hatchling (about two days old) – entirely self-reliant and without protection.

Gisela Kaplan

A brush turkey adult male stays near his mound as long as there are eggs in the mound.

Robyn Burgess

An emu male and offspring in the outback (north-western NSW).

Gisela Kaplan

The southern cassowary male does more than just protect his offspring. He will help them cut up fruit to a manageable size and even show his youngsters how to handle difficult fruit.

Gisela Kaplan

Australian (or common or eastern) koel nestling. Its tail feathers are still short and the plumage is like that of the female, well camouflaged, but this parasitising cuckoo chick is likely to already be much larger than most of its potential hosts.

Bobbi Marchini

Striated pardalotes, *Pardalotus striatus* (pair, next to each other, and juvenile with its back to camera) belong to the cooperative species.

Bobbi Marchini

One of the most outstanding examples of female songsters among songbirds worldwide is the Australian magpie. The female's repertoire may be slightly larger than the male's, develops earlier than in males and is used throughout much of the year (here: juvenile female close to moult).

The zebra finch male is an international star in the study of birdsong and has been extensively used as a model for brain and song development. The male learns a special breeding song.

Noisy miners belong to the cooperative species, have complex social structures and rules and are one of the few species that will aid other species in predator defence and take in lone orphans of their own species.

Gisela Kaplan

Grey fantail (*Rhipidura albiscapa*) males protect breeding sites and will actively mob anyone, including humans.

Gisela Kaplan

In pied butcherbirds (*Cracticus nigrogularis*), closely related to magpies, females also have song. It is generally agreed that pied butcherbirds' songs are extraordinarily beautiful.

Gisela Kaplan

Chiming wedgebills (*Psophodes occidentalis*) have male and female song. Picture taken between Uluru and King's Canyon.

Gisela Kaplan

Black-faced cuckoo-shrikes (*Coracina novaehollandiae*) have no visible sex differences at all. Parents share nest-building and raising of young and have the same vocal range. They sometimes leave the area post-breeding but tend to return to the same site.

Bobbi Marchini

Mating in white-bellied sea-eagles. The considerably lighter weight of the male is of great advantage when copulating; because of the bird's size, he has to step right on top of the female.

Gisela Kaplan

Rufous whistler (*Pachycephala rufiventris*) males have a breeding song.

Robyn Burgess

Galahs flock in relatively large groups when moving about locally in search of food and water.

Robyn Burgess

Brolgas in their favourite wetland environment, foraging in pairs – but too many wetlands have been converted to dry land and brolgas can now be a rare sight.

Gisela Kaplan

A little wattlebird, fiercely territorial for its food patches; extraordinary in its courtship.

Bobbi Marchini

Crimson rosella (*Platycercus elegans*). Gift feeding by the male of his female partner is often considered a sign that he promises to be a good provider while she is brooding. A magpie male will also feed his female while she is incubating the eggs.

Bobbi Marchini

Beak-touching tenderness. Kookaburras also have a gift-giving ceremony: he brings her an edible gift but he won't release it until she makes a specific low-intensity growling sound. Once she has taken the gift, the union is sealed.

Bobbi Marchini

Red-browed firetails (finches) mating. This species is one of twelve species of finches without notable sex differences in appearance (see also Table 2.1).

Bobbi Marchini

Scaly-breasted lorikeets (*Trichoglossus chlorolepidotus*) house hunting. House hunting is done jointly by the pair and is both a stressful and exciting time for them. The excitement is palpable when they have found a potential nest hole. Their bodies are stretched and they sway from side to side as shown here.

4

The 'heartache' of finding a partner

For a bonded pair to be successful and remain together season after season may depend on how well matched the parenting partners are and to what extent they can rely on the other's best efforts in defending young and providing adequate and nutritious food. Finding such a partner, perhaps with a good deal of choosiness involved, may well be based on social and cognitive factors, as in humans.

Modern dating agencies for humans apparently use a grid of some 200 qualities with which they try to match people. Many of these 200 matching points are related to character, social interests, education, hobbies and world views, but there are a few that relate to physical aspects, such as appearance, height, eye colour and ethnic background. A photo attached to these points might supply subtler information such as physical attractiveness. I have no idea how successful such dating agencies are, given that most criteria are rational or descriptive, and, as has been studied in humans in great detail, actual attraction often functions at subconscious, hormonal and chemical levels. As Grammer and colleagues explained (2004), pheromones, conveyed by a sense of smell, have the potential to influence human behaviour and physiology. The major histocompatibility complex (MHC) is a large chromosomal region containing closely linked polymorphic genes that play a role in immunological self/non-self recognition, in other words, the recognition of foreign bodies. This genetic information is relayed by androgen-based pheromones. We know that most species of birds, although not all, by and large do not have a sense of smell equal to that of humans (Roper 1999), but there are birds that have been shown to clearly distinguish between noxious and innocuous smells (Burne and Rogers 1995).

But what are the assumptions about mate-choice in birds? Birds have created a very special niche in their partnerships because they form relationships beyond courtship and copulation and are the only animal model of exclusive bi-parental care, apart from humans. According to Timothy Clutton-Brock (1991), only about five per cent of mammals, including some primates, meerkats, wild dogs including dingoes, and certain species of mice, form lifelong pair bonds or even short-term pair bonds while nearly all breeding avian species, at least 97 per cent of more than 10,000 species pair bond with a mate!

And the five per cent of mammals that also practise bi-parental care typically still live in a troop, pride or pack in which the breeding pair typically consists of the alpha male and the alpha female. Their social life tends to be organised as a hierarchy including a number of permanent members that might eventually leave and be replaced by offspring (adult males or females leaving to find or to found their own group) but as long as possible, the alpha pair will be the only one breeding. In wild dogs, the pair counts on complete cooperation from its pack to help feed the offspring. In some canine species, as in Arctic or Ethiopian wolves (*Canis simensis*), food is so scarce that every adult pack member is needed just to provide enough food to raise the pups of one pair (Rogers and Kaplan 2003). In meerkats, the alpha pair expects of its gang members total fidelity and support for its offspring, as well as satisfactory job performance of sentinel duties of the tutors to their offspring teaching them new skills of foraging. In some of these close-knit groups, ranking order is matriarchal, as in bonobos (*Pan paniscus*) or in hyenas (Hyaenidae).

Perhaps surprisingly, the alpha position does not necessarily reflect the best in overall quality, something so vehemently stressed in the literature on birds. In wolves (*Canis lupus*), apparently confidence and consistency in behaviour are highly important qualities that safeguard the alpha pair's rule (Schassburger 1993).

The majority of birds have chosen a very different path and one that is, in fact, most similar to the social and partner arrangements in humans. From my own observations on how birds fare in the partner game, one of the striking features is that some of the partnering games often look very similar to those played by humans, including ceremonial aspects valued in human societies. Birds are often seen as a valuable model for vocal learning comparative with human vocal learning of speech. What is sometimes overlooked is that, on matters of partner choices and matters of sex, humans and birds may have so much more in common than was once believed, despite millions of years of distance in evolution.

Childhood sweethearts

How birds meet and how many preliminary encounters there are is not very well known. We usually study mate-choice at the end of this process, namely, when they have their courtship rituals and when they mate. There are some unusual examples, as in human society, of childhood friends turning into long-term bonds, presumably because both partners share a joint history; perhaps their parents were friends or neighbours. In almost all cases, familiarity helps in bonding and quite often, childhood sweethearts were friends in primary or high school or were at least in the same schools, sometimes in the same year. At least in some cockatoo species, it is not far-fetched to draw comparisons to humans.

Sulphur-crested cockatoos, and perhaps most cockatoos, may be somewhat unusual in the bird world. We know that youngsters stay with parents and get fed by them up to three months post-fledging, even though they are already part of a flock of immatures. The parents can find them easily, recognising their youngsters by their own begging calls. In such flocks, one source claimed (Billabong Sanctuary, online) that immatures seem to form some smaller group alliances early or, one might say, friendships develop within these flocks. Unmatched by most other avian species (except, among others, bowerbirds and albatross), sulphur-crested cockatoos reach sexual maturity only after seven years (five to seven years among all other cockatoos). Among the largest South American counterparts, the blue and yellow macaw, *Ara ararauna*, reaches sexual maturity between three to four years of age, hence body size alone does not determine age of sexual maturity. Surely it is an extraordinarily risky biological strategy to wait at least seven years before matings can be successful. In the Galapagos albatross, the young leave the island of their infancy, returning for the first time after six to eight years, but often do not begin breeding until they are twelve to fourteen years of age, and thus reproduction is significantly delayed. It is a risk also shared by humans and some of the great apes: late maturity buys time to physically grow up and get valuable life experiences. However, such a general statement isn't sufficient to explain the delay.

Biologically, cockatoos are not in a hurry to reproduce. They spend their time in a flock, often with the parents remaining close by. The role of a friendly flock cannot be underestimated. We class cockatoos as pair bonding birds but the effects of such substantial time spent in a familiar group has probably been underestimated, if it has been considered at all.

Indeed, in such groups or subgroups, friendships and close alliances get readily formed and even pair formation may begin in the second or third year post-fledging. Such pre-mature pairs are easily identified because they roost together and are seen sitting very closely next to each other (as can be seen in Fig. 3.8).

What makes this so unusual in corellas and sulphur-crested cockatoos, and possibly others, is that the trigger for pair formation may not be sex and it is certainly not mating. Indeed, a pair may have been together for the best part of five years before they are even ready to mate. It is only when they are physiologically ready and do decide to have offspring that the male performs a courtship ritual, and this ritual is somewhat delayed and even interrupted because at the same time, both male and female engage in nest hole searches and nest preparation. They usually choose hollows in trees but also 'prepare' the nest site at the base of the hollow by chewing the woody substrate until it forms a good layer of wood dust, at times adding dry leaves and twigs.

When the male finally 'proposes', it is with body movements, head-bobbing and turning, erect crest, tail feathers splayed, sometimes also wings stretched out, making low grunting sounds. Such displays may be repeated over several days and be awkwardly expressed amidst the nest site preparations. They prepare their future home that may be used for decades, and while such activities are interspersed with the male's displays, apparently no mating occurs until the nest preparation is complete (Billabong Sanctuary, online). A video sequence has actually recorded an entire mating sequence of sulphur-crested cockatoos in the wild (*The Green Eye*, 2013) and while copulation is longer than in most birds, on average 90 seconds, there was no apparent solicitation, no rush and no display or sound of any kind. The pair was obviously clear as to what they wanted to do, or what the female wanted to do, flying to him and landing on a branch where he was preening.

Pair formation and experiences of wedded bliss

Indeed, in many birds, a commitment to breed is frequently preceded by a commitment to each other, signified by elaborate wedding 'ceremonies', some of which have been used as symbols of love. The swan's ceremonious swim together, for instance, has been forever immortalised in wedding card designs (Fig. 4.1).

Many permanently pairing birds have extensive rituals (Fig. 4.2). Albatrosses spend their lives separately at sea, but the pair comes together at breeding time. When they meet for the first time, they go through quite a lengthy and complicated beak fencing/display ritual, not unlike the scissors-paper-rock game. Facing each other, they usually first do some beak fencing but from thereon in, the sequence seems to be quite specific to a pair.

Next steps in the sequence (always facing each other) may involve head-bobbing or swaying, followed by left and right head movements, each partner in the direction opposite to the other, and may then conclude with a series of silent beak fencing (Fig. 4.2) concluded by another round of fencing, gaping or swaying. Once all this is done, the pair may mate immediately or may just sit down together, usually roosting very closely to one another and allopreening (allopreening refers to one bird preening another). They tend to uphold at least a short version of the ritual as a greeting while they are engaged in

Fig. 4.1 Image taken of a pair of black swans (*Cygnus atratus*) by author near north coast, Tasmania. Part of their ritual involves head-bobbing and neck arching at close distance, together with the beak forming a pattern of a heart that has been commercially exploited as a symbol of love.

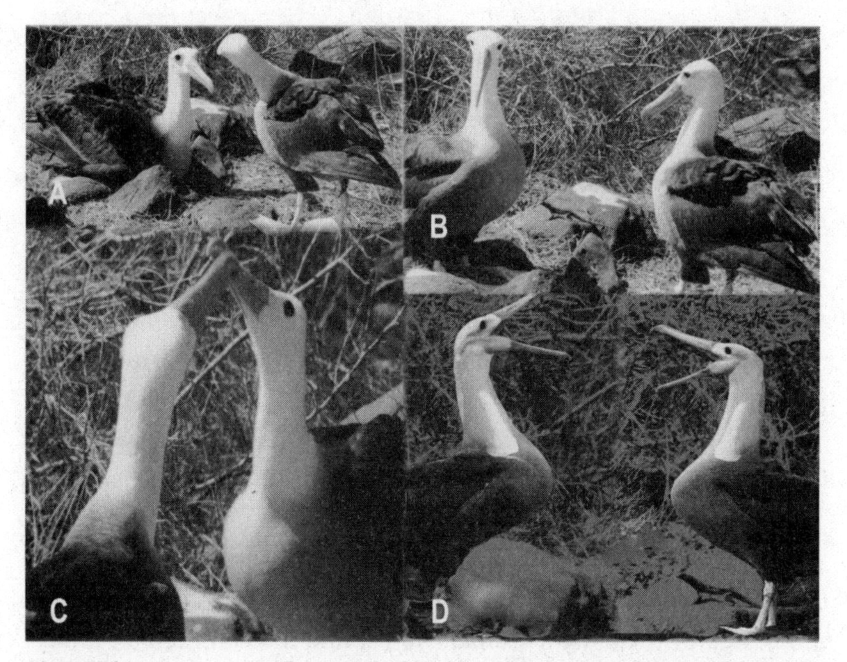

Fig. 4.2 This sequence was photographed by the author on the Galapagos Islands (Española Island) from some distance away. The Galapagos albatross (*Phoebastria irrorate*), also called the waved albatross, is the only member of the family Diomedeidae located in the tropics. When not breeding, they are usually near the Ecuadorian and Peruvian coastline. Their mating dance is very well known and there are a number of such dance/beak fencing sequences available online. A: A waiting albatross is approached by another with waving neck and head movements. B: Recognition and vocalising, waiting bird gets up. C: Beak fencing. D: Gaping. All part of a ritual that cements and reinforces an unbreakable bond for life.

raising a single chick. To memorise the sequence exactly is not an easy task. In grebes, ritual dancing before mating is similarly involved, but there is no memory task involved in this: one simply follows the example of the other. Great crested grebes, *Podiceps cristatus*, conclude their display with a spectacular 'walk on water', a very difficult physical feat, first described by Julian Huxley (1914).

Some of the rituals are extensive, involved and often graceful or even slightly funny to the human onlooker. For instance, unattached flamingos, tightly packed into groups, stroll in one direction, and another group strolls right next to them in the other direction so that the birds can see and meet face-to-face. Since there are usually large groups involved in one of these walks, this is quite a commotion to watch. The flamingos hold their heads up high as if practising for a fashion parade and during this wave of walking, birds quietly pair off, leaving the mate market. After a few hours, it is all over. The parade ends and pairs begin the serious business of finding or building a large, raised mud-nest. Cranes are noted for their brief hopping dances with flight feathers extended that lift them off the ground by not much more than a foot. Their beautiful wing markings are exposed and some head movement and footwork give the birds a graceful appearance. In Australian brolgas, *Grus rubicundus*, head-bobbing and swaying, and stretching the head right back while emitting loud trumpeting calls are interspersed with symbolic feeding dips of the beak downwards. When brief wing flutters are included, they nicely expose the black tips of their flight feathers and frame the considerable wings, about 2.4 m wingspan. Brolgas are unusual in that they perform many of the separate movements of their courtship dance largely outside the breeding season. So, occasionally, one can see an individual brolga jump a little and spread its wings, toss a bit of grass around or sway the head and neck. This does not indicate a courtship dance performance on its own, nor is it necessarily a practice session for such a dance but may have a multitude of other contexts. It is possible that individual segments of their dance serve distinct functions in everyday life. For instance, I have observed brolgas stretching their wings as a threat display followed by the eviction of smaller birds. Jumping up can be a predator avoidance move. After all, they prefer to feed in wetlands and snakes are abundant in such contexts.

In the courtship dance, two individuals have to be together and entire sequences are played off against and with each other. However, the way it has been described in the literature is that the actual courtship dance is less a pas-de deux but a sequence of events in which both birds do not face each other but stand next to each other, and the male performs more movements of wings than the female who keeps her neck and head very erect. In the finale, the male inflates the large gular sac and issues particularly long, broken and low-pitched calls (Johnsgard 1983). Brolgas are thought to mate for life and jointly raise their chicks but usually do not start breeding before the age of four of five. These days, not many see pairs of bush stone curlews, *Burhinus grallarius*, or hear their nightly wailings, let alone see their unusual and multimodal courtship dance. Strictly speaking, it is not a dance because the birds more or less remain stationary, but they have their wings outstretched, necks stretched and, very unusually, feet stomping from one foot to another and vocalising loudly (Fig. 4.3).

The only other Australian birds I know that use feet in advertisement related to courtship are the palm cockatoo and the two lyrebird species. The fabled palm cockatoo uses his foot to hold a stick which it drums on a branch, preferably hollow, to get his message of availability

Fig. 4.3 Brolga photographed in north-western NSW; an iconic bird and one of the two crane species in Australia (the other is the sarus crane). Close-up image: the darker area around the eyes extending to the back of the head is a bright red, the eyes are a mellow yellow and most of the plumage is grey except for the black wing-tips. Image on the right: a pair of bush stone curlews – rarely seen. The pair mates for life. Their vocalisations are somewhat haunting – a low whistle growl as warning and wailing at night.

known. The others are the Albert lyrebird and the superb lyrebird. Their extraordinary performances have been described in great detail by Sydney Curtis and later also by Norman Robinson (Robinson and Curtis 1996). The fascinating and unusual part in the Albert lyrebird's display is the rhythmicity of the dance, and the vocalisation is reinforced by the use of one foot for an action that is not unlike that of a bell ringer. The bird will seek out a performance platform that also has hanging lianas and climbers, using these to pull on them rhythmically to add a surprise element to the vocal and dance performance. These vine rattlings can be quite loud and add an unusual element to the performance (Curtis 1972).

Mutual pair displays, as has been discovered recently, especially those that are indeed song and dance, also tend to have an attentive audience. Ota et al. (2018) studied the multimodal courtship behaviour of the cooperative life-bonding blue-capped cordon-bleu (*Uraeginthus cyanocephalus*), a small finch native to East Africa. Apart from mutual song, male and female cordon-bleus perform a 'tap dance–like' display by stomping rhythmically with their feet whilst hopping, adding visual and even vibratory signals to the song. And their performance is most vigorous when they are close to each other and have an audience.

We are all familiar with public declarations of love and marriage in human societies – many birds have these too and it is difficult to see how they differ in intent from those rituals so well established in human society.

Courtship displays of songbird pairs, apart from those of water and shore birds, have rarely been described in Australia. A very interesting one is the courtship display of the little wattlebird, *Anthichaera chrysoptera*, from 1947. I doubt whether many people have read it recently. This small entry in *Emu* is a reminder that we probably do not know and may have missed many such mutual displays in Australian songbirds because they may occur in trees and are therefore far more difficult to see than dances and mutual displays in open landscapes and on water, and because they tend not to last long. The observer, HE Tarr, was attracted to a strange whistle and lifted his eyes towards the canopy of trees and here is what he observed:

> We then noticed two of the above birds [little wattlebirds] facing each other on a small branch of a banksia tree. Suddenly the presumed male (the slightly larger bird) raised his wings a little, fluffed up his feathers, elevated and spread his tail fan-wise and made an attempt to peck at the other. She fluffed her feathers and immediately swung under the branch and, suspended by one foot, kept swinging from side to side, the body being held rigid all the time. The swinging bird then commenced to 'claw' at the air and the male bird started swaying in unison whilst on one leg and began to 'claw' the air also. Occasionally their feet would meet momentarily and both birds would tremble intensely when that took place. Then they both stood on the branch again and after a few seconds repeated the performance. While the birds were on the branch together, they bowed to each other a good deal. During all the five minutes' display, both birds kept up a musical high-pitched whistle (Tarr, 1947).

I was struck by the unusual elements of this courtship and grateful to the journal when it still printed short observations of unique behaviour. The manner in which the little wattlebirds used so many aspects of possible displays is astounding and certainly varied and multifaceted. The bobbing of the head, the fluffing of plumage, the whistles, and particularly the hanging upside down from a branch by one leg in order to have one leg free to search for the foot of the other, is highly original, yet has components of bird of paradise male displays. The clutching of feet, so far only described in juvenile magpies (Kaplan 2019) as an affiliative gesture and in eagles as part of a courtship display, seems to be a relatively rare part of the repertoire of mutual courtship displays.

Then there is a variety of bird species with elaborate gift-giving ceremonies, some of which last throughout a 'honeymoon period'. Ravens have gift-giving occasions, as do kookaburras and grebes, just to name a few. Many species search for and select a home together (kookaburras, palm cockatoos) and then they live 'happily ever after' as do most cockatoos and ravens. Hence elaborate preparations for breeding by such rituals are usually found in species with long-term bonds. Long pair-bonding, as well as often extensive rituals preceding such commitments, are very special and even unique in the animal kingdom. The only comparison possible is again with humans.

Whatever the routine the couple has chosen, and however different the routines may be, physical coordination is a central feature of all the dances and displays. One repeats the movements of the other, and in many such dances and rituals, the timing of the physical activity is often near perfect. The same is true of song, which is often synchronised between partners. Juvenile brolgas can give dances a bad name because most of these little practice jumps, flutters and dips of the beak into the water look clumsy and far too excited to be coordinated.

The idea that these bonds are always 'a happily ever after' is as false as it is when referring to human bonds, but possibly less so than among human pairs. A now seemingly dated hypothesis, called the incompatibility hypothesis (Coulson 1966), argued that some bonded bird pairs are incompatible and reproduce poorly but the individuals do well later when they link up with a different mate. Catry and Furness (1997), however, provided examples that contradicted Coulson's hypothesis. They observed great skuas, *Catharacta skua*, and found that the abandoned males were simply poor providers. The female had found a better option for partnership, referred to as the 'better option hypothesis' (Kaplan and Rogers 2001).

Some pairs may squabble and eventually divorce, going back on the market for a new partner, although there may be fitness consequences (Heg et al. 2003). It happens often enough, and an entire review paper was published just on divorce in birds (Choudhury 1995), a term that has since become more acceptable in scientific circles. Indeed, new work has further confirmed the idea of divorces in birds and provided some probable causes (Liker et al. 2014). According to Liker and colleagues, adult sex ratios exert pressure on pair bonds: divorce rates are higher when females outnumber males and males may become more polygamous. When adult sex ratios show an oversupply of males, infidelity increases in socially monogamous birds. Hence, according to their findings, sex ratios can influence the quality of pair bonds and even of mating behaviour in wild populations. A very different interpretation was provided by Culina and colleagues (2015) when they examined the results of all available studies on monogamous bird pairs that divorced. They came to the conclusion that divorces were adaptive in the sense that, in territorial birds, the female often became part of a better territory and reproductive success increased in species that produce more than one egg (Culina et al. 2015).

Other couples have affairs on the side (both male and female) but stay together and raise the ill-gotten offspring together (such as blue fairy-wrens or magpies). Some lose a partner through a mishap and may grieve deeply. Some, like tawny frogmouths, cry and may even die of their grief (Kaplan 2018b).

It is important to remember these family affairs both in terms of often cruel culling programs (also very relevant to duck shooting), and what this might mean to bird families. Careful reflection should take place before a nest site is destroyed or a single adult bird shot that may have had a bond with a partner for many years, or may be central to a pair's or family's territory and future safety and wellbeing.

Dance rituals for long-term bonding birds seem to be more common in water and shore birds than in land birds, but there are notable exceptions. Topknot pigeons, *Lopholaimus antarcticus*, once at home along the entire eastern seaboard and flying about in flocks of hundreds, are now very reduced in numbers but can still be found in patches of rainforest. They never come to the ground throughout their lives despite their large size; they are as mobile as parrots and corellas and can hang upside down even on one leg, to reach a fruit such as bangalow palm nuts or any other rainforest berries (Frith 1982). Very few have seen them or their performance, but they apparently dance and intertwine their necks as swans do.

However, is pair bonding the best option? One can readily see that in similar pair bonding mammals, such as jackals and foxes, the total reliance on an exclusive pair bond can make the pair extremely vulnerable. For instance, if the female is forced to stay behind to suckle her young and the male goes out, either one could come to grief when dealing with a hostile world alone. But, if the female joins the male in a hunt, they may find all of their pups killed, or gone, on return.

Innovations and changes in nesting sites

Yet the persistence of the model of just two individual birds raising offspring suggests that it may offer some significant advantages, though they are hard to see at face value. Most birds were probably originally ground nesters, using scrape nests (just indentations on the ground) or burrowing some way into the ground (as bee-eaters and some pardalotes may do to this day) and were precocial, meaning that hatchlings were feathered and walking within days of hatching. Joint parenting enabled one to stay with the offspring but that may not always have been enough. Most penguin species today have a similar vulnerability to foxes and jackals. When taking to their watery feeding grounds, they often have to swim the gauntlet of predators and if one parent does not return, the other rarely manages to successfully raise offspring on its own.

However, birds have taken significantly innovative steps to improve their chances of raising offspring. As only a few other vertebrates have managed, chief among them primates, most parrots and songbirds left the ground and shifted breeding to trees early in evolution, a serious advantage over the parental situation of a fox or jackal pair. Shorebirds, when given the opportunity, will use cliffs to minimise access for predators. Tree holes are utilised by all parrot and cockatoo species and also by kookaburras and some owl and nightjar species, and, distressingly, also now by the introduced Indian myna, distressing because they evict native birds from nest holes and even kill nesting parrots of the size of eastern rosella.

Choosing tree nest holes was as significant for birds as the invention of making fire or making tools for humans and, most likely, nest holes in trees changed life fundamentally. Apart from some small gliders and possums evolving much later in Gondwana, birds had few competitors for tree nest holes except among each other. For forest species, the choice of nesting sites was likely in rich supply and that is possibly a reason why cockatoos and other parrots were never forced to switch from nest holes to nest building.

The next, even more fundamentally important, innovation was not to wait and find a nest hole but to build a nest. The idea, probably put into practice as early as 40 million years ago, was to revolutionise the rearing of offspring and even the size of a species.

Some non-songbirds continued to nest on cliff ledges or remained on the ground, as is the case for most shorebirds. Interestingly, the species mentioned that remained ground nesters are mostly those in which parental care is absent or limited to one adult such as malleefowl and pheasant coucals. Actually, the nightjars as a whole (Caprimulgidae) are interesting and a little exceptional as a group. Some nightjars, such as the spotted nightjar, *Eurostopodus argus*, never made the transition to a tree nest site but its own colour and that of its single eggs are extremely well camouflaged on the ground, especially among leaf litter. Others, such as owlet nightjars, *Aegotheles cristatus*, nest and roost in tree hollows and cliff caves while the tawny frogmouth has taken to nest building. Platforms are built by waterbirds such as jacana and ducks. There are also ground burrow nesters such as short-tailed shearwater, *Ardenna tenuirostris*, or rainbow bee-eaters, *Merops ornatus*, and even grass owls, *Tyto longimembris*. Some species have never progressed much beyond the level of placing a few sticks precariously across parallel branches, such as tawny frogmouths and most pigeons, or they may take over someone else's nest site.

Most songbirds, however, moved themselves and their breeding sites off the ground and with this major innovation, they took a huge positive step forward in parental care. This point cannot be over-emphasised because it revolutionised the birds' ability to breed and raise offspring probably more safely and successfully than might be possible on the ground.

They invented nest building, and with some further ingenuity, birds increasingly learned to build impressive and safe homes in which to raise offspring, constructing their own nests from natural materials such as mud, twigs or leaves, interlocking them or tying them together with vines or even spider silk. They also learned to tie down structures in such a way that the nests were firm and strong enough to withstand storms and even protect against predators. The ground was filled with reptiles (lizards, snakes) and small mammals ready to take bird eggs, and even the adults. Birds now had ways to camouflage their breeding site and remove it from the immediate access of ground predators. By hiding away from most predators, birds could be small and still have a chance to survive the most vulnerable period of their lives, sitting on eggs and raising nestlings. Some very small Australian songbirds have never made that transition to trees and stayed amidst grasses, as most finches and wrens do, or have graduated to only low shrubbery. Still, most of them have learned to build nests, some relatively basic, whereas some native species have well-designed and often very well camouflaged nests. One of the most beautiful of the camouflaged tree nests is perhaps that of the varied sittella, *Daphoenositta chrysoptera*, with its perfect symmetry and the outside of the tubular nest perfectly mimicking the tree bark and appearance of the tree to which it is attached. Their nests high up in trees are almost impossible to spot (Beruldsen 2003). Every generation of bird has to learn this task anew.

This major innovation of nest building was most likely of crucial importance in the successful expansion of avian species, and even in speciation. Among vertebrates, birds are among the most accomplished of architects. In some cases, as in several African weaver bird species, males alone build the nest and use the finished product to advertise for a female, and when one is willing to approach, she will inspect it in detail and then decide whether to take the male as her partner. Weaver nests are not tied to branches but free-hanging intricate structures that have only a small opening. The male first has to pass the test regarding the quality of the nest site and if she is satisfied, the partner comes as part of the package (Szentirmai et al. 2005). The female behaves more like a tenant and does not even look at him but will inspect the nest very thoroughly. Consideration is first and foremost given to the nest site and its quality and the territory (where applicable). This may seem a little callous but the fact that the male is able to build such a nest or have a good territory is a statement of desirable qualities, experience and assets.

Nests in tree forks need to be tied down but nests that hang need to be carefully woven, like a complex piece of tapestry or basket weaving, all just done with the beak, so that wind and the landings of larger birds on the construct do not rip the structure apart. Such skills are learned, and young African weaver males, for instance, make many basic errors, sometimes even comical ones, such as sliding down individual strands and taking the whole construction with them. This rules them out completely from getting a partner. In Australia and South East Asia, the yellow-bellied sunbird, *Nectarinia jugularis*, also builds a very finely constructed hanging nest, complete with roof. The birds are still vulnerable. Something like 80 per cent of nests get torn down near urban areas (Maher 1992) where cats abound and do serious and increasingly devastating damage to all songbirds, no matter how accomplished they are at nest-building (Woinarski et al. 2019).

Building, even just building a bower, is a surprisingly complex feat. Male bowerbirds usually have to serve a seven-year apprenticeship under an accomplished adult male just to get it right. He will be surrounded by jealous or keen juvenile males who try to find out his secrets and may even try to steal some of the ornaments in the false hope that these will entice a female. But they are mistaken. Juveniles are simply not contenders. The European house wren male also builds a nest as enticement, but does not improve on one nest he has built, instead he will continue to build nests, sometimes ten to twelve nests, before a female may consent to join him.

In Australia, there are only a few examples where the male actually builds and prepares the nest largely on his own and then uses this as an advertisement to entice a female. One, already mentioned, is the jacana. The brush turkey male may qualify although he does not build a nest but a mound. Brush turkeys can be seen in many backyards (to the chagrin of gardeners), collecting and heaping up nest mounds of some metre height and width, or even higher. The mound becomes very impressive and consists of any loose leaf litter, small twigs and some soil. Males are very meticulous. We watched a male in our garden who was taking weeks over his construction. The male had already amassed a considerable amount of material when the neighbours forced him out of their garden. Mercifully, they went on holidays and did not see what happened next. The male dismantled his mound and moved it bit by bit right across their driveway, scratching more material (in an absolutely straight line) until finally our garden was reached. Once he had decided on a suitable position for the mound, he continued raking the material from the other property to ours, the slim train of leaves becoming more and more voluminous. Eventually, the major part had been shifted over to the grassy area in our backyard. The driveway was finally clear again. It showed method and attention to detail and perhaps also suggested that the substrate of leaf litter in suburban gardens is hard to come by, since most backyards tend to consist of well-groomed lawns. He then spent another month finalising the mound. After that, we saw and heard nothing more until some considerable time later, when there were three very small brush turkeys running about in our garden. Years later, the mound is still there and quite obviously still in use since we regularly have brush-turkey chicks and juveniles of different stages of development, height and maturity.

In some songbird species that may pair for life, females alone build the nest, and in some cases, as in female magpies, females also do all the incubating while the male gets food and guards her but then the pair jointly raise the hatchlings.

Oddly, many of the species in which couples may pair for life and in which the male help in raising young are not nest builders but nest hole users. Whether this was always the case in kookaburras is not known but kookaburras do not only use existing nest holes but may also enlarge small nest holes or shape them if the wood happens to be soft/rotten enough at a particular tree node. The pair, once they decide to proceed with breeding (after a gift-giving ceremony that I describe in *Bird Minds*, 2015), then flies around and inspects possible sites. If he thinks one site may be suitable, the male starts cleaning it up while she sits on another branch, watching. This can be quite hard work and may go on for hours. If she does not like his efforts or the site, she will fly off and he has no choice but to follow her and start working on the next nest hole. One pair I observed was going through these routines for several days and he seemed to get quite bad-tempered, expressed in cackling and looking at her repeatedly over his shoulder. They squabbled almost all day but when she finally inspected their latest site, she seemed satisfied and peace returned at once. He even brought her a small gift of a large moth, which she accepted and then disappeared in her new home.

Rainbow bee-eater pairs, as already mentioned, have to dig burrows with a nest chamber at the end. They may use the side of a gully or river bed but, in its absence, they will also just dig holes and burrows in the ground that are likely almost a metre in length. The problem is that in the large areas of increasing suburban occupation of humans, good grass areas can be scarce and confined to golf courses or parks, putting the birds in a very precarious position with lawnmowers running over their (hard to see) entrance, crushing the tunnel and killing nestlings inside, for instance. The male usually does most of the digging by using his strong feet and anchoring his beak in such a manner that he has his legs free to shovel. The female stands guard very close by, watching at the entrance, and will not even move when she gets showered with sand.

Another similarly complex and almost human-like interaction of male and female can occur as in palm cockatoos. They inspect sites together, head-bobbing and swaying, vocalising and looking at each other. The site he proposes strongly, seemingly with her approval, leads the male then to do some nest preparation, creating an inner lining or platform for the open nest hole. While he cuts twigs to size and drops them to the bottom of the nest, she watches intently, often sitting almost right next to him but without helping. The raised inner platform is very important when they nest during the wet season. The nest hole could get water-logged and the very methodical build-up of a raft-like structure inside, fashioned to the exact length of the hole, ensures that at the level of the egg there is no wetness. Apart from the aspect of tool use here, the 'conversation' between the pair is intense, and when that issue is finally settled, he tends to feed her as a further goodwill gesture.

In osprey pairs, *Pandion haliaetus*, for instance, it is still qualified help. The male starts the nest by bringing all the large branches needed and dropping them near the proposed nest site. The female stays at the nest site and actually builds it, showing an incredibly intricate skill in weaving the large branches together in such a way that they are safely wedged in the tree or on a bare patch of rock, using the material he provides in many trips (Fig. 4.4).

If the structure is good and proves successful, they will return the following year, using the same nest but adding a substantial new layer each year so that, over the years, osprey nest sites can become very large elevated structures, sometimes being built on by several generations (Fig. 4.4). In magpies, the female builds the nest by herself

Fig. 4.4 A pair of ospreys in their nest on the banks of the Ord River in the Northern Territory. Judging by the size of it, the nest was already a good many years old.

without any assistance from the male while he guards the territory (Kaplan, 2019a).

Most Australian land birds, however, build their nest jointly. Apostlebirds, *Struthidea cinereal*, are a cooperative species and live in close-knit family groups engaging in nearly all tasks together. Even nest building is seen as a significant group effort (Fig. 4.5) and one I have been privileged to witness at very close quarters on several occasions. Apostlebird nests are mud nests, as are those of white-winged choughs.

Fig. 4.5 Three apostlebirds finding mud near Copeton Dam, NSW. They were so engrossed in their activity that they paid no attention to me sitting just half a metre away. Left in the image, the bird repeatedly jabbed its beak into the moist sand/clay mix (head seen from above). On the right, it has collected a beak full of mud held together by a few twigs and the bird then flew off directly to the nest-building site. Note that the bird just next to it is also collecting mud.

The laying female decides on the site and then stays at it, high up in the tree. The rest of the group, including her male partner and as many other helpers as the group has, all look for mud (Fig. 4.5) and return with tiny portions of it in their beaks to the nest site where she is waiting to put it in place and to stop any mud from simply dripping or sliding down the side of the branch. Oddly, such activity, as I observed, occurred only, somewhat pedantically, between the hours of 6.30 am to 9 am, then all nest-building activity stopped abruptly and the group started feeding. The next morning, it was back to mud collection and the same frantic activity and chatter. There was one apostlebird that did not pull its weight and was repeatedly reprimanded not just by cackles, but by being pushed in a bodily fashion (literally shunting the individual back to the mud spot by bumping into the reluctant bird). By the second day of this treatment, even this recalcitrant individual bird complied. This suggests a certain mutualism and agreement of basic procedures necessary for building a home.

Still, all these special cases aside, most Australian species choose each other, live in pairs and stay together. Males and females consenting to mate also tend to put in a joint effort in raising offspring. Hence, further discussions will concentrate on those that do.

Worldwide, 92 per cent of all birds live in pairs and are socially monogamous (Jouventin et al. 2007). In Australia, it may be nearer 97 per cent. Socially monogamous refers to the fact that a pair is exclusive and stays together but some of the offspring may have a biologically different father (called extra-pair mating).

Species that bond for life may even be largely monogamous and dedicated to each other for life; see Fig. 4.6 (Bried et al. 2003). I find it particularly telling that in such bird pairs, the bond is never taken for granted but reinforced and renewed almost daily either via grooming, feeding or communicating. Instead of spending time competing, such pairs invest in their own relationship even under difficult circumstances such as enforced and long-term separations, as is the case in the various species of albatross. Indeed, albatrosses (of any species

Fig. 4.6 Pair of peaceful doves, *Geopelia striata*, in the MacDonnell Ranges. Fidelity to each other as a socially monogamous pact may partly be separate from reproduction.

but classically the wandering albatross, *Diomedea exulans*) provide possibly the most extreme example of fidelity despite separation. They belong to the few species that may have to separate for most of the year, flying the oceans in search of food and only meeting again during the breeding season, yet breeding with the same partner. As was discussed in Chapter 2, they have developed such intimate forms of greeting that, one suspects, they may also ensure that a stranger will not be showered with affection.

Even a superficial scanning of the literature will reveal a never-ending enthusiasm for giving biological reasons for cheating on a partner while the literature remains rather scant on explaining monogamy (Jouventin et al. 2007).

Extra-pair mating

Studies of the superb blue wren have shown a high rate of cuckoldry, in which both females and males quietly disappear and mate with someone else, even quite far away, and then come back and stay with their partner (Double and Cockburn 2000). Many of these mating excursions are far from private. The question has always been why would the male raise offspring that are not his own? This is a question that could well also be raised in human society. Birds, it seems, can even be less certain of the fidelity of their partner than humans, despite some males using mate-guarding techniques to keep an eye on their female. Astonishingly, as in turtles, avian females can store sperm and keep the donors separate (more of this in the next chapter).

Today, we dare speak only of social monogamy (especially in species from which DNA sampling has not been taken) since we know from countless studies that in many species, both males and females may have extra-pair flings that produce offspring. The best studied and most notorious are the superb fairy-wrens. In some areas, it seems, Australian magpies have also been discovered to have offspring from different males, at least in specific study areas and to varying degrees

(Durrant and Hughes 2005). Yet some Australian species may have been falsely suspected of extra-pair affairs and even some smaller species may not cheat as often as is now thought. We still have far too few examples of DNA testing of Australian birds to confirm whether extra-pair matings are common across the board or are clustered in some families or some species within a genus. As stated before, I suspect that the incidence of extra-pair mating is higher in species defending permanent territories than in non-territorial birds.

A recent study has indicated a strong correlation between the quality of a relationship and the incidence of extra-pair fertility. Ouyang and colleagues argued that infidelity dropped off sharply when the bond between the pair was strong. In fact, any brood produced by very close partners was most likely their own (Ouyang et al. 2014). Ravens and cockatoos certainly might well rank among the most monogamous of any species, by forming stable lifelong relationships which are broken only on the death of a partner. Both species are long-lived. In some permanently bonded seabirds, DNA sampling has shown that offspring are 100 per cent their own (Ouyang et al. 2014).

Those who do not breed – what happens to them?

One wonders what the career options are of birds that do not mate, do not raise offspring or follow other life paths. If only six to fifteen per cent of a species breeds at any one time (at least we know this of magpies), we have not accounted for the vast majority of birds that cannot be defined by their breeding. To be sure, many die too early but that may still leave as many as a third of birds and their social activities unaccounted for. What is often also not said is that mating systems designed purely for mating and not joint parenting are typically accompanied by a glut of males, of which the vast majority are unable to contribute genetically to the next generation over a lifetime. There is one consolation price for those males that lose out: they tend to live longer than those that enter the mating game (Kervinen et al. 2012).

Many birds end up in flocks and roam the countryside. To distinguish here between migratory birds and those that fly long distances, migratory birds are defined by their choice of breeding area in one geographical region and, once that is achieved, they fly back to wintering quarters where they will not breed. Their wintering quarters usually mean avoiding either extreme cold or, in Australia, extreme heat or rainfall. Welcome swallows, *Hirundo neoxena*, are migratory birds between Tasmania and mainland Australia. They are monogamous pairs but usually make the long and arduous journey across the vast body of water of the treacherous Bass Strait within small flocks (Fig. 4.7).

Fig. 4.7 Pair of welcome swallows just arrived in north-eastern Tasmania from the mainland in early September, the beginning of the breeding season. They do not have a nest built yet and do not need to rush because, unlike similar species in high latitudes, they have considerably more time to raise their young, nearly five months. Importantly, as they are a pair already, they are not looking for partners, saving time, energy and potential stress.

Then there are species, such as currawongs, that are locally nomadic. They do not have fixed territories but may just develop favourite nesting sites which they defend. They are permitted to breed almost anywhere, including in someone else's territory, such as that of magpies. Not once in over twenty years of fieldwork have I witnessed currawongs being prevented from breeding in a magpie's territory but, over the years, I noticed that currawong nests tended to be at the furthest distance from the magpies' nest and tended to be located towards the edge of a magpie's territory rather than in its centre. Currawongs are not classed as migratory birds because the geographical locations of their breeding sites are not dependent on seasonal variations (although indirectly they are) and they roam to where the food is.

Finally, there are a substantial number of fledged birds that have left their home (natal territory) or familiar nesting sites and are now expected to make it on their own. In so many native species, we have no idea where they actually go or how far afield they may have to travel to find reasonably safe conditions for feeding and roosting.

We may have substantially underestimated the amount of bird movement that occurs across the Australian continent (Griffioen and Clarke 2002). One reason fledged birds move may be the enforcement by parents to leave. Magpie and tawny frogmouth youngsters, two species I have studied in detail, most definitely do not want to leave their natal territory. In some cases, they only fly as far as over the territorial border and hope to stay near familiar ground. This does not usually succeed. Real estate is highly sought after in good areas and neighbouring areas are usually already occupied. The youngsters are permitted to fly over such areas but are not permitted to land, let alone feed (Kaplan 2019a). Hence, they are pushed on and on until they have to stop somewhere, exhausted. If they are lucky, they find other juveniles and together look for a spot where they can land and roost and get some food. Some of these leftover patches of land that no other magpie wants can be of very poor quality and often cannot provide enough nourishment to allow them to stay (Veltman and Hickson 1989).

Such a circumstance leads to roaming. Particularly adults may move, possibly due to declining food and water supplies, searching for better conditions if one area or environment suddenly does not provide the necessities of life as it might have done just a year earlier.

Indeed, except for some birds of prey that must of necessity often hunt on their own, there is hardly a species found in outback Australia that does not move about in flocks. It is also instructive to look at *The New Atlas of Australian Birds* (Barrett et al. 2003) and compare tables that provide breeding site data with those that provide data on mere numbers of birds present at a given time. In so many of these tables, it becomes obvious that birds of the same species tend to be clustered around the rim of Australia at breeding times, while in the winter months, bird numbers swell substantially inland.

So where do these birds appearing inland come from and why are they there? We do not know. It used to be the case, and still is largely so, that most studies on breeding biology of native birds were carried out in coastal areas and largely focused on sedentary species, as Clarke rightly pointed out in 1997.

However, it is perhaps relevant to mention that wanderings and temporary relocations have been recorded in small native inland mammals. Over a period of eighteen years, Dickman and his team (1995) monitored the movements of two species of rodents, the sandy inland mouse, *Pseudomys hermannsburgensis*, and spinifex hopping-mouse, *Notomys alexis*, in the Simpson Desert. The results showed that both species disperse widely and are highly mobile during bust periods, but sedentary and more social during population increases and collapse. In their case, it seems, sociality here is a by-product, ironically, of both extremes: of scarcity as well as plenty, while periods of low food availability (as distinct from population collapse) is a period of high mobility. Perhaps similar principles apply to native birds, but we don't really know. The detailed information on rodent movement gained via this excellent longitudinal study of native desert mice provides some insight into external factors affecting species behaviour. As its location and timeframe amply illustrate, such field studies (especially in the Simpson Desert!) are exceptionally difficult to conduct, let alone sustain.

But why raise this here? It is simply to remind us that coastal activities and the evidence of breeding might lead us to believe that all birds breed. It is well possible that non-breeding birds flock together inland for mutual safety and to find enough food to survive. Although such flocks might largely consist of unrelated individuals, dominance relationships tend to develop. Indeed, they appear to be almost ubiquitous in flocks. High rank implies priority to contested resources.

We have very little information on temporary alliances in Australian birds, but countless studies of high latitude birds have demonstrated how birds, normally living in pairs, may flock together in lean times. For example, Ekman (1990) provided a detailed account of winter flocks of willow tits, *Poecile montanus*, and showed that despite some disadvantages for lower-ranking individuals, survival was improved by decreasing the risk of starvation and of predation. One might add that learning opportunities gained under relatively unfavourable conditions but under the protection of a group alliance would ultimately benefit surviving members later, when and if they had the chance to breed themselves.

Same-sex affiliations

Many authors have now confirmed that same-sex associations between birds exist across taxa and genera. The behaviour is indeed far more widespread than has been admitted or believed but has often been ignored as irrelevant or abnormal and misdirected behaviour (i.e. as an aberrant outcome of captivity), despite a steady trickle of scientific publications since the 1950s. For whatever reason, social opinions were divided. Erik Holland wrote as recently as in 2004 that homosexuality in animals was 'extremely rare', a claim that had already been disproven (Bagemihl 1999) and led to a rush of publications to prove otherwise. When Tina Adler wrote a brief piece in *Science News* (1997), 'Animals' fancies: Why members of some species prefer their own sex', she created a storm that said more about the protesters' human stance and anti-gay sentiments than about biology.

Whether these are alliances for safety or for friendship, cooperation and help in raising a brood, and whether they are sometimes or largely sexual, is not always clear. However, many confirmed examples of same-sex sexual behaviour have now been published in book form and in papers. The results obtained so far would suggest that there are major differences between males and females. In a paper we wrote some years ago (MacFarlane et al. 2006), we found that male–male sexual behaviour occurred across all mating systems but mostly in polygamous species, while female–female sexual behaviour occurred most frequently in socially monogamous species. Both expression and frequency of female sexual behaviour were strongly related to the precocial state of development at hatching. The 90 species we identified included Australian examples (such as swans, kookaburras and zebra finches).

Male–male associations are perhaps more common in waterbirds than in land birds, i.e. in precocial rather than altricial species, but the jury is still out on this. The most familiar waterbirds are ducks and swans. They are precocial, meaning they are feathered and can feed themselves once hatched. Altricial hatchlings, by contrast, are very under-developed on hatching and depend entirely on adults caring for and feeding them.

Black swans, for instance, well known for forming primarily monogamous, long-term pair bonds between males and females, also form adult male–male pair bonds both in captivity and in the wild. For temporary bonds, a third of all black swans are known to be in such bonds. For about five per cent of males, they form long-lasting male–male pair bonds. In the latter, males engage in greeting ceremonies, pre-copulatory displays and mountings. As a pair, they may even seek to raise an offspring. To do so, they have been known to force a female off her nest and jointly raise an offspring and do so successfully. Male pairs tend to be more aggressive and succeed in maintaining larger territories than male–female pairs (MacFarlane et al. 2006).

Young and colleagues (2008) have shown that female–female pairing is common in Laysan albatross, *Phoebastria immutabilis*, and found in over 30 per cent of all breeding albatross pairs of that species. While female–female pairs fledged fewer offspring than male–female pairs, they did so in more than one year. Interestingly, they also found that at least one offspring was genetically related to each female, indicating that both females had opportunities to reproduce. Other species, particularly females, may form lifelong bonds with or without raising offspring on their own.

Our knowledge of same-sex pairs suffers from one very limiting factor. Many bird species that form such relationships are monomorphic – they look exactly the same – and the sex of the bird is not revealed just by looking at them. Only studies that managed to get large sample sizes for sex identification were able to reveal the actual level of same-sex pairing, and even then it was often restricted to those instances when same-sex pairs were actually engaged in breeding.

There have been a few studies manipulating parent involvement in raising zebra finch. In one study, young zebra finches were raised without fathers (Adkins-Regan and Krakauer 2000), and in another adult females were removed (Banerjee and Adkins-Regan 2014). In both cases, same-sex pairings increased dramatically. Still, these are artificial manipulations not reflecting likely scenarios in the natural environment.

In all forms of partner formations, it becomes clear that reproduction, sex and partner choice are not necessarily occurring in one predictable order. There are pairs without reproducing, same-sex pairs that do reproduce and an army of birds that have no partners at all. Moreover, it is of some interest that male and female birds may reach sexual maturity at different ages and often quite late. The most extreme cases are probably the bowerbird (six to seven years for males, five for females) and seven years for sulphur-crested cockatoos, at which time they may already have a partner. Those bird pairs that do both, live together and reproduce, may go through rituals every year to reconfirm the bond. Territorial birds may have a substantial advantage because of the constancy of their environment. None of these facets of their social and partner relationships necessarily tell us whether birds actually have sex and whether adaptations for enjoying sex is one of the motivators to stay together rather than reproduction.

5

The sex life of birds

There are two contrasting perceptions of sexual activities in animals. One was expressed most forcefully by the philosopher Thomas Hobbes (1588–1679) who, in *Leviathan* (1651), characterised all natural life as nasty, brutish and short. Strangely, it was not just the supposed lack of thought and rationality, but the belief of an unbridled, unrestrained and shameless display of sexual activity that contributed to the view of animals as dirty, even disgusting, and amoral beings to which humans were so obviously superior. We have preserved such attitudes by describing people engaging in antisocial and criminal conduct as 'behaving like animals'.

We have many strange expressions that compare human activity with animal activity, such as 'sweating like a pig' – actually, pigs do not have sweat glands and hence never sweat. In most cases, comments of undesirable or repulsive behaviour or appearance tend to refer to mammals. Birds are generally left out of the vocabulary of bodily denigrations because, presumably, birds are not thought to have any sexuality or repulsive physique, although reference to birds' supposed stupidity, worthlessness and lack of character (silly goose, drongo, stupid galah, 'chicken out' or 'being for the birds') are relatively common.

Not much is known about sexuality in birds. Of course, we know about imprinting, a process that occurs in two stages, the first of which is an acquisition phase when birds learn about their social environment, called filial imprinting (Oetting et al. 1995). Experiments with zebra finches have shown that raising them with Bengalese finches in a cross-foster experiment made the zebra finches later choose Bengalese finches as partners (Sonnemann and Sjölander 1977). At the same time, Patrick Bateson (1982) had shown that the second stage sexual imprinting is a regulatory mechanism to strike an optimal balance between inbreeding and outbreeding. It was thought that learning about immediate kin would lead to mating with a member of the opposite sex slightly different from the imprinted bird's immediate kin. When tested experimentally, Japanese quail, *Coturnix japonica*, of both sexes, having been reared with their siblings, subsequently preferred a first cousin of the opposite sex, therefore lending support to the hypothesis (Bateson 1982).

In reproduction, it is presumed that hormones may automatically start the breeding cycle, triggered by temperature, length of daylight (called photoperiod) or other environmental variables and that for the rest of the year, birds have apparently no interest in sex.

The role of hormones is not disputed but the assumption that sex is always based on genetically pre-programmed hormonal change over which the animal has no control may be a simplified view. Equally, the view that all evolutionary processes into more and more complex behavioural and social partnerships can be dismissed merely as genes asserting their survival, would make little sense. It is the differences between the phenomena that we have to account for and that cannot be done by claiming the same cause for each phenomenon. And then there are the ghosts of Descartes that ultimately reveal beliefs that animals are automatons and entirely under the control of their genes. As late as 1995, a published letter in the *New York Review of Books* by the then-president of The National Association for Research and Therapy of Homosexuality (NARTH) stated in its conclusion:

> ... in man the enormous evolutionary development of the cerebral cortex has made motivation – both conscious and unconscious – of overwhelming central significance in sexual patterning and sexual-object choice. Below the level of chimpanzee, sexual arousal patterns are completely automatic and reflexive.

It is one of the less admirable traits of humans to make summary claims without the slightest hesitation or knowledge of the subject at hand, although of course the above fits well with the type of thinking that Descartes had introduced.

One immediate observation may put the above comment in perspective. It is now known that common ravens, *Corvus corax*, as well as a number of other avian species, have nearly the same overall number of neurons in the brain as chimpanzees (Olkowicz et al. 2016) and that the 'cerebral cortex' to which the writer refers has thus some crucially important similarities, enough at least to doubt the sharp distinctions being made between apes and large-brained birds, such as ravens or the cockatoos. Who is to say whether sexual-object choice in birds is not also guided by brain activity at the level at which chimpanzees or humans supposedly operate?

Responding directly to the assertion above that sexuality is purely mechanistic was made in the absence of any evidence. Interesting, too, is that humans and chimpanzees are singled out as superior while all other animals, regardless of class, order, family or species are uniformly judged to be incapable of differentiated responses to reproduction and sexuality generally. Clearly, to claim so wholesale for about 40,000 species of vertebrates is so unlikely that the statement can only refer to prejudicial thinking, by no means unusual. Descartes would also have agreed.

Hormonal adaptations

Most of the very detailed knowledge we have is of birds that inhabit temperate and boreal (far north/arctic) latitudes and experience marked seasonal changes. Their bodies are calibrated by choosing the most favourable time of year for reproduction, as countless papers have shown. The calibration is largely undertaken from the brain, by the action of hormones. For instance, Kriegsfeld and colleagues (2015) identified an important hypothalamic neuropeptide, GnIH, that is also present in humans, which acts directly on the pituitary to inhibit luteinising hormone (LH) and follicle-stimulating hormone (FSH) release. GnIH, or gonadotropin-inhibitory hormone, is part of a large family of RFamide peptides (Tsutsui 2009; Annette 2011) that has known regulatory effects on a variety of physiological processes such as food intake, pain perception and endocrine activity. GnIH has emerged as a major regulator of the reproductive axis and seasonal control of reproductive function across vertebrates.

There are many variations in its direct function: inject a human with a GnIH infusion and appetite for food will rise. Do the same to a hamster and it will inhibit sexual motivation but retain the same food intake. And there is another factor in how or whether these actions will be realised, and that is stress. The stress hormone corticosterone (cortisol in mammals) may act directly on GnIH cells in the brain, as well as directly at the level of the gonads to alter reproductive function, i.e. by decreasing testosterone and estradiol secretion from testes and ovaries. Of course, hormones do not act in an environmental vacuum. A very simple behavioural experiment showed a depressive effect of aversive stimuli on gonadal function. The researchers simply placed a mirror in a budgerigar's cage and measured the effect on reproductive readiness (Ficken et al. 1960). Interestingly, the mirror (suggesting that budgerigars do not recognise themselves in a mirror) inhibited ovarian development in females but not testicular development in males. Carrick (1963) argued and demonstrated in Australian magpies that external circumstances, such as the intervention of a strange magpie in a pair's territory, determined or, in this specific case, delayed maturation of testes and could even prevent full maturation. This is not entirely unusual in nature. In our study of orang-utans in Borneo, sub-adult males did not develop the full set of secondary sexual markers (the huge side-flanges surrounding the male's head) until an adult male had vacated the area, and such delays in full sexual maturity were maintainable for years (Kaplan and Rogers 2000).

Testosterone is known to regulate reproductive behaviour, both sexual and aggressive. However, John Wingfield, Distinguished Professor of Environmental Endocrinology at UCL Davies, has spearheaded many such investigations of the interaction between avian hormone responses, reproduction and environmental factors and warns of oversimplification. In a study with colleagues, Wingfield had already pointed out that levels of testosterone do not always correlate with mating systems, and testosterone levels are not always indicative of reproductive state (Wingfield et al. 1990). Testosterone levels in the blood can vary markedly among populations and individuals, and even within individuals from one year to the next.

The uropygial (preen) gland – for good looks or more?

The uropygial or preen gland in birds has a great deal to do with the overall health and good appearance of plumage. The preen gland is a heavyweight second line of defence against the growth of fungi (melanin acts as the first line of defence; see Chapter 6) and helps against other assailants such as chewing lice, ectoparasites which mainly feed on feather keratin. Depending on the degree of infestation, they can cause rapid feather deterioration and affect a bird's overall fitness but, it seems, the cocktail of fatty acids and long-chain alcohols of the preen gland waxes are designed to limit the effects and success of ectoparasites.

The question is what and where is this gland and which species have it? Not every bird has a uropygial gland, but most do. The gland varies enormously in size among species and its chemical composition

Fig. 5.1 This Australian raven, *Corvus coronoides*, is touching the preen gland with its beak. Reaching the preen gland is not easy. It requires the bird to twist its head right back, drop its left shoulder and wing, raise the right shoulder and twist the tail towards the beak in order to reach the base of its tail. The viscous fluid that is extracted is taken up by the beak and spread across the feathers. Each tail feather is picked up individually and wiped through the beak. The feathers on the wings and all other reachable feathers also receive the same attention while the head is typically swiped across the preen gland in vigorous motions.

may differ among species but is always extraordinarily complex. It is positioned at the base of the tail (Fig. 5.1).

The excretions vary with seasons and, interestingly, social species have been shown to exhibit a larger increase in gland size during the breeding season compared to non-social birds. Non-migratory birds also have larger glands than migratory birds (Vincze et al. 2013). Although there are various adaptations to different social and ecological conditions, the main functions of this gland appear to be the same: cleaning and waterproofing the feathers, as well as protecting feathers and skin against parasites. However, how such protection works and whether the gland's functions are universal is by no means entirely clear (Moreno-Rueda 2017).

The best proof of the importance of the preen gland is when it is not working. In rare cases, the uropygial gland gets blocked. I was once handed a thin, shabby-looking magpie for rehabilitation. The feathers were matted and appeared dishevelled and some feathers had broken off barbs, leaving gaps in wing feathers. The bird's posture was hunched and its wings were drooping, the preen gland enlarged and inflamed. After treatment, the bird recovered rather swiftly, but the feather quality took a good deal longer and only the next moult (replacement of all feathers) would entirely remove the past evidence of this medical problem. The tail feathers also had a faint line across showing a section of thinner feathers, often called a stress line when birds have been through a traumatic experience. In the case of this specific bird, it was not clear which came first, malnutrition, stress or the inflammation, as all three can cause blockages. Still, after recovery, the bird's feathers were once again thoroughly supplied with preening oils.

There is one alternative to the preen gland and that is found in cockatoos and cockatiels, *Nymphicus hollandicus*. They produce feather dust instead of having an oil/preening gland. They do so by means of specialised 'powder-down' feathers that shed a very fine white, waxy powder composed of keratin, and it is this powder that is spread through the feathers when the bird preens itself. This powder seems to have the same function as the oil gland, as it forms a waterproof barrier for contour feathers. One might add that this powder is lightly perfumed and exudes a smell that is very attractive to humans. Why this is so is so far not known. In some species and especially among brooding females, their preening gland produces a foul smell that fades once the nestlings have hatched but, in such cases, it is thought that this specific chemical response is a predator deterrent (Hagelin and Jones 2007).

The relationship of the preening gland to social status and sexual selection may also become clearer. If the system works and melanin and the preen gland excretions fulfil their function, the difference in plumage brightness and sheen may be evident even to the human eye. For conspecifics, such health differences are likely to be obvious and may have far-reaching consequences for the affected bird. For instance, it is unlikely that a bird with a poor health status would have a hope of social inclusion, let alone mating. Chewing lice can be passed on and so can microbes, which can even infest eggshells, leading to a poor prognosis for the clutch's survival.

Preen gland and chemo-signals

It may well be that we have overlooked quite a number of subtle signals that birds might use in partner choice and even in social communication in larger groups. The fact that social birds have larger glands than non-social ones would support the idea that this may be important.

The view is also being revised now that it is not just the plumage colour that matters in sexual selection but the entire bio-chemical background evoked by the uropygial gland. The preening gland might do more than just keep feathers in good condition. Indeed, in a detailed review of the evidence, it was suggested by Caro and Balthazart (2010) that uropygial gland secretions have a socio-sexual function and, like pheromones in mammals, stimulate brain areas implicated in the control of sexual behaviour.

Obviously, if any chemo-signals are actually produced from that gland we would expect that such olfactory signals would have to be detectable by the birds themselves. We have some evidence now of smell being important to the survival of some birds, although this seems to be largely limited to birds of prey. However, Canestrari and colleagues (2014) made an interesting discovery when they studied the relationship between the great spotted cuckoo, *Clamator glandarius*, and carrion crows, *Corvus corone*, in the north of Spain (Canestrari et al. 2014). Neither crow parents nor the cuckoo hatchling evicts any eggs. Hence, crow offspring and the cuckoo parasites are raised together. The researchers noticed that the parasitised nests had more successfully fledged crows than those nests that were not parasitised and started investigating how this could possibly be so. They discovered that the cuckoo hatchlings produce copious amounts of a foul-smelling cloacal secretion, a mix of caustic and repulsive compounds, chiefly consisting of acids, indoles, phenols, and several compounds containing sulphur. Canestrari and colleagues concluded that this habit of excretion in cuckoo hatchlings during the nest period repels mammals and birds of prey, and fosters the survival of the crow offspring. Survival of offspring in this case is thus closely tied to a sense of smell, also in would-be avian predators.

Until some twenty years ago, there was relatively little interest in olfaction in birds and the general scientific view was that, for the vast majority of birds, olfaction played a minor role in reproduction and generally (Balthazar and Taziaux 2009). The studies that were available concerned individual species among seabirds, vultures, and also chickens and pigeons, all non-songbirds. However, interest has been steadily increasing and it is becoming more and more apparent that olfaction may be far more important than once thought.

Corfield and colleagues (2015) conducted research to establish variations in the olfactory bulb across all orders of birds. The diversity in the olfactory bulb, responsible for detecting smells, is enormous. Basic size differences in volume varied from 0.06 mm^3 in spotted pardalotes, *Pardalotus punctatus*, to 217.63 mm^3 in emus, constituting a 3627–fold increase in size. However, emus may weigh anywhere between 18 kg and 60 kg (females are heavier and larger), but this does not tell us much because of the different body weights. Spotted pardalotes probably weigh no more than 10 g (the smallest are the hummingbirds, some weighing as little as 2 g, finches around 8–10 g and the largest flighted birds around 12 kg, such as swans or condors (Clark 1979). Hence the increase in body weight and size between a spotted pardalote and an emu is at least 4000–fold, meaning relative to the weight of the body, the emu's olfactory bulb is smaller than that of the pardalote. Since the size of olfactory bulbs vary hugely between avian species and do not always co-vary with body size, it is often difficult to even guess in which species olfaction might be important.

To get some measure that may be more meaningful, Corfield and colleagues (2015) assessed the sizes of the olfactory bulb against overall brain volume, which can at least pinpoint how much brain space is given over to olfaction. Their results showed enormous variations in functionality, even if the olfactory bulb was small. It has been argued that all the senses of the bird compete for very limited space in the brain, possibly explaining why corvids with high cognitive capacity have relatively small olfactory bulbs. One would need to examine each species separately. It is at least interesting that the olfactory bulb in Australian magpies is larger than in Eastern rosellas but that alone does not tell us anything about the functions and the range of olfactory abilities (Fig. 5.2).

Why is it important to know about a sense of smell in a discussion of feathers, preening and mate-choice? First, once the sense of smell is biologically confirmed, it is then also possible to discuss the possible

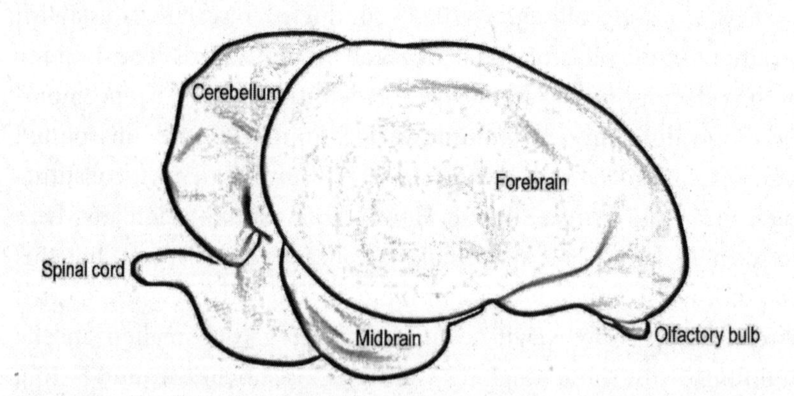

Fig. 5.2 Magpie brain. Olfactory bulb (head facing right; spinal cord left, leading to the neck). The small protrusion attached to the forebrain is the olfactory bulb, in which scents are pre-sorted and inputs generated by some of the molecules entering the nares (nostrils) then continue to be assessed in specialised nuclei in the brain (redrawn from Corfield et al. 2015).

role of chemo-signals emanating from the preen gland. The colour of the feathers and good feather condition may play a role in mate-choice. Indeed, in some cases, it is likely that a female (or a male) will receive signals that are multimodal as mentioned before, thus involving not just one sense but at least two. In some cases, three senses may be engaged in assessing a potential partner – song (auditory), plumage colour (visual) and scents (olfactory) (Candolin 2003; Partan and Marler 2005).

A recent paper was titled 'The perfume of reproduction in birds' (Caro et al. 2015) and another, studying dark-eyed juncos, *Junco hyemalis*, a North American bird, found that males with larger and specific kinds of excretions from their preen glands had greater reproductive success than those with less and fewer kinds of excretions (Whittaker et al. 2013). Among Australian birds, it is certainly the musk duck, *Biziura lobate*, that has attracted particular attention, partly because of the male's unique displays (Fig. 5.3) and splashes (Fullagar and Carbonell 1986) but also because of the male's preen gland.

When Captain George Vancouver first reported on the musk duck in 1798 during one of his voyages, he wrote in his diary of the duck: 'A very peculiar one was shot, of a darkish grey plumage, with a bag like that of a lizard hanging under its throat, which smelled so intolerably of musk that it scented nearly the whole ship', a sentiment that was echoed by Frith (1967) but not shared by McCracken, who wrote his PhD on the musk duck in 1999. He claimed that the scent was 'more subtle, definitely pleasant musky fragrance'. Apparently, not all musk duck males have the same strength of odour, and it dissipates very rapidly. No one has yet trumped Darwin's original speculation (1876) that the musk duck's odour was likely part of trying to attract a female.

There may also be functions of the preen gland that have nothing to do with mate-choice directly. During the breeding season male and female sandpipers, Scolopacidae, fly long distances to their mostly sub-arctic breeding grounds and then the compounds of the preen gland change in both males and females. They exchange a preen wax with lower molecular weight, called monoesters, for one with higher

Fig. 5.3 Display stages in the male musk duck. The drab greyish/brownish-looking musk duck male certainly makes up for his lack of plumage contrasts with an elaborate display involving vocalisations. A: Pre-display mode, but announcing display by raising tail feathers. The unique flap under his bill is an ornament worn permanently. B: Full display, arching back down to expose full size of the flap and raising the rear to raise the tail feathers above his head; when looking at the bird from the front, the tail appears like a crown around the duck's head. (A: Photo courtesy of David Cook Wildlife Photography; B: Photo courtesy of Nicholas Tomney, IBC1050088. Accessible at hbw.com/ibc/1050088.)

molecular weight, called diesters, which is far denser (Reneerkens et al. 2002) but this might well be due to the environmental conditions they will encounter when nesting on the mosquito-infested tundra. Obviously, much more research is needed to establish how many odours birds can detect and what functions specific scents may have. However, it is clear already that in some cases olfactory messages may also be important in mate-choice but such choices may not be specific to male or female.

The role of hormones in life histories and climate change

The other important point Wingfield raised, in 2008, is that the cycles determined by seasons can be subdivided into life-history stages of birds in which different abilities, activities and hormonal actions come to the fore. For an adult migratory bird, for instance, there are six distinct annual (life-history) stages: winter (non-breeding), spring migration, breeding, post-breeding moult, autumn migration and winter (non-breeding) (Fig. 5.4). The significance of this is that the more life stages there are, the lower the flexibility in timing becomes. At the other end of the scale are those birds (many of which are in

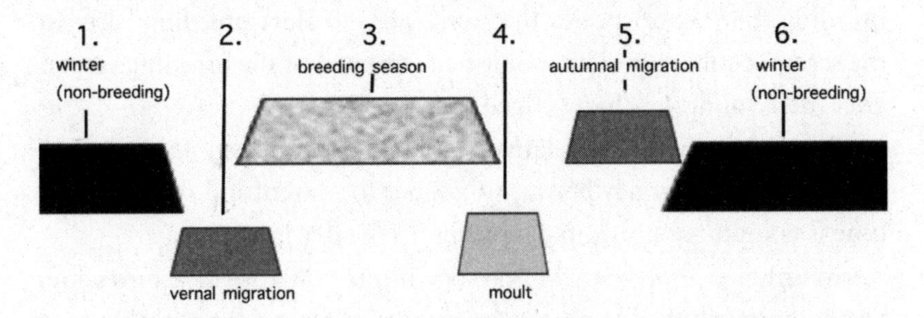

Fig. 5.4 Timeline of annual life cycles of migratory birds – the six life stages contract the time for breeding substantially; non-migratory birds have just four stages, not only lengthening the breeding season but having fewer hormonal changes (redrawn from Wingfield 2008).

Australia) that have fewer life stages and greater flexibility to plan their activities, including breeding. There is a downside to this – while maximising flexibility on timing, it reduces tolerance to environmental variations. Wingfield uses as an example coral reef fish that have among the highest flexibility among vertebrates, but have a marked intolerance for any environmental variation, such as temperature.

Unfortunately, we do not have many detailed studies of Australian land birds of the kind that Wingfield and colleagues produced. The behaviour of those species that have some migratory activity (altitude migrants) and those that markedly change climate zones, such as dollarbirds, *Eurystomus orientalis*, Eastern or Australian koels, *Eudynamys (orientalis) cyanocephalu* or even many of the silvereyes, *Zosterops lateralis*, are likely to be very similar in their life stages to those described and included by Wingfield and colleagues.

However, some early studies up to the 1950s and 1960s endeavoured in fieldwork to collect some basic data on moult periods in inland birds. These are surprisingly stable (see Table 5.1). Keast (1968), the author of the paper, noted that moult was not just related to hormones but to climate. Drought prevented breeding even if the gonads were live. Moult and breeding are physically demanding events and therefore typically separate events in time. Breeding commenced when the rain arrived. Drought could thus delay both moult and breeding, but those species that were able to start breeding early in the season could then start moulting at the end of the breeding season after their youngsters had fledged.

Table 5.1 shows the relative stability of moulting, according to Keast, occurring largely between October to March, and the length of time it takes to moult from data taken in the dry inland.

Maintenance of feathers plays an important role in a bird's life. Feathers contribute directly to thermoregulation and their quality may undermine or enhance chances of predator avoidance and even reproduction. The essential process of moulting to renew feathers takes energy.

Family	Common name	Latin species name	Moult time (months)
Campophagidae	Black-faced cuckoo-shrike	*Coracina novaehollandiae*	≃ 3
Muscicapidae	Willie wagtail	*Rhipidura leucophrys*	≃ 3
Muscicapidae	Weebill	*Smicrornis brevirostris*	3–3½
Muscicapidae	Grey shrike-thrush	*Colluricincla harmonica*	4–4½
Muscicapidae	Jacky Winter	*Microeca leucophaea*	3–3½
Muscicapidae	Rufous whistler	*Pachycephala rufiventris*	≃ 3–3½
Meliphagidae	White-plumed honeyeater	*Meliphaga penicillata*	3½–4
Meliphagidae	Yellow-throated miner	*Manorina (Myzantha) flavigula*	4–4½
Meliphagidae	Striped honeyeaters	*Plectorhyncha lanceolate*	3–3½
Pardalotidae	Striated pardalote	*Pardalotus substriatus*	≃ 3
Corcoracidae	Apostlebird	*Struthidea cinerea*	≃ 4–4½
Grallinidae	Magpie lark	*Grallina cyanoleuca*	≃ 4
Artamidae	White-browed woodswallow	*Artamus superciliosus*	> 3

Table 5.1 Moult period for select inland species (Source: Keast 1968).

Researchers have long since discovered that moult, breeding and seasonality lead to trade-offs between corticosterone (the stress hormone) production and moulting and even breeding because of the energy demands. Species with a short moult (e.g. at high latitudes where climate conditions strictly enforce migration departure dates) may need to suppress the hormonal stress responses. Most species in low latitudes presumably have a longer moult cycle, particularly those that are opportunistic breeders such as in the zebra finch or the budgerigar. We know that in zebra finches, the moult may take as long as eight months which, no doubt, may also have to do with the unpredictability of resources. Zebra finches have thus adapted to retain an ability to maintain stable corticosterone responses and the ability to reproduce and still continue moulting, while high latitude birds show increased corticosterone and can generally not moult and breed at the same time.

Australia, though, is full of 'opportunistic' breeders, i.e. they have great flexibility in timing when and how often they breed and this probably means that there are different triggers other than season per se (such as rainfall) that bring about the ability/decision to reproduce. And somehow it works. Everything in most Australian birds is geared towards flexibility, and this also means that other physiological processes such as moulting and stress hormone levels, for alertness and vigilance, have to be maintained throughout the year (Cornelius et al. 2011).

However, since this general and impressive flexibility with its relevant hormonal adaptations allows the birds to breed when conditions are good, it is now beginning to be a trap of a new and troubling kind. It was pointed out above that there is a trade-off between breeding flexibility and tolerance of environmental variations. Hence, current climate change events and temperatures that are higher for longer than they have ever been before could have devastating effects, ironically and specifically on species with great breeding flexibility. This, in other words, is a disaster. Breeding flexibility would now catch out these resilient species with nothing to throw at this climate change precisely because the change is too sudden to have time for new adaptations to develop.

The new climatic changes worldwide, noticeably reflected in prolonged heatwaves in inland Australia, can thus turn the impressive adaptations, namely being able to wait for the best time of year to breed, into its worst and non-survivable weakness.

Increases in temperature and drought may not just cause major food supply disruption but also become a problem for thermoregulation. We know that there is a direct relationship between number of breaths per minute and ambient temperature. This is about basic survival of adults. The young will die but the adults may also have a problem. Breeding in prolonged and hotter droughts is then completely out of the question. Weathers and Schoenbaechler showed long ago (1976) how such thermoregulation works in budgerigars. They have approximately 50 breaths per minute at a comfortable 30°C. Breathing rates begin to rise sharply at 40°C, doubling to 100 breaths per min, at 41°C again doubling to 200 breaths per minute and then, importantly, every single degree of temperature increase seems to matter: at 42°C, it is 200 breaths per minute and at 46°C, number of breaths rises to 300 and then keeps increasing to 350 even without further increase in temperature. It is obvious that there are limits to how much a body can take and the birds often die of hyperthermia or severe dehydration. The birds may also be forced or choose to self-cull when appropriate breeding environments are not available. That is often the job of the female who chooses and assesses the nest sites.

Sexuality outside breeding

There is a strong assumption that birds do not have a sexuality outside reproduction. Even when some primates were observed to have an active sex life, there was silence and coyness around the issue for a long time. Indeed, the discovery of promiscuous sex in great apes in general was hushed up for years. Initially, the most research-neglected but probably most sexually active of all primates, the bonobo (a chimpanzee), has sex often, regularly using sex for bond confirmation but also for appeasement when conflict breaks out in a troop (De Waal 1995). In other primates, copulatory patterns and frequencies may vary widely, according to the primate mating systems (Manson et al. 1997). They may display sexual behaviour in the wider context of social communication and exhibit same-sex mounting in a variety of socio-sexual and bisexual contexts. Teenagers in orang-utan society can be very promiscuous and experimental in their approach to sex. Juvenile males may even ambush-rape females or try to get a sneak mating with an adult female under the very nose of a consorting territorial male (Kaplan and Rogers 2000), meaning these events are outside a breeding season and do not often lead to pregnancy.

The little we know about sexual behaviour in birds generally comes via pet birds and veterinary practices and via a serious medical condition called cloacal prolapse. One avian specialist veterinarian told me point blank that parrots masturbate (Rosen 2012). The cloaca is the common chamber and outlet where the urinary, intestinal and genital tracts open. Cloacal or vent prolapse is the name for the inner tissues of the cloaca protruding from the vent and thus exposing the tissue to infection, tears and exposing the inner cloaca and intestines to such risks as well. Untreated, it can lead to death. It has been shown to be particularly prominent in parrots and cockatoos (including also the Goffin, Umbrella and Moluccan cockatoos). Birds can be sexually imprinted on their human carers. Sometimes such sexual imprinting is mistaken for tameness or for friendship but the real reason may be that the bird has a misdirected sexual fixation. Bird owners often treat their birds as they would a cat or dog, lots of patting and cuddling. Patting a bird on the back has two meanings in the natural context – it indicates either that a predator has got hold of the bird, causing the bird high stress levels, or that the one doing the back touching is ready for mating. Hand-feeding and constant cuddling can have the same effect of sexual arousal in the bird as expecting sexual activity. What cockatoos and parrots do is masturbate against a solid surface and the more often they do it, the more likely they are to get such a prolapse, which can be the result of constant strain. Masturbation would suggest that sexual arousal exists independent of seasonal mating at least in some species. If it is linked to mating, the pet bird might choose the human companion, find an anchoring point, preferably the head or a shoulder, and actually go through the process of copulation.

There are two variables here, the sexual fixation versus the need to satisfy a sexual desire even if there is no partner on whom to fixate. The former could be part of sexual imprinting and come to the fore at breeding times, the latter suggests a sexuality independent of breeding and reproduction.

The lovebird (*Agapornis*), a small African parrot, is called 'love' bird for a reason. For many years, we owned a pair of lovebirds that was housed in a large aviary with two alternative sites for nesting.

I spent a good deal of time recording their vocalisations and generally watching them and was absolutely astounded at the number of times they had sex with each other. Each such act took about 10–20 minutes (most bird fertilisations are over in a few seconds) and the male performed continuous thrusting copulatory movements but this did not result in egg laying or brooding activity. She laid an egg once a year and raised one offspring, but the rest of the time sexual activity seemed divorced from reproduction. As they grew older, such sexual activities occurred less frequently but each time, copulations were just as vigorous. When they were about nine or ten years old, I noticed that his behaviour changed markedly during coitus. He had his beak half open, tongue separately hanging out, panting and eyes bulging a little. He showed signs of hyperventilation and stress. Clearly, at age ten, the stamina to perform to her satisfaction was beginning to be a problem. Later that same year, he dismounted, panting heavily, and she looked around at him and then cackled in annoyance. In later incidents, she even pursued and pecked him, accompanied by some short sharp sounds of rebuke. He obviously had not performed to her standards! Of course, this is speculative, but their behaviour over the years strongly suggested that the pair had a sex life that was as much part of their bonding as preening and feeding together, while breeding was incidental and happened only when she was ready to do so. 'Readiness' was expressed in her collecting nesting material and letting him know what she was doing.

We do not have any details as to whether Australian parrots or Australian songbirds have such an independent sex life. The candidates to investigate, I would think, are the opportunistic breeders, i.e. the species such as a budgerigar or the grasswrens and many others, that time breeding with the onset of rainfall and the reemergence of resources. If they are so flexible, it may take very little to bring copulatory behaviour to the fore. Of course, external triggers can also affect hormones and act on the brain to get individuals into breeding condition for producing fertile eggs. But, as the lovebirds showed, it seems that in some cases copulation does not always result in reproduction nor is reproduction necessarily the goal.

The point here is that any division of sex as an activity independent from reproduction immediately changes the nature of the questions of mate-choice and creates very different dynamics when other adults get involved on the margins. Religious cultures knew this well and tried to turn 'nature' around, either by prescribing that sexuality be reintegrated into reproduction (i.e. the expectation that sex was only permissible for the sole purpose of reproduction) at a time and place to be determined by the legal husband, or by severe mate-guarding and circumscribed access to public life. In other words, human society has always struggled with an independent sexuality and endeavoured to socially contain it.

Evolution as a gain and loss game

A very tricky part of evolution is that traits in an organism are not necessarily kept forever. One general evolutionary rule is simple: use it or lose it. For instance, colour vision is a special attribute that can be pinpointed across the animal world as a relatively fickle attribute. Some species that once had colour vision evolved into species that did not. But there are attributes that seem so central and integral to a class of animals that its capacity to be 'lost' seems almost improbable. Flight, for instance, is one of the most defining abilities and characteristics of birds, yet there are birds that cannot fly. The flightless cormorant, *Phalacrocorax harrisi*, of the Galapagos Islands has only vestigial wings. It seems that the loss of flight came about because there were no predators from which the bird had to flee. A similar explanation can be given for the inability of flight in New Zealand's kakapo, *Strigops habroptilus*, a nocturnal parrot, and the kiwi. Again, current explanations are that until the introduction of humans and ground predators, such as rodents, stoats and cats, they did not need flight as New Zealand originally contained no mammalian ground predators.

In a way, both the kiwi and the kakapo took over the ecological niche of ground mammals.

In emus and cassowaries, it was not a matter of loss of wings but of not fully evolving. Their wings are used for fanning, displays and temperature control but are not enough for total lift-off. The brush turkey has an interesting interim position. Since the hatchling is on its own and has no protection from the day of hatching, the wings can perform some vital function of fleeing to a nearby tree during stages of juvenile development, keeping young brush turkeys also safe from any dangerous pursuit of adults. Once they become adults, their ability to fly diminishes considerably.

If flight has been retained in the majority of species, it is because of ongoing use and sufficient environmental pressure. One is migration, an astounding feat of flight of sometimes thousands of kilometres. Many things can happen on such a journey and many birds do not make the two journeys successfully from breeding ground to wintering quarters and back. We know this of waterbirds and even of raptors but in land birds, the evidence tends to remain relatively slim. One can not be sure how many survive these migratory feats and how beneficial it is for a species to maintain migratory behaviour. Moreover, for practical reasons, nearly all results on songbird survival come from populations studied during the two- to four-month breeding season in high latitudes. We know that natural events such as weather conditions, physical conditions and nest parasitism have significant effects on migratory songbird populations. Then there is the huge range of human-instigated disasters that end in tragedy for many migratory birds, such as poaching and trapping, disappearing waterholes and habitat alteration. An area that was known to provide suitable habitat one year may have turned into a suburb the next, with the trees gone, driving exhausted birds on, well beyond their expected range and capacity. Technology, ranging from cars to wind turbines and, no doubt in future also including drones that invade airspace, has been a consistent killer, increasing in magnitude every single year. As has been shown in wind turbines, the blades leave a grizzly harvest of millions upon millions of documented dead migratory land birds each year (Kaplan 2016; Martin 2017). At the time of first radiations, birds 'only' had to contend with natural barriers and events. Whether so many disastrous events will eventually alter specific migratory behaviour is not known, but there are signs that this might happen.

Even if one disregards the human-made risks and disasters for birds, birds are not as free as the previous personal choices of females suggest. The environment, as Järvilehto (2009) reminded us, working in the relatively new field of Ecological Psychology, is not a passive backdrop to the decisions of living organisms. It creates its own rules and imposes challenges to which the organism may need to respond. One of the most basic forms of an organism's response to threatened survival is to reproduce at a faster and higher rate.

The matter of quantity versus quality of eggs per clutch (or even several clutches) is a constant see-saw between environmental conditions, including climate and time factors. Small Australian songbirds have a major problem. Their eggs are of a size and composition that makes them ideal food, be this for snakes or a wide variety of larger native birds. They simultaneously raise their offspring and need plenty of protein to satisfy fast-growing youngsters. Such larger birds as kookaburras, ravens, currawongs or shrikes and butcherbirds will raid the nests of small songbirds which often leads to the loss of the entire clutch. However, since modern birds had about 20–50 million years to co-evolve, there are compensations. Small birds can re-nest, not just once but perhaps even several times in a season if a nest had been discovered and raided, and they will usually succeed in raising one clutch of three or four offspring per season (with an investment of as many as twenty eggs actually laid). The raiding birds, by contrast, usually do not re-nest at all and just raise one brood per season – hence the persecution stops as soon as their own nestlings have reached adult size, usually before fledging. That gives small birds the chance to re-nest, although, as a precaution, they often then nest in a different location.

Yom-Tov (1987) confirmed in his detailed study that small Australian passerines have longer breeding seasons, breed more frequently and have bigger clutches than larger birds.

The special issue of the penis

Losing flight in birds, as already noted, indicates the loss of something intrinsic to birds. The penis (also called phallus or intromittent organ) would certainly be considered an intrinsic and seemingly an essential part of a male bird's anatomy. Ducks and geese have it, as do emus, but more than 97 per cent of all modern male birds do not have a penis (Briskie and Montgomerie 1997; 2001).

There is at least one important exception in the loss of the penis in birds generally. Perhaps the most convoluted and complex male–female relations have been found in a Madagascar native parrot, called the greater vasa parrot, *Coracopsis vasa*. In this group, males have re-evolved a penis and have very different interactions with females than elsewhere. Females are substantially larger than males (up to a quarter larger), and they entertain as many as eight boyfriends at a time and are classified as promiscuous. The female defends a nesting territory competitively against other females. Their copulatory practices are reminiscent of dog copulations. Copulation can take a remarkably long time (up to 90 minutes) and it ends in a copulatory tie, meaning, as in canine copulation, that the sexual partners cannot separate due to the swelling of the male's penis. However, this parrot remains unusual within modern birds and, as with many other evolutionary developments, this may well be attributable to the long separation of Madagascar from any other landmass (Ekstrom et al. 2007).

Most water-dwelling organisms have fertilisations taking place externally and also do not have penises, with a few exceptions such as sea mammals. This is not just a natural progression from one form of insemination in one class of species to another. We have known of the absence of the penis in most land birds for a very long time and now also know that such loss did not occur just once in evolution (Briskie and Montgomerie 1997, 2001). In 2008, Brennan and colleagues reported two novel and phylogenetically independent reductions in phallus complexity by examining the non-intromittent phallus in the genus *Crypturellus* (Tinamidae), another bird in the ratite group. They rightly concluded that phallus evolution has been more dynamic than previously thought, both qualitatively and quantitatively.

How this absence could be accounted for as a process in biological and evolutionary terms has at least partially been answered, thanks to research by Ana Herrera and colleagues (2013). They found that the penis was actually lost by active intervention of hormones in early development of a bird's embryo. They compared those ancient avian lineages that still do have a penis (just over 240 species) such as ducks, geese, and flightless birds such as kiwis, ostrich, emu and cassowaries, with another ancient lineage, the galliformes, to which all species of chicken belong.

For the vast majority of birds, a protuberance develops while still in the egg. Male genitalia are indicated in the embryo but then a hormone is activated that not only suppresses further growth but actively kills off any new growth (called apoptosis, meaning cell death). In the early stages of embryonic development, the beginnings of a penis are visible but then regulated by a hormone to have any further development arrested. Notably, the same hormone, named Bmp4, was not detectible in those avian species in which the male has a penis to this day (Herrera et al. 2013). This clearly indicated that in most species, quite early in bird evolution, males actively lost the penis.

How is such a profound change possible, especially for such an important and basic activity as reproduction, central to the survival of a species? One convenient answer lies in the 'lock and key' hypothesis that has been quite popular in arguing that no penis offered cross species or subspecies opportunities when the precise lock/key obstacle was removed. Expressed differently, the 'lock and key' hypothesis argued that rapid evolution of genitalia facilitated speciation through breeding incompatibility (i.e. only males of the same species can fit their genitalia to same species females). Other writers, such as Mayr (1963), thought these were effects of incorrect transmission of signals at hormone level leading to unintended consequences.

There have been many others but they either seem convoluted or not very convincing. In the present climate, the explanations that win tend to be those that explicitly refer to competition between males, competition between females and competition between males and females, arguing in one way or another that males and females evolved adaptations and counteradaptations to gain control over copulation and fertilisation. This can certainly be demonstrated. The hypothesis that a phallus exists for paternity insurance, however, was blown out of the water when studies began to demonstrate that male parenthood had no more guarantees of paternity when the penis was present or absent. In emus (with penis) it was shown that most incubating males sat on eggs of which roughly 50 per cent were not his own, varying from 0–100 per cent – i.e. at the extreme end of 100 per cent paternity and nil paternity are rare, but they occur (Taylor et al. 2000).

A significant step towards cooperation

Instead of arguing that the loss of the penis in birds was indeed a loss, I would like to propose the very opposite, namely that the abolition of the penis was the most advanced evolutionary step against competition between the sexes. Rape, as has been observed in waterfowl, often with substantial penis sizes, is impossible without a penis. Without the male's penis, the female has to actively participate in the copulation by tilting her cloaca up and sideways to meet his. Hence sex, be it for reproduction or not, became a negotiated mutual event.

One can immediately object and say that this was not an essential step. Females already had the last word in reproduction. It is in the ovaries where it is decided whether and which male would not or would succeed in fertilising the next generation. If the reason for forced copulation is to have more offspring, male birds have a disadvantage. Because female birds ovulate and fertilise just one egg at a time, they have the ability to abort an embryo without having invested much energy in it. An egg may take a day or two to develop and its abortion is a minor physiological stress compared to mammals with their long gestation periods or reptiles with their simultaneous fertilisation of many eggs. Male birds generally gain little advantage by forced insemination since the female can abort an unwanted egg within a matter of days.

There is also the matter of sperm competition. In a sense, females can carry on their infidelity well after it has happened because females still have choices post-copulation. This is referred to as sperm competition, a competition between spermatozoa of different males to fertilise the eggs of a single female, and many females have been shown to deal with such eventualities. Sperm competition occurs in a wide range of species (Kaplan and Rogers 2001), among species as different as the cattle egret, *Bubulcus ibis* (Fujioka and Yamagishi 1981), the bobolink, *Dolichonyx oryzivorus* (Gavin and Bolinger 1985), and in swallows, Hirundinidae (Moller 1987), including also the zebra finch (Birkhead et al. 1988).

Hemming and Birkhead discovered recently (2017) that after the female zebra finch has been inseminated, very fine discriminations between sperm deposited by different males can be made. Remarkably, sperm from separate ejaculates can be stored differentially by female birds. Sperm from different inseminations are sorted and stored in different storage tubules within the female reproductive tract, resulting in almost complete segregation of the sperm of different males. While these are cryptic and unseen processes, they are powerful. Apparently, the 'sorting' is done by sperm length – the longest are more likely to be able to fertilise.

I am not altogether certain whether the term 'competition' is the correct one here if sperm gets sorted by origin and held, a point clearly made in the excellent review of the field by Firman et al. (2017). It is indeed not competition but post-mating female control (called cryptic female choice). In this method, after all, it no longer matters whether a male was there first or last, whether some ejaculated faster than others. The choice is neither judged by speed, nor on a first come, first served basis. Indeed, it could be that the slower or the faster is chosen since ejaculates of both males were stopped at the gate. Quite often, the outcome is that a mixture of both ejaculates will be selected so that the fertilised eggs represent a mix of both males.

Moreover, in humans the sex of the fetus is determined by the male. In birds, it is the female who can control the sex of offspring. Legge and colleagues found, for instance, that kookaburra females produced largely male clutches if helpers at the nest were predominantly female (Legge et al. 2001) and largely female when helpers were largely male. Generally, in this asynchronous laying process, kookaburras usually produce a male first, a female second. According to Jenny Graves (2019), zebra finch females respond to environmental conditions and produce more females when times are tough (Graves 2019).

In eclectus parrots (*Eclectus roratus*), as Heinsohn and colleagues (1997) have shown, the choices for the sex of offspring can be extraordinary and extreme. The authors cite the case of one eclectus female at Chester Zoo producing 30 male offspring before the first female hatched. Eclectus parrots are perhaps also among the very few, if not the only parrot, that breed cooperatively in the sense that a number of males will guard one nest site.

The idiom 'putting all the eggs in one basket' as an expression of high risk is literally deflected in such cases. An interesting bind can occur in superb blue wrens, one of the world-famous cooperative Australian species that has been studied for about 150 years now and still holds surprises. A recent paper has shown that female wrens choose males early in the season who make commitments to raising their offspring and these males may not even have their breeding plumage yet. Having settled the question of parenting with a plain male, the female may then turn her attention to unattached males that had either changed into the attractive blue breeding plumage very early in the breeding season or, increasingly, even try to keep it all year round (McQueen et al. 2017). It is these males to which females make pre-dawn flights for extra-marital matings.

Obviously, the 'blue' plumage is very attractive to females and thought to indicate good health (Mulder and Magrath, 1994). The problem is that the blue makes the birds, otherwise of brownish colour in the non-breeding season, very conspicuous and the response of the wearers of such bright plumage spots all too often has been to hide, be cautious or even fearful and not show up in the open. As providers of offspring, this could make them rather useless – hence the female's choice to allow a few of her clutch to be fathered by such a high-quality male but to have the confident and capable male who is not necessarily fearful and not always in full colour help provide the food.

In summary, then, the evolutionary biological developments concerned with reproduction have set birds on a substantially different social path from the one taken by most mammals. The loss of the penis, the manner in which sperm can be stored in the reproductive tracts of females, and the option of spontaneous abortions together would suggest that females have a substantial level of independence.

In mammals, social organisation is often described in terms of matriarchy or patriarchy. Matriarchy, as in elephants and hyenas, is the rarer form. Patriarchy is the dominant form and includes also various human societies, meaning the ultimate power of social organisation tends to rest with the male, as in gorillas. Most human societies have constructed their social life around patriarchy and despite the fact that western societies profess supposed gender equality, there is a great failure rate to make such equality work at any level. In extreme cases, husbands kill their wives or physically abuse them to reassert their dominance. However, while social hierarchies in birds living in larger groups may also centre on a male, generally, the evolution of pair formation in birds has prevented such hierarchies from being the main form of social organisation. Birds are thus an ideal class of animals to study in terms of bonding and relationships and to what extent these offer benefits.

6

The colour of the sexes

We all know that birds can be very colourful and the question has always been why this may be so. Mammals, by contrast, have very cryptic colours. There are no mice with purple stripes or antelopes with red patches. Instead, there are endless variations of white to greys and black, wheaten to muted oranges and all shades of brown. Of the vertebrates, only tropical fishes, amphibia and reef fishes have developed colour ranges similar to birds, and although there are some primates with contrasting or striking face markings, these are usually still within the limited colour palette of mammals. The rich kaleidoscope of colours in birds have intrigued people for thousands of years. Some birds even acquired the position of status symbols, and many were found in paintings and sculptures (Mynott 2018).

Apart from its aesthetic value and human appreciation of bird ornaments and colour, the question of colour may be biologically of great importance to birds, not least in mate-choice. Colour in birds is a topic that has been of great interest to scientists and has produced myriad papers ranging from pure physics to molecular hormonal studies to those that focus on the perceptual apparatus of birds. This can be very technical and difficult to follow for the uninitiated, but in some ways can help decipher the complexities of mate-choice – if it is colour (be this depth, iridescence, brightness, ultra-violent markers) or ornament that has been stipulated as one of the possible triggers for mate-choice.

The topic of colour in birds cannot be divorced from the question of what colours birds can actually see and what importance might be attributed to colour in their plumage, their beak, their legs and even their eyes. Although it may not be altogether wise to start a discussion about the exciting subject of colour with the technicalities of colour vision, it is useful to remember that theories of mate-choice cannot be explored meaningfully unless we know something about a bird's sensory perception.

How and what birds can see

Bird vision has been subject to substantial research (Martin 2012, 2017) and there are many important aspects that are different from human vision. One of the most notable external differences between human eyes and those of birds is their relative position. Except for birds of prey and frogmouths, with eyes placed frontally, all birds have their eyes placed laterally (one each side of the head). This changes their visual field to be much wider than that of humans and determines their attention to things in front and to the side, depth perception (stereopsis) and has many other consequences. There are several ways to determine depth. A common one in mammals is eye convergence in the frontal binocular field, used also in birds but less so. Another is by comparing the inputs to each eye in the binocular field – the brain figures out the amount of discrepancy and determined depth from it. Determining depth in some sense also relies on motion parallax, which uses the differences in the amount of movement of images of objects relative to each other – for example, while moving, distant objects appear to remain almost stationary whereas those nearby seem to speed past. By using these differences, the brain can determine depth (Miles 1998;

van der Willigen et al. 1998). Birds also use head movements to estimate depth, called parallax. Especially juvenile tawny frogmouths move their heads in very obvious and exaggerated ways, almost through full circles. They do so by keeping their eyes looking forward and always in the horizontal plane (Iwaniuk and Wylie 2006; Kaplan 2018b). Birds can watch out for aerial predators and monitor the ground for sources of food or as landmarks on its flightpath more or less at the same time.

In fact, bird vision is superior to that of humans in so many respects. Speed of perception is also faster than in humans, enabling them to fly rapidly through a maze of obstacles (such as branches in forests) or catch insects in flight. This is significant because, as in humans, vision is perhaps the most important part of the entire perceptual apparatus.

The emphasis here will be on colour vision, because plumage colour or coloured ornaments have been regarded as crucial for sexual selection and female choice in many species. Varela and colleagues (1993) preface their chapter on bird vision by saying that birds have arguably the most elaborate and interesting colour vision of any land animal.

Diurnal birds, that is, birds that are awake during the day and sleep at night, see the same objects human eyes can see but, as far as colour is concerned, human eyes can only see part of what birds can see, based on the same architecture of rods for grey range and cones for colour range (Fig. 6.1).

By contrast, nocturnal birds, as is also true of nocturnal mammals, are equipped with a larger number of rods than cones and substantially more rod cells than humans. Rods discriminate between shades of grey; cones are designed to respond to wavelengths of colour. We have described this in great detail elsewhere (Kaplan and Rogers 2001).

Movement of eyes, while there are substantial differences of degree of movement across avian species, is less than in humans. Intriguingly, birds can control the size of each pupil separately, whereas mammals cannot. While this has long been known, I discovered this by myself

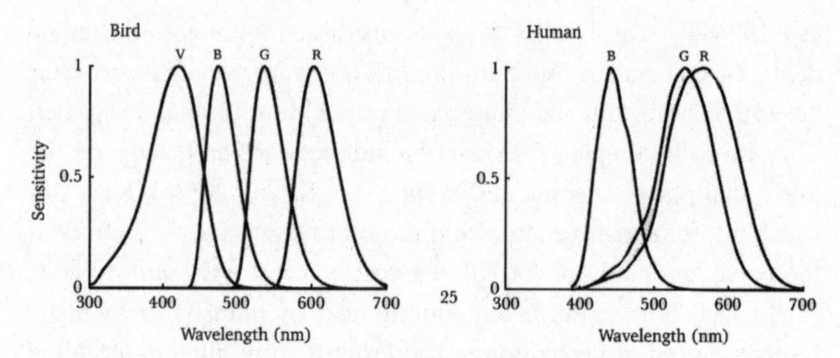

Fig. 6.1 Comparative colour perception in birds and humans. V: violet (also called NUV=near ultraviolet, 300–400 nm is the upper range of ultraviolet spectrum); B: blue; G: green; R: red. Note the wider spread of peaks in colour perception in birds and the clustering of colour perception in humans. Note also that there are no receptors for ultraviolet in human eyes. X axis: nm=nanometres (cf Olssen et al. 2018).

in close encounters with a tawny frogmouth. The bird was sitting on a branch and the pupil exposed to the sun was reduced, while the pupil on the shaded side was wide open as the bird actually looked at me directly (Fig. 6.2).

This control over how much light enters the eye can be an excellent protection against glare and also allows the bird to retain a sharper image of its environment without it being washed out by intense sun rays.

Some native birds also have the ability to see in fine detail in two directions at once (summarised in Rogers, 1995) and this is so because the most sensitive concentration of cone cells (called photoreceptors) is located in an area at the back of the retina called the fovea. Humans have one fovea but some birds may have two foveae: one strategically located for frontal vision and the other directed towards the side of the head so that birds may have sharp images to the side and to the front at the same time. Since most birds have eyes placed at the side of the head, these dual foveae are a highly useful adaptation for feeding, predator detection and even for roosting next to a partner.

Fig. 6.2 Tawny frogmouth roosting during daytime. Its right eye, exposed to the sun, shows pupil contraction while the pupil in the bird's left eye (in the shade) is of a wider opening. Human eyes cannot contract and expand the pupils independent of each other.

Most importantly, the visual system of birds has been described as the most richly endowed visual system of any vertebrate (Bennett and Théry 2007). What humans see of colour is based on three types of cone cells, whereas what birds see may be based on four different types of cone cells (call tetrachromatic) and some may even have five different types of cone cells. Some species also have the ability to see in the ultraviolet range, an ability that seems widespread among birds (see Fig. 6.1).

Ödeen and Håstad (2003) categorised colour vision in birds into two classes: one with a short-wavelength sensitivity biased towards violet (VS), including raptors, and the other biased towards ultraviolet (UVS), especially parrots and songbirds. Colour vision is not just an ability of vertebrates or an evolutionary adaptation to living on land – there are some arthropods and fishes with outstanding colour vision. It is also true that many species have no or very limited colour vision. Yet it is mostly thought that the colour vision in avian species evolved separately and the UVS variant has evolved at least five times from the (ancestral) VS form, including in parrots, most songbirds, and even in some gulls and rhea (Osorio and Vorobyev 2008). Stoddard and Prum (2011) thought that the plumage gamut of early lineages of living birds was probably small and dominated by melanin-based colours. Over evolutionary time, novel colouration mechanisms allowed plumages to colonise unexplored regions of colour space that involved pigmentary innovations evolving as possible communication signals, be this as health indicators or sexual signals.

Two attributes make the bird eye really special; one is a structure called the pecten that projects inside the back of the eyeball, because it supplies the retina with nutrients (Pettigrew et al. 1990). The other special feature concerns oil droplets that filter light before reaching the cone cells. These oil droplets come in various carotenoid pigmentations that are derived from carotene in the diet of birds. In some birds, not all cone cells are so protected across the entire retina (Fig. 6.3) and these are the species that also have sensitivity to ultraviolet rays, for instance zebra finches, budgerigars and some pigeons (Bowmaker et al. 1997).

Another extraordinary variable has been discovered in the colour vision of birds and that is the perception of colour according to light intensity. A study by Lind and Kelbe (2009) showed that colour vision can be compromised by light and that it varies between different species. They examined the threshold of colour vision in budgerigar and Bourke's parrot, *Neopsephotus bourkii*. Human eyes also lose some colour vision in bright light but not by as much as these parrots. The optical sensitivities of single cones are similar in both birds but Bourke's parrots have more, thinner and longer rods and fewer cones than budgerigars. These are important findings because the assumption is sometimes that mate-choice is based on colour and that the male will seek a bright spot to display such colours to advantage. At least in

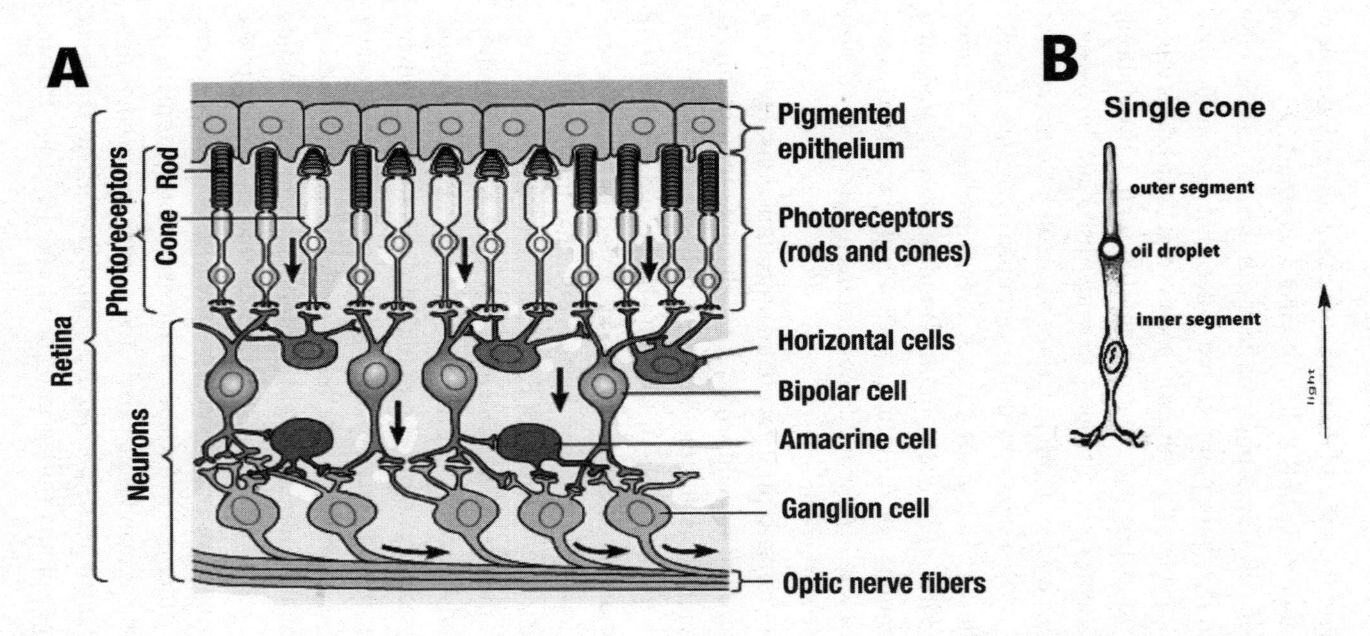

Fig. 6.3 A diagrammatic cross-section of the retina. The eye is a truly remarkable construct. This figure presents only the layer at the back of the eye, called the retina (shown in all its layers in Panel A). Light enters the eye from below in this diagram and passes through the retina to reach the outer segments of the photoreceptor cells. The latter generate nerve impulses that are transmitted to the rod cells (and the horizontal cells) and then to the ganglion cells (and the amacrine cells). The axons of the ganglion cells make up the optic nerve that leaves the eye and goes to the brain. Panel B presents a single cone and shows where the oil droplet is located which modifies light input before it even gets to the outer segments of the cone photoreceptors. (Pearson Education Inc.)

some cases, bright light would do a disservice to a displaying male if the onlooker can perceive only dull or washed-out colours.

Thus, in sexually dimorphic species with sexual selection by plumage colour, it is both plumage and vision that need to be considered: the male evolving the plumage colours and the female's vision capable of discriminating and determining what is attractive. Indeed, Friedman and Remes (2015) found that in Australian fairy-wrens (Maluridae), the rapid evolution of elaborate male colouration was driven by the visual system and this is certainly intriguing. Equally intriguing is the fact that most parrots, overall probably the most colourful of all birds as an order, are not colour dimorphic, meaning that in a vast number of Australian species, males and females are barely different in their plumage colour, confusing the problem even more – why have all this colour?

Vision is of course central for many other functions, including detecting and recognising landmarks, especially important in migration and feeding. In short, it is one of the most essential single parts of the perceptual apparatus without which no bird could survive. Here it is only important to establish that colour vision in birds is excellent and considerably better than in humans. That insight, though, is of rather recent history. In 2005, Eaton published an article in the Proceedings of the National Academy of Science with a headline titled: 'Human vision fails to distinguish widespread sexual dichromatism among sexually "monochromatic" birds.' For those studying sexual dimorphism and plumage colour, it was probably as revealing and surprising as it was after the much earlier discovery of echolocation, inaudible to humans. Eaton's announcement was a major moment (and shock) for scientists, learning that their perception had been inadequate for proper identification. In fact, 91.6 per cent of 166 North American passerines that were monochromatic in plumage from the human visual perspective were found to be dichromatic from the avian visual perspective (Eaton 2007). This is largely because plumage colours shifted into the ultraviolet range that the human eye cannot see. There are also wavelengths that do not emit or separate into colours, called achromatic.

Another recent discovery has also shown that vision in birds is not necessarily the same across all songbirds or parrots. We would expect this to happen between species living in different environments but it can also apply to individual birds within the same species. Carotinoid pigments are essential to bird colour. Carotinoid pigments in oil droplets in the eye act as optical filters. Lima and Pike (2016) used dietary manipulations, in which juvenile Japanese quail received either a high- or a low-carotenoid diet, and then tested the effects on the ability to perform a colour discrimination task. Only birds that had received the high-carotenoid diet were able to make chromatic discriminations (Lima and Pike 2016).

In other words, fine discriminations of plumage colour in others can only work if the onlooking bird, especially a female, is in a good state of health and has a high carotenoid intake. Subtleties will be lost on other birds when these basic dietary needs are not met.

Why some females are 'drab'

When Alfred Russell Wallace (1877) was writing about colours in birds, he said that female birds could not afford to have coloured plumage until birds built hidden nests (presumably, he would have included nest holes as well). There is some truth in this. Parrots do not build nests but raise young in tree holes, so presumably the female is protected and can raise her offspring without being detected while sitting on eggs. In eclectus parrots, *Eclectus roratus*, with extremely strongly dimorphic plumage, the female is a bright red over most of her body while the male is largely green. She spends considerable time in the nest hole while he does not. Wallace, although he was just north of Australia on one of his travels, unfortunately never made it to mainland Australia or he might have reconsidered this statement in terms of the actual evidence of the colours of Australian birds and also as to the role of coloured plumage in birds. In thick rainforest, for instance, colour may in fact be quite cryptic because of the low dappled light making reds and yellows look like breaks in the foliage. I keenly remember walking through the rainforest of the Guatemalan highlands and listening to the sounds of parakeets and parrots, often right above me, but failing to spot them. And they were plentiful, species such as orange-fronted parakeets, *Aratinga canicularis*, red-lored amazon, *Amazona autumnalis*, or yellow-headed parrots, *Amazona oratrix*, enough red and yellow in these species' plumage, one would imagine, to make their discovery and tracking easy. The second point, implied by Wallace, is that the female of the species cannot 'afford' to wear colours. If the male is colourful, then he is at great risk, but if he does not share incubation duties, he can fly away. If the female has to fly away to save herself during incubation, it tends to result in the loss of a clutch.

There are two problems embedded in the assumption of colourful plumage for the male only. First, such a claim is not well supported in Australian birds. Only 27 per cent of Australian land birds have plumage-related markers of sex difference and even some of these may be miniscule to the human eye. If one added shore and sea birds to the mix, the percentage of colour markers in Australian birds would decline even further. Second, by having implied that the female is 'drab' (for whatever reason) why is an evolutionary adaptation to increased colour desirable or superior to a move away from colour?

Pinning down sexual dimorphism of body size but especially of plumage colour (or sexual dichromatism) has resulted in a multitude of excellent studies that show how sexual dimorphism might work in support of Darwin's theory of sexual selection. It has also given us an indication of how climate and ecology may affect plumage colour. For instance, Bailey (1978) investigated latitudinal variation in colouration across 787 passerine species in North and Central America and found that sexual dimorphism is more pronounced in high latitude species and that females as well as males were more ornamented at higher latitudes.

We do not have any studies of similar magnitude in Australia, but we do have a very important study by Friedman and Remes (2017) of three species of honeyeater of the genus Gavicalis, often called by the alternative name, Lichenostomus. These three species, by Australian standards of distance, are in relatively close proximity to each other. One is the varied honeyeater, *Lichenostomus versicolor*, at home just in a narrow strip from about Cooktown along the east coast, all the way up the Cape York peninsula and in New Guinea. Another is the mangrove honeyeater, *L. fasciogularis*, which occupies a narrow coastal strip starting around Cooktown and all the way south to northern New South Wales, while the third species, the singing honeyeater, *L. virescens*, is widespread across Australia, inhabiting much of the inland. All three species of the same genus are about the same size, but they have plumage colour and pattern differences.

While it is not unusual that birds of the same genus have similarities in plumage colour and patterns, Friedman and Remes had drawn our attention to the fact that plumage colour may be dependent on specific variables in the environment.

The interesting aspect on which the researchers' analysis focused was not on latitude or altitude but on rainfall, a pivotal climatic factor in Australia (Friedman and Remes 2017). The habitat of the three species is subdivided by rainfalls received: from the highest rainfall of an average of 2045 mm (varied honeyeater) on the Cape, to 1275 mm (the mangrove honeyeater) at the coast and, finally, for the singing honeyeater, to the much lower annual rainfall of 20–430 mm inland. Their findings show that these gradients are mirrored in a gradient of plumage colour. The lightest is for the species in the driest area and the darkest is in areas of the highest rainfall (Fig. 6.4). This is entirely consistent with Gloger's rule, named after the zoologist Constantin WL Gloger (1803–1863), stating that birds in climates with high relative humidity were darker than conspecifics in climates with low relative humidity and that in turn has to do with the amount of melanin stored in the feathers.

Fig. 6.4 Left: the singing honeyeater and right: the varied honeyeaters of the same genus. I photographed this singing honeyeater in the Bungle Bungles, the famous and unusual mountain formations south of Kununurra, a town in the top end of Western Australia, close to the border of the Northern Territory. It moved about in a relatively large group and was not shy, hopping quite close on the ground. This species can be found throughout Australia except the eastern seaboard. The varied honeyeater, by contrast, is very confined in its habitat to the Cape York region of the tropical east coast. This bird was hidden and a long way away in tree foliage and dappled light, and seemed to be on its own. Despite the differences in light quality, the plumage differences are quite remarkable. The distracting background was removed in order to focus on the actual bird.

Sexual dimorphism, as expressed in plumage and ornaments, tends to favour the male in intensity and brightness of colour, but not always. There are species in which ornaments are equally developed in males and females and sometimes these ornaments tend to become more elaborate with age rather than be determined by sex (Kraaijeveld et al. 2007). In those cases, as Tarvin and Murphy (2012) pointed out, ornaments may be socially selected status signals without necessarily increasing mating success.

However, as said before, even when ornaments do play a role in sexual selection, they may not be as common as was once thought and there are also examples of species in which colour brightness or intensity is more pronounced in the female. In a few cases, such as the emu, this is related to a necessary role reversal (because she will exhaust her energies by having produced among the largest eggs known). In their mateship dance, both male and female raise the feathers on their necks, exposing a bare patch on the front of the long neck, and the area behind and below the ear is often of a slight blue tint but, actually, the colour on the neck of the female turns a deeper blue but only around breeding time. She also makes more varied vocalisations. In the dance, they both contribute slow semi dance-like steps, perform beak dips into the feathers, little symbolic preenings and snake their necks. In the outback, I have seen splendid performances of females that suddenly started running in large circles with wings half raised, looking elegant and as light as the wind. The male has to be careful how and when to approach her because she can become very aggressive towards him if he does not fulfil her expectations. When her eggs are deposited with the male, she leaves altogether while he will continue to invite females to his nest site. Unlike other males that mate with several or even many females, this male takes full responsibility and will both brood and raise on his own the offspring of the females with whom he has mated.

Rarely is the female brighter than the male without such role reversal but there are some stunning exceptions. One example is the shining flycatcher, *Myiagra alecto*. In this species, the female is splendidly adorned by highly visible and contrasting colours: glossy black-blue for the crown, sides of face and nape, while the upper part including the long tail is a rich rufous chestnut, set off by the white underparts and belly. By contrast, the male is unpatterned and is uniformly a shiny and iridescent black-blue. In Snares penguins, *Eudyptes robustus*, the female's yellow crest feathers contain more colour and fluorescent pigment content than that of the male (McGraw et al. 2009).

How colours are made

The question is how are colours made and why? In an Aboriginal dreamtime story, all birds were once black and that is actually not a bad way of thinking about colours in birds, because melanin that produces black is common to most birds with the exception of parrots.

The colours in the visual spectrum are traditionally described as red, yellow, orange, green, blue, indigo and violet. Red has the longest wavelength and violet has the shortest. The longer-wave colours (red, yellow, orange) are produced using pigment and the shorter-wave colours (green, blue, purple) are created by the structure of feathers. Carotenoids, or psittacofulvins in the case of parrots, produce colours rich in long wavelength reflectance (red, yellow). Structural colours are single-handedly responsible for all colours rich in short wavelength reflectance (blue, violet, UV) and account for nearly half of the occupied colour space. Colour in Australian birds is concentrated at the shortwave end of the colour space (Delhey 2015) and thus structural colour plays a major role in the way we perceive them to have colour. Finally, the combination of structures with carotenoids or psittacofulvins creates colours rich in middle wavelengths (greens).

Bird feather colour is a complicated business in several ways. First, the number of pigments involved have different evolutionary trajectories and distributions. In mammals, pigmentation is largely based on melanin. Skin or feather colouration accumulates from pigments that can be produced via dietary intake (endogenous production). Melanin is the most common endogenous pigment and accounts for nearly 75 per cent of all measured plumage patches in Australian birds. Strictly speaking, there are two forms of melanin: phaeomelanin in most birds and eumelanin in parrots. Phaeomelanin produces rusty red and tawny yellow colours and is present in black plumage. Melanins are often considered ancestral and can be synthesised by the birds themselves. Indeed, melanin has been credited with a multitude of functions, not all well documented or at least not all applying universally. Melanin is said to be favoured in humid environments, offers protection against UV radiation, protects the skin from harmful biophysical agents and can even provide increased resistance to oxidative stress.

Melanins produce the major form of cryptic colouration because they match the colours of a large part of natural backgrounds (such as soil, bark, etc.), which is useful for camouflage. The nightjars, among them the tawny frogmouth, are past masters in camouflage. Their mottled greyish brown feathers make them almost impossible to spot, even during the day. Of course, such colours make poor visual signals. Visual signals are usually associated with other mechanisms of colour production (Delhey 2015). Further, melanin is important for thermoregulation and may play a role in defence from pathogens. Melanins can also contribute to expressions of sexual dimorphism when modified and used in combination with other pigments (Saino et al. 2013) and can determine the expression of certain colours, and appear differently as a result of the distribution of a pigment in the actual feather (close to surface, middle or close to shaft), also changing the perception of intensity. While it may not have every function in every species and circumstance, as a structural colour, melanin is a very important pigment.

Perhaps its most important function is the health benefits it provides. These are related to feather upkeep. A typical vaned feather is organised like a branching tree crown: there is a main shaft, called the rachis, and from this main stem, and fused to it, arise a series of branches, or barbs. The barbs themselves are also branched and form the barbules. In other words, branches support sub-branches and even the sub-branches support further smaller sub-branches. The difference between the distribution of branches from main branches to smaller and smaller ones is that the branches arising from one branch symmetrically overlap with the branches of another and these are held together firmly by little hooklets. Under the microscope, these fine structures look like tapestry and are so tightly packed and secured by the hooklets that even the pressure of air or a downpour of water will not separate them (Figs. 6.5.1 and 6.5.2).

Impressively, the architecture of a feather remains complex even at the most miniscule level. The *Australian Journal of Forensic Science*

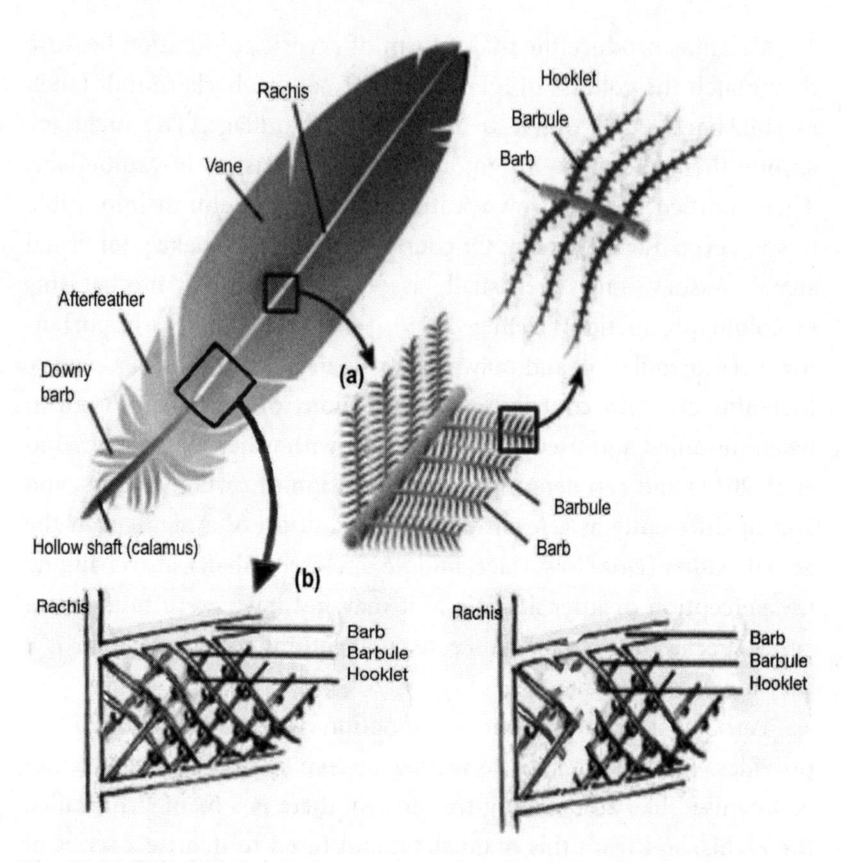

Fig. 6.5.1 A flight feather: a true masterpiece. The rachis as the main stem has fused to it all the branches called barbs and from these derive further smaller branches, called barbules, equipped with hooklets to interlock crosswise with the barbules from branches next to them. a) enlargement to show barbs and barbules; b) further enlargement to show where parasite damage typically occurs, Lower panels: Left: enlargement of interlocking barbules. Right: microbic activity can damage or destroy the interlocking barbules as shown here, or even break barbs entirely. (Upper panel source: Venz 2016; lower panel drawn by author.)

recently published a paper on Australian bird feathers. This may sound surprising but in the context of the allegedly high traffic in poached native birds, and the idea of finding ways of producing evidence of any native birds being illegally traded, it makes sense to see feathers in a forensic context. Importantly, their point was that they rarely have

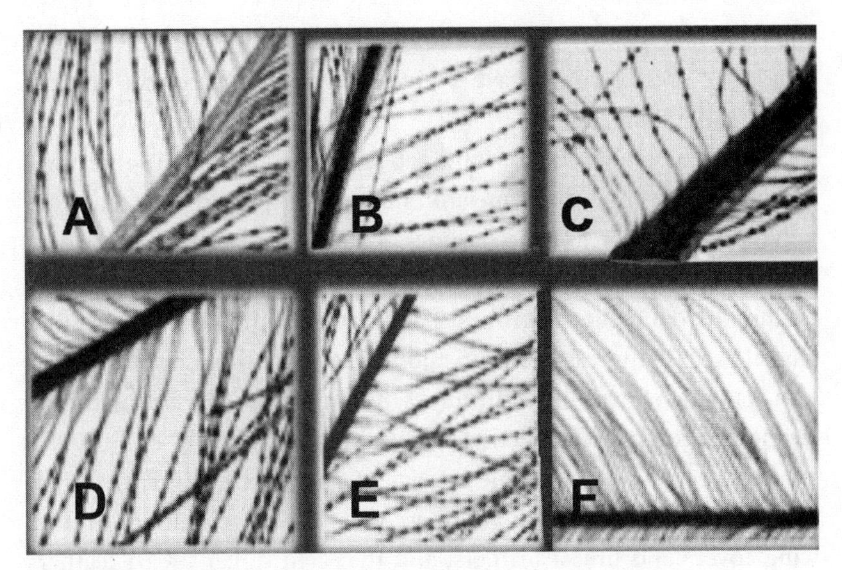

Fig. 6.5.2 Barbules under the microscope, showing microscopic feather characteristics of downy barbules using auto-montaged light microscopy: A: Glossy black cockatoo; B: Rainbow lorikeet; C: Crimson rosella; D: Australian magpie; E: Spangled drongo; F: Light-mantled albatross. The barbules of the downy feathers are sufficiently different in structure and in the number of nodes on each strand (note that the albatross has no nodes at all) that they can reveal the identity of a species (excerpts taken from Lee et al. 2015).

the luxury of gaining as much evidence as an entire feather, but they may get small fragments, particularly of the more fragile segments of downy feathers. As their microscopic work has shown, species can be identified from such small segments. The information obtained in the paper by Lee and colleagues (2015) can also be used effectively for science. Indeed, their work is new and provides an insight into the intricacies of bird feather construction (Fig. 6.5.2).

Such perfection is under constant threat from microbial organisms that will chew through some of the connections in the barbs and become visible as flappy out-of-place bits of feathers and, to the birds, would become very noticeable in flight. These microbes come from soils that tend to contain a variety of feather-degrading bacilli, such as *B. licheniformis* and *Streptomyces pactum* and fungi *Chrysosporium* and *Fusarium sporotrichioides*. The combined action of several feather-degrading species could have a great and lasting effect on feathers (Burtt and Ichida 2004).

When these microbes become active (particularly so in some environments with humidity), melanin becomes important. Melanins are polymers that increase the hardness of the biological tissues where they are embedded. Hardening of the feathers protects to some extent against the damaging microbes. The first experimental evidence that parasites can suppress the expression of structural plumage colouration was first shown in wild turkeys, *Meleagris gallopavo*, which have strong iridescent UV-reflecting structural plumage (Hill et al. 2005). When injected with multiple species of coccidial oocysts, the birds suffered coccidial infection and there was less UV reflectance in their wing covert and breast feathers, and they had duller breast feathers (Hill et al. 2005). These results exemplify that health problems become visible and thus become a signal of overall health.

Apart from melanin, birds have carotenoid pigments as well as structural colour. The carotenoid group has recently drawn renewed interest because of its complexity and conserved status. The majority of carotenoid compounds and reactions are utilised in biological functions unrelated to plumage colouration, including vision and the immune system (Toomey et al. 2015), assuring their evolutionary retention (Lu and Li 2008). Morrison and Badyaev (2018) were struck by the realisation that carotenoids as a biochemical structure of an ancient carotenoid network have persisted through avian diversification and are likely to play an important role in the evolution of contemporary adaptations.

We tend to think of evolution as having gone from the most primitive to the most advanced through major changes. There are moments to give pause for thought that in order for organisms to develop, there need to be some basic building blocks at genetic, microbiological and molecular levels that are essential, remain constant and are deeply engrained in extant species. Morrison and Badyaev (2018) compared structural and historical associations in 467 carotenoid networks of extant and ancestral species and uncovered the overwhelming effect of pre-existing metabolic network structures on carotenoid diversification over the last 50 million years of avian evolution. Apart from the historical nature, what their study shows is a remarkable convergence of complex pigmentation patterns among (phylogenetically) very distinct species. Apparently, once formed, these patterns can be preserved even without being expressed for millions of generations, suggesting that their genetic and developmental organisation allow these patterns to appear intact in distinct lineages (Badyaev 2006). Despite the enormous malleability in nature and the ability of birds to adapt and change, even speciate, this is an important reminder that at least some of the basic biological building blocks have to remain and become indispensable ingredients throughout evolution and they may also place certain constraints on evolution.

Psittacine or, more correctly, psittacofulvin, is a pigment that is unique to parrots worldwide. Parrots have unique red feather pigments (McGraw and Nogare 2005). Amazingly, it is not found at all in any other bird group and despite the diversity of about 350 parrot species worldwide, all parrots have it. Why? Nobody knows. No single other species has it and it is one thing that binds the group of parrots (of all three major groups) together around the world. It is responsible for the bright red, orange and yellow colours and is produced in the parrots' bodies. The puzzle is also that these unique psittacofulvin pigments of parrots occupy an essentially identical red/orange/yellow region of colour space as the carotenoid pigments found in the passerines (Passeriformes) and yet parrots have ample concentrations of carotenoids in their blood to colour their feathers (McGraw and Nogare 2005), but still evolved this distinct alternative for expanding their colour palette into the long wavelength regions of colour space (Stoddard and Prum 2011).

When parrots from any group produce reds from the light-pink hue of several cockatoos to the deep red of red lories, *Eos bornea*, they all use the same set of five lipochromes to colour their feathers (McGraw and Nogare 2005). They can also produce yellow that can fluoresce under UV light. As in melanin, the pigment has other functions. Feathers with high levels of psittacofulvin resist feather-degrading bacilli such as *Bacillus licheniformis* better than white ones (Burtt et al. 2010). Indeed, in certain species, plumage patch sizes have been linked to health and positive social attributes, but such studies have usually been confined to males (Boves et al. 2014). Thus, most birds outside the parrot group that have red and yellow pigments derive these colours from the carotenoid complex, and it is partly introduced by diet.

Finally, apart from psittacofulvin, melanin and carotenoid pigments, structural colour is very important as well. Structural colour is perhaps a misnomer because it is not a colour-producing pigment. Structural colouration involves the selective reflectance of incidental light, be this containing reflectors, or structures causing scattering of light waves. The structure that enables such refraction can even be transparent but have micro structures that refract light. The colour effects can appear very bright, even brighter than those of pigments.

The production of colour via light refractive structures in the organism is just about as old as life itself (Parker 2000) and in invertebrates of sea and land, it has been identified as having a number of very important functions. The efficiency of refraction may also indicate a state of health and stress. In a sense, such colour is an optical illusion created by very specific feather structures whose exposure as colour or iridescence depends on feather exposure and on the way light falls on that feather. What we see in structural colour is usually in the range of blue, green and purple (short wavelength reflectance), and is most dramatically shown in displays by some hummingbirds and birds of paradise. In some cases, it is dramatically highlighted under ultraviolet conditions. For dramatic greens (middle wavelengths), it requires the combination of structural colour with carotenoids or psittacofulvins.

Some of Australia's birds that seem just a boring black in fact have structural colour and UV reflectance. When viewing black spangled drongos, *Dicrurus bracteatus*, in sunlight, the wing feathers suddenly reveal stunning deep purple and dark green hues, merging into dark blue and green in the tail feathers. The mature male satin bowerbird's wings sport a hue of dark blue. In Victoria's riflebirds in the Atherton Tablelands, an Australian relative of the birds of paradise of New Guinea, male plumage has an iridescent purple sheen turning into blue-green on the head and more bronze on the lower breast. The throat is velvety black with a metallic green and blue triangular patch in the centre, which is used to full advantage in courtship displays (Frith and Cooper 1996). In riflebirds, plumage is an example of strong sexual dimorphism because the female is a patchy and patterned tawny and brown. while in spangled drongos it is not dimorphic. Males and females have the same plumage.

Hence, the presence of structural colour may not define a sexually dimorphic signal. In the shining flycatcher, the male is entirely black and very shiny because of structural colour reflecting a strong dark blue all over his plumage. The shining flycatcher is also one of the most sexually dimorphic native birds in plumage. The female only has black in the upper part of the head, extending to the neck, but her belly and neck are white and the wing feathers are a very bright rust to chestnut colour. She could barely be more conspicuous, a case in point against the argument that females have to look 'drab' to provide camouflage while nesting.

Some yellow plumage colour is created both by reflection of light from white structural tissue and absorption of light by carotenoids. Thus, structural components of feathers contribute substantially to yellow 'carotenoid' displays, or, expressed the other way around, as Shawkey and Hill (2005) did, carotenoids need structural colours to shine. Interestingly, black cockatoos, gang-gang cockatoos, galahs, cockatiels (all part of the cockatoo/Cacatuidae family) have no structural colouring (Tielfan 2015). White cockatoos, incidentally, have no visible melanin in their feathers.

If this were not complicated enough, the pigments can be modified and each of those altering mutations has a trigger which is different for each pigment. Moreover, the genetic assignment into dominant, recessive, or progressive determines the expression of certain colours, and the distribution of a pigment in the actual feather (close to surface, middle or close to shaft) are changes that alter the perception of intensity. This is even further complicated by the fact that different pigments can be layered on top of each other. For example, iridescence can be produced by alternate (hummingbirds) or single (satin bowerbird) layers of a feather as an ultraviolet-blue plumage colouration (Doucet et al. 2006). Finally, and importantly, colour in birds is influenced, if not determined, by lifestyle, plant environment and climate, as was shown above in the study by Friedmann and Remes (2017).

7

Plumage and eye colours in Australian birds

What are they?

We are lucky that, apart from studies such as Friedman and Remeš (2017) discussed in Chapter 6, plumage colours have been investigated in all Australian land birds (Delhey 2015) and a study specific to Australian parrots by Taysom and colleagues investigated parrot plumage as sexual signals (Taysom et al. 2011). Such studies are very laborious to conduct because each individual bird of a given species has to be sampled in all areas that typically could have specific colour patches. These might be specific to a species or subspecies and also different between male and female. For these reasons, as many as seventeen sampling points had to be selected in each bird in Delhey's study of more than 500 Australian avian species (Delhey 2015).

Delhey showed that Australian birds are not all that flush with colours and argued that most colours are unremarkable. Of the entire theoretically possible colour space that could be occupied, more than 70 per cent of that space is, in fact, unoccupied by Australian birds. As for special colours, those that push the boundaries of colour space, they are extremely rare. This also means that colour variation is uneven in native species. A quick look at any bird guide book makes this obvious. The finches, manakins, parrots and lorikeets are the main contributors to colour and possibly provide more than the majority of birds, meaning that a few selected clades of birds are much more colourful than expected for their number of species (Delhey 2015). This becomes clearer when the distribution is broken down into percentages (Fig. 7.1).

When comparing males and females in different clades, Delhey found that male colours almost completely surround female colours in some groups, hence the argument for sexual dimorphism is supported,

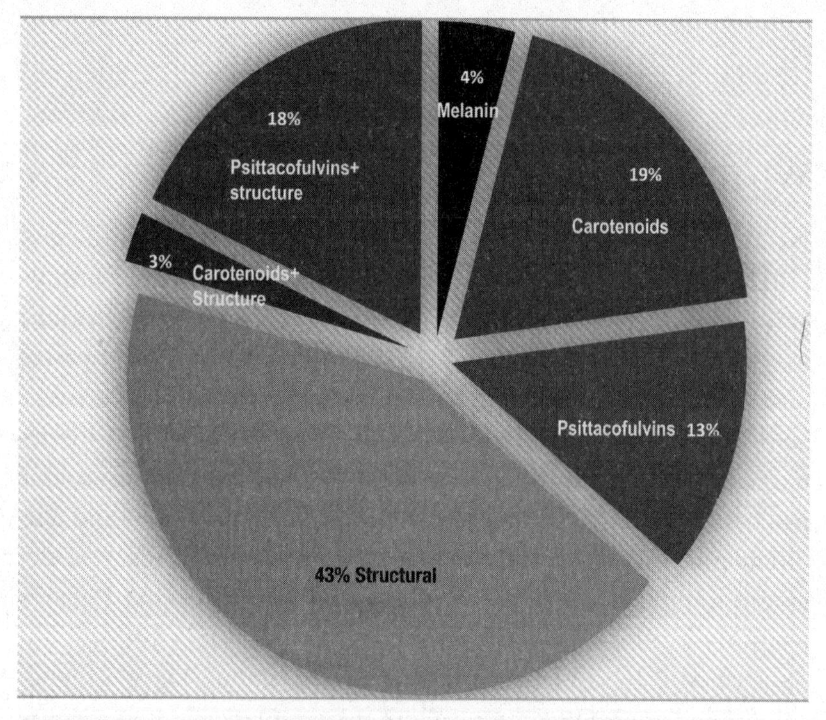

Fig. 7.1 Colour spectrum used. Structural colour makes up a good deal of the colour ranges identified and the percentage is even larger when all components with structural colour are included (more than 60 per cent). In terms of the colour spectrum, parrots dominate the colour palette in Australian birds. They represent about ten per cent of land birds but psittacofulvins (also including structural colours) make up more than 30 per cent of the colour palette (based on data by Delhey 2015).

but much more weakly, than one might have supposed. This becomes apparent when all land birds are compared for signs of weak or strong differences in appearance (Table 7.1).

Taking only the species the Delhey study used but omitting birds of prey because they tend to have little or no colour dimorphism, one arrives at a picture that gives a good indication of the lack of importance of sexual plumage differences between male and female songbirds and parrots in Australia.

As Table 7.1 shows, strong sexual dimorphism via plumage colour affects only 28 per cent of all native birds examined and this percentage, one suspects, is largely influenced by the parrots and to some extent by finches and manakins.

Australia has been described as the land of parrots and they are very colourful, but songbirds and certainly most seabirds, while not very colourful, also show little to no plumage diversity between sexes. The way the above summary was arrived at was by defining sexual dimorphism in plumage in accordance with the *Simpson & Day Field Guide to the Birds of Australia* (any edition). Note that such field guides always provide an image of juveniles (because juvenile plumage is almost always different from that of adults) but list male and female adults separately only when there are plumage differences between the sexes, even slight ones, such as an additional mark on the neck or head. Species which are only represented as adults in one image are deemed to have no visible differences (to the human eye) that could serve as identifiers to differentiate male from female. Table 7.1 on page 168 follows this published ornithological convention and in the order of families presented in the Field Guide rather than relying on personal observation.

Hence, this finding presented in the table is in itself quite important. Further, Taysom and colleagues (2011) found no strong evidence for a widespread role of melanin-based colours in sexual signalling, and could find only mixed evidence for the role of psittacofulvin-based colouration in sexual signalling, the very pigment that evolved

Families	No of species	Cooperative	Pair	Weak dimorphism	Strong dimorphism
1. Pigeons/doves	18		18	14	4
2. Cockatoos	14	1	13	10	4
3. Parrots/Lorikeets	36	3	33	24	12
4. Cuckoos	13	--	--	9	4
5. Owls	8		8	6	2
6. Nightjars	9		8	9	--
7. Kingfishers, bee-eaters, dollarbirds	11	4	7	9	2
8. Pittas	3	--	3	3	--
9. Lyrebirds/Scrubbirds	4	--		--	4
10. Swallow, Martins, Pipits, Wagtails	10		10	--	10
11. Cuckoo-shrikes, trillers, robins, bellbird, whistlers and shrike-thrushes	16		16	9	7
12. Monarchs, fantails whip-birds to babblers	35		2	24	11
13. Fairy-wrens, grasswrens and bristlebirds	23		2	10	13
14. Pilotbird to gerygones	15	--	15	14	1
15. Thornbills and whiteface	12	6	6	12	--
16. Honeyeaters, miners, friarbirds	37	2		37	--
17. Honeyeaters, orioles,	25			20	5
18. Chats, figbirds	5			--	5
19. Drongos, bowerbirds, chough, apostlebirds	10	2	8	7	3
20. Riflebirds	3	--	--	--	3
21. Magpies, currawongs, butcherbirds, woodswallows	13	2	11	13	--
22. Ravens	6		6	6	--
23. Sunbirds, white-eyes, mistletoebird, pardalotes, silvereye	10		10	6	4
24. Finches	10		10	8	2
TOTAL	346			250	96
Totals, expressed in per cent				72.3	27.7

Table 7.1 Sexual dimorphism and social organisation.

specifically in parrots. The average chromatic contrast between the sexes for yellow to red colouration was less than for structural blue colouration and less than the birds' calculated threshold for colour discrimination. Although the male-biased sexual dimorphism in patch size indicates that yellow to red colours are often ornamental, the other findings suggest that this is not a prominently sexually selected type of ornamentation.

We do not know whether these Australian results are exceptional or if they would be comparable with other continents or apply at higher altitudes. I suspect that the figures might not differ by all that much worldwide, suggesting from the perspective of Australia, the cradle of songbirds and parrots, that strong sexual dimorphism in plumage may concern only a minority of birds. Yet as recently as 2014, in another landmark publication on comparative genomics, the discourse was almost unchanged from decades earlier, implying that sexual plumage dimorphism is central to the debate on sexual selection in birds:

> We investigated the genomics of plumage color, a behaviourally important trait and longstanding example of sexual selection. Male birds have frequently evolved extravagant plumage color in response to both male–male competition and female choice resulting in remarkable sexual dichromatism (Zhang et al. 2014).

I have quoted this in full partly because I do not believe that we have any overall figure worldwide showing that males have 'frequently' evolved extravagant plumage. At least in Australian birds, this refers to a rather small proportion of birds. Hence such biased theoretical positions on which a good many other assumptions rest may not only not ring true in the Australian context but, inevitably, must be exposed as opinion. Yet opinions like this are reinforced and reiterated as if such statements were anchored in well-known facts and required no further critical and sceptical review.

Of course, there is a further addendum necessary. Even if birds show little obvious sexual dimorphism, they may still make decisions about mate-choice based on visual cues. The starling is a case in point. Males and female look alike, but there are cues in the refraction of light in the feathers that are revealed only under ultraviolet light. Fluorescent pigments appear to glow because ultraviolet light is absorbed and reemitted at longer wavelengths. In budgerigar males, it is a splash of colour next to the beak and on top of the head. While we are unable to see ultraviolet and cannot really imagine what the influence of exposure to ultraviolet may do to perception of the male's feathers by an avian female, we can conceive that iridescence of these feathers is enhanced. In budgerigars (Fig. 7.2), the patches on the side of the head may reflect ultraviolet light and the female can see these enhancements of the patches. It could well be that we make some incorrect assumptions, at times only by degree, about the visual signalling that may occur in mate-choice because we read colour from the perception of human eyes and thus outside the ultraviolet.

Andrew Bennet and colleagues (1996) conducted a series of experiments with zebra finches by allowing the female to see the male through a series of filters of two types, ultraviolet blocking filters and ultraviolet transmitting filters. The females strongly preferred viewing the male through the ultraviolet transmitting filters. Males may choose females solely on the radiance provided under ultraviolet light. In several other studies, similar conclusions were drawn. Hunt and colleagues (1998) announced that blue tits were not blue but ultraviolet. The announcements concerning the blue tit were a real surprise at the time. Blue tits are typically monogamous and considered to be classified as sexually monochromatic, i.e. only very slightly dimorphic, with large overlaps between the sexes in colouration. To find that they were visually sensitive to wavelengths in the near-ultraviolet (300–400 nm) range and then testing the birds in this spectrum, it became obvious that there were strongly sexually dimorphic signals that influenced mate-choice in both sexes.

Choice of partner may be guided or influenced by ultraviolet perception and other visual criteria that we may not as yet have discovered.

A study by Hausmann and colleagues (2002) on fluorescent signalling in Australian parrots found that just about all parrots they tested, and even most of the Australian songbirds and corvids, had UV colours. They then tested whether there was an association between UV colours and display areas. Again, this association existed for most. They tested UV-suppressed budgerigars against those whose UV reflectance was not impeded and they found that both male and female budgerigars preferred partners with higher UV reflectance. It appears in mate-choice that UV rays, invisible to humans with the bare eye, may play an important role, and this may be for both males and females.

In budgerigars, as was discovered some years ago, it is the colour of the nares (the fleshy saddle on the beak that accommodates the nostrils, see Fig. 7.2) that is pinkish in females and blue-grey in males. Males also have tiny dashes of dark blue on each side of the beak and

Fig. 7.2 Wild budgerigar pair photographed near Alice Springs in their typically green body colour and yellow head. The male is in front, the female behind (her nares are slightly lighter and vaguely of pinkish hue).

that colour begins to shine only under UV light. The UV exposure, if within the perceptual capacity of a bird, may be very telling and persuasive. Staffan Andersson and colleagues called ultraviolet differences in plumage the first, but probably not the last, example of hidden sexual dimorphism in birds (Andersson et al. 1998).

One hastens to add, however, that the very idea that mate-choices would be made on one criterion alone (such as plumage colour) may be reductionist in the extreme. In important cases, as indeed discussed in more details in the coming chapters, plumage may be just one facet and not the only or even the main criterion of choice.

Clearly, at least, there is a correspondence between the evolution of the visual system, or rather visual perception, and the colour scheme of conspecifics and of the environment generally. How this can work in evolution has been explained by examining the genes responsible for regulating opsin-based visual pigments. Bloch (2015) studied four cone opsin genes: Lw, Rh2, Sws2 and Sws1. Interestingly, opsin gene coding sequences and associated visual pigment spectral sensitivities are known to be rather invariant across birds, while the actual expression of opsin varies very widely across birds. Only one of these genes, Sws2, was found to be associated with sexual dichromatism and thus sexual selection, but this is only in females. Gene expression is adaptive and can respond rather quickly to sex-selection pressures. That is, if male colourations change, female visual perception can co-evolve.

Juvenile plumage and eye colour

Perhaps no special introduction is needed to point out that most juvenile birds have plumage that is different in colour and/or patterns from that of adults. It is rare for juveniles, however, to have entirely different plumage colour and markings than the parents, as happens in some finches (star, red-browed and Gouldian finches) and in white-breasted woodswallows, *Artamus leucorynchus*. The juvenile is more cryptic and brownish in colour but heavily striated across the mantle while the parents are white on the breast and uniformly dark grey from head to the back. In birds with predominantly black plumage, juvenile plumage may be greyish brown, as in currawongs and magpies, and may have more scalloping of feathers or markings. There are exceptions, as in crested pigeons, a species in which the juvenile looks like a miniature replica of the adults. Parrots have the adult plumage almost immediately once the sheath has broken surrounding their pin feathers. Kookaburras and parrots are the same, going from no feathers to pin feathers and directly into adult plumage at least on the wings and head, while many songbirds go through a plumage stage that only changes into adult form after the first moult. Plumage differences can also be in colour or in patterns and these differences are clearly indicated in bird guide books. Most of the colour differences, when they occur, tend to be less colour intensive or colour contrasting and are usually within the range of cryptic colours that help camouflage the young birds.

Age differences can also be detected in the colour of feet and legs (usually grey or pale or black) regardless of the colouring in adults, as well as in beak colour. In kookaburra offspring of the same plumage as the adults and quite quickly even of the same size, the upper and lower mandible are slate grey in juveniles, while in adults, the upper mandible is a dark brown and the lower mandible a light bone colour. In dollarbird juveniles, *Eurystomus orientalis*, the beak is a slate colour while in adults, it is a bright orange-red. Juvenile feet and legs are grey while they are a red/orange in adults. Beak colour changes from dark grey to light in Gouldian finches, *Erythrura gouldiae*. Sometimes there are additional colour differences on other parts of the body. The pink on the gape at the base of the bill of young ravens and currawongs was already described above (Fig. 7.3) and this can be seen from some distance away.

Rather intriguing is the fact that eye colour plays a particularly prominent role in Australian birds. Some time ago, Craig and Hulley (2004) investigated the presences of iris colour in hundreds of species in Southern Africa (355 species), Australia (299), Europe (164),

Canada (182) and Venezuela (654). To my great surprise, 35.1 per cent of Australian species have brightly coloured eyes, far above the level of light irises in any of the other regions. Southern Africa was next with 25.6 per cent while the rest, even with Venezuela's rich bird life (11.8 per cent), was substantially lower: 7.9 per cent for European birds and just 6 per cent of Canadian birds. This is obviously a phenomenon of particular relevance to Australian birds and, even more surprisingly, is reflected in the colour changes some birds undergo from juvenile to adult stage.

In magpies and currawongs, birds that are just black and white, the most obvious change from immaturity to maturity is indeed the colour change in the eye – juveniles of both species have brown eyes and after the first moult, magpie eyes turn into a reddish light brown or a light red, while those of currawongs turn yellow (Fig. 7.3). In currawongs, in which adult males and females are indistinguishable to the human observer, juveniles may have a dark grey plumage

Fig. 7.3 Currawong adult on left, fledged juvenile on the right (brown eyes). The signal of status as adult or juvenile is very prominent in birds with dark plumage and unmistakeable even from a distance. Note also the light (pink) colour at the corner of the beak/gape which is still very malleable to allow wider beak opening and shows that this bird has only recently fledged. This area will harden and darken by the first moult into adult plumage.

and may be recognised as such by the slightly greyer shade of the feathers. However, the clearest indication of whether a currawong is a juvenile is by eye colour alone. Australian ravens, *Corvus coronoides*, also black-plumaged, start with brown eyes that turn white. In various cuckoo-shrikes (Campephagidae) eye colour also changes from brown to yellow. In ground cuckoo-shrikes, *Coracina maxima*, the adult eyes are yellow while those of juveniles are black and particularly conspicuous against the light grey plumage. And then there are the incredibly intensely blue, almost shimmering eyes of satin bowerbird males or the largest deep red eyes I have ever seen in a bird, those of the letter-winged kite, *Elanus scriptus*. The juvenile kite starts life with brown eyes and brownish plumage while the adult has snow-white plumage and very large bright red eyes. The colour red as an iris colour is not all that uncommon in Australian birds. The wompoo fruit-dove, *Ptilinopus superbus*, already colourful throughout its plumage, with very dramatic contrast colours of violet and yellow on its belly, also sports a light blue head, red nares and red eyes. In helmeted friarbirds, *Philemon buceroides*, juvenile eyes are brown while those of adults are reddish brown, similarly in red wattlebirds. In blue-faced honeyeaters, *Entomyzon cyanotis*, however, it is not the eye colour that changes but the featherless patch around the eyes. In adults, it is a bright blue while in juveniles it is a light and iridescent green.

Why these changes occur is not really known, but all sorts of suggestions have been put forward including developmental ones concerned with the bird's own visual perception (Burtt 1986), environmental factors to do with visibility in a given environment (Davidson et al. 2017) or socio-sexual reasons. The latter, my own idea, is that difference in eye colour might be the most visible immediate difference that protects such juveniles in the sense that they will not be regarded as competition or sexually available and it may prevent any sexual harassment as well as possibly making some adults in some species (red wattlebirds are definitely not among the tolerant) some leeway if they find themselves in neighbouring territories or another adult family of the same species. In such cases, their identification as juveniles may also protect them from attacks from other avian species. Even magpies are a little more lenient when juveniles of another family wander into their territory – it may be a short truce but enough for the young bird to get away with a warning.

Finally, another surprise is the fact that many Australian avian juveniles have long periods of dependency. Indeed, as was shown and discussed in Chapter 1, compared to northern hemisphere birds, they are unusually given many months of post-fledging parental care. In some cases, as in satin bowerbirds, there may also be unusually long periods of a sub-adult pre-breeding stage. Male bowerbirds, as mentioned, practise for about seven years before they are considered serious contenders for mating. In magpies, there is a gap of four to five years between reaching sexual maturity (at about one year of age) and breeding. The blue-faced honeyeaters, *Entomyzon cyanotis*, I hand-raised and then released two years ago have successfully integrated with another pair and their juveniles. All juveniles still wear the near iridescent green colour around their eyes and not the bright blue of the adults and that is fifteen months after release and nearly seventeen months post-fledging.

Delayed plumage maturation

There are yet other important aspects to plumage variation, discussed in detail in a review by Hawkins and others (2012). In quite a few avian species, change to adult plumage can be delayed. I want to refer here only to a more rarely studied aspect in delays in juvenile plumage change, particularly when the young male's plumage is near identical to that of adult females. Such delays may have to do with sex and sneak matings. The phenomenon has been studied in the South American tawny-bellied seedeater, *Sporophila hypoxantha* (Facchinetti et al. 2011), the central American long-tailed manakin, *Chiroxipia linearis*, (Doucet et al. 2007) and in the northern or Baltimore oriole, *Icterus galbula*, a migratory bird of North America (Flood 1984).

In Australia, we have studies on delayed plumage maturation in such different species as the red-backed fairy-wren, *Malurus melanocephalus* (Karubian et al. 2013), and the satin bowerbird (Collis and Borgia 1993). A very recent study, unfortunately not of an Australian species but of the green-backed flycatcher, *Ficedula elisae*, of China (Chen et al. 2018), examined the wavelength of plumage of the female and that of juvenile males and concluded that the juvenile plumage was indeed mimicking that of the female. They showed convincingly that the delay in plumage change (from mimicked female to adult male plumage) made these young birds gain considerable reproductive benefits as well as superior quality food and water resources. Hence, still in female garb, they succeeded in fertilising females and had clutches of similar size and success rate as the fully adult plumaged birds. Under the mantle of 'femaleness', they were not fighting and competing. The female imposter is also a very nice example that the supposed rule that females will choose the best, the strongest and most experienced is not always true. They may choose the youngest, the least aggressive and more unisex male than all the macho on display in the adults.

Indeed, one might easily find parallels in human behaviour. The idea of sexual attraction in humans, as we wrote elsewhere (Kaplan and Rogers 1990), is only predicated on the notion of strong masculinity or femininity. There are covert signals and biological attributes that may either run counter to culturally acceptable notions of masculinity and femininity or have nothing to do with either. Cultural fads have either emphasised more unisex or more oppositional traits. A new age male in the 1950s and 1960s, such as Elvis Presley (feminine face and soft lips) or Boy George played on mixed signals, and for several decades unisex was a fad in fashion and hairstyles. Cross-dressing in theatre, transgender displays and males impersonating females are as old as humanity and such representations have had unfailing appeal. One cannot speak with ease about sexual 'attraction' among birds but one can certainly say that the often human coyness about gender-appropriate appearance, enforced largely by culture and religion, may not be shared by birds. Interestingly, these same-sex appearance cases, also known among fishes, are quite inbuilt into a number of species as alternatives, hence showing that the female/male divide can be quite fluid in nature when the hiding of the true sexual identities of players can be an advantage for survival or present opportunities for breeding.

Notes on theoretical perspectives concerned with visual signals

The great detail in which colour has been described here has some solid theoretical reasons. Science is always looking for the simplest (most parsimonious) explanations. It has sometimes been felt that there is no pressing reason to investigate additional signals – be they visual, auditory or even olfactory – if one signal alone may indicate preferences in mate-choice. Such other signals may be used simultaneously or sequentially. We now know that multimodal signals may indicate a set of different and important variations in the sum total of the message intended and it is this total package that may lead to a choice being made. In other words, it is now clear that a message can be complex and such complexity needs to be unravelled by the recipient. But before even this level of signalling is identified, we also need to understand whether a recipient is perceptually capable of viewing or hearing and interpreting such signals and we need to know that they work in certain environments (Endler et al. 2005). According to the sensory drive hypothesis, and this applies to vertebrates generally, signals likely to be favoured are those that are easy to detect by the intended recipient (Kaplan 2015a). Particularly in visual signals, there are a range of inherent characteristics, such as colour, colour contrasts, intensity and structural colour reflection that affect signal conspicuousness and detection.

As Boughman (2002) rightly pointed out, such signals need to be evaluated in the context in which they occur, but so do at least three other interrelated processes: (1) habitat transmission (passage of signals through the habitat); (2) perceptual tuning (perceptual adaptation to local habitat); and (3) signal matching (matching of male signals to female perception). And all these variables can be tested separately, be this spectral sensitivity and even UV perception and habitat circumstances that can add or subtract from the signal. If the environment subtracts from the signal, the individual may even move on to a more suitable spot and there is evidence that habitat conditions can lead to habitat partitioning between species so as to maintain the most effective environmental niche for a male bird to show off his wares (Leal and Fleischman 2002).

Habitat as a variable in signal display is a very plausible hypothesis and has found wide application in species. However, it may not fully explain the colours in Australian birds, especially not in Australian parrots and lorikeets and also not in such brightly coloured birds as bee-eaters (Fig. 7.4) because in so many species there may be little to no difference in colour, however bright, between male and female.

Fig. 7.4 An immature, yet already beautifully coloured, rainbow bee-eater: bee-eaters are colour monomorphic and are thought to mate for life, and they are a rare combination of a cooperative species that is migratory and often nests colonially. Only the one species (of about 25) occurs in Australia. It may overwinter in northern Australia, but usually in New Guinea and most islands west to Lombok and as far north as Sulawesi. The rainbow bee-eater's two central tail feathers are longer in males than in females. The crown of the head, the stomach and breast, and the throat are pale yellowish in colour, and the adult rainbow bee-eater has a black bib (missing in immatures) and a black stripe through its red eye (brown eyes in juveniles). (Boland 2004)

The question is, where has this excursion into colour and into sensory perception got us? To a position of being able to decide what the dynamics of partner choice actually are. It is vitally important to know what birds can perceive and how their vision is actually deployed in mating contexts. Still, caution is required so as not to arrive at premature conclusions. For instance, for years we were satisfied with the explanation that zebra finch females respond to the courtship song males had to practise for so long and then a paper is published telling us that zebra finch females prefer redder bills, regardless of the song rate (Simons and Verhulst, 2011). The implication is that female choice in the case of zebra finches is a little more complex than first thought, at least relying on more than one modality (audition) by including visual cues as well. Hence caution is required in making assumptions on the triggers for mate-choice.

To assume that the basic biology of the sensory system translates directly into behaviour and that actual choices on which often lifelong bonds are forged might depend on just one specific signal could well also be a false premise. Neither in birds nor in humans would such a premise hold. Market research understood very early in the twentieth century that, whatever is considered desirable is not always enough to take an object home. Even if a Jaguar and a Holden were sold at the same price and the desire to own a Jaguar had been substantially greater than to own an average Holden, chances are that most people will end up buying the Holden. Vance Packard's books of half a century ago still make insightful reading today (such as *The Hidden Persuaders*, 1957 or *The Status Seekers*, 1959). The reasons are complex, having to do with friends and family, with status and neighbourhoods. Equally, while sexual prowess in college males judged to be particularly good-looking (Little et al. 2008) may be high and the individual may have no difficulty continuing to make sexual conquests, marriage is an entirely different matter. The same guys with high scores in sexual victories may find it difficult to find a marriage partner. It seems that agreed signals of beauty, power and status may not always determine with whom humans choose to procreate (Buss and Schmitt 1993) and it is at least worth asking whether similar processes might occur in birds.

There are also plenty of tragic cases in humans and birds of falling for the wrong guy on the basis of seemingly desirable traits. One is called a sensory trap, meaning that a male may display traits that are familiar to the female but just resemble signals/stimuli that belong to other contexts. Another is sensory exploitation, meaning that a pre-existing bias of the female is detected and exploited by the male in order to make himself more attractive to the female (Ryan and Cummings 2013). A third one, at least in humans, is that traits a particular female actually values may be ones that she is not aware of and would normally not think of in the context of mate-choice. A fourth, quite common in humans, is for the female to choose a partner with features similar to some of those of her father, even if he had been a poor provider, a negligent or even abusive father.

To borrow a legal term from the coroner's office, an open verdict may have to be returned as to whether colour is a major or, in some cases, the only variable in mate-choice. In science, the law of parsimony has to be upheld. If there is a simple explanation, then there is no need for more convoluted arguments. This is undoubtedly one of the cornerstones of good scientific research. However, say, if colour comes up as a variable for sexual selection in a high number of cases, we cannot be certain that colour does not happen to be a co-variant of something else that is the essential focus of which the colour happens to be a by-product, a concomitant feature or even almost incidental in a range of other features. Simply because colour is an obvious feature does not make it the only or the main one. Testing colour and responses to UV by itself may give us an indication of preference, but a preference for what? The simplest answer may also be such a reductionist answer that it can distort the fuller meaning of an event even if the stimulus gives clear results.

Research has shown the flexibility and response time of the perceptual system of birds to environmental change, and has verified specific components from genes to oil drops capable of relaying important nuances in colour. Research has therefore come a long way towards understanding how changes in colour perception work and how colour changes are met by a perceptual apparatus that can also well adjust to changes.

However, there are gaps in our knowledge and these could be crucial. One concerns the emphasis of research on sexually dimorphic colour and ornamental traits. As Ken Kraaijeveld and colleagues argued quite rightly, mutual ornamentation (male and female that have the same ornaments) has often been neglected and explained away in general terms. They present good evidence that mutual ornaments can have a signal function in both sexes and give the example of social status signalling. Status signalling, under the right social conditions, may likely be especially important, because competition over nonsexual resources is more balanced between the sexes than sexual competition (Kraaijeveld et al. 2007).

Plumage, of course, can also have signalling functions quite apart from mate-choice but often may be of great importance for birds living in close proximity to each other. Facial expressions and expression of emotions in birds have gained more prominence since Homberger and de Silva (2003) showed that there are mechanical forces in the feather-bearing skin that enable birds to move feathers across their entire body and also in the head and face region. It is this physiological process, at once good for thermoregulation and other physiological processes, that enables birds to express emotions (these feather expressions and their subsequent behaviour have been discussed in detail in Kaplan 2015). How deliberate and intentional any of these movements are is not the point here. They are clear signals to other birds, and even to humans, to express a warning or fear and possibly a whole range of subtler emotions.

Studies in birds have certainly appraised and confirmed the expression of emotions by feather postures around the head and neck. In fact, birds, songbirds and parrots alike have a multitude of emotional expressions almost exclusively conveyed by feather position (see Kaplan 2015). We also know that birds respond appropriately if a conspecific generally or a partner specifically expresses overt and agonistic emotions such as anger or aggression.

There is another gap in our knowledge and one that may be crucial. We don't know how the birds will actually react in real-life situations. The assumption is that the right signals will produce the most desirable outcomes without considering a wider net of criteria that may play a role in mate-choice. The next chapter will delve more deeply into a possible range of criteria that are not only valid in human mate-choice but also, in some species, may apply to birds.

8

Attractions and motivations in pair formations

Pairing up and jointly raising offspring and then staying in long-lasting or even lifelong pair bonds is a most remarkable reproductive choice most birds have made, shared only by humans and a small group of other animals. What evolutionary advantages can be derived from having one social partner long-term? We may think we have answered all of Darwin's observations on sexual selection, but far from it. What we have done, largely, is pick and choose the species in which it can be most easily demonstrated that male plumage, song or performance are relevant, even if not key triggers, for sexual selection and female choice. A nagging question remains whether there is not a whole set of other, perhaps subtler, criteria associated with partner choice, and we have managed to identify only one or two of such criteria. If birds were anything like humans, one would imagine that each partner has at least vague conceptions about an ideal partner and that bonding partly depends on individual preconceptions, exposure, experience and personality. In long-bonded socially monogamous pairs, the partners may also have made mutual choices in which sexual dimorphism plays only a minor role. As was shown in the last chapter, reliance on sexual dimorphism as the sole explanation for mate-choice would probably fail to explain partner choices in about three-quarters of Australian land birds. The question is, what enticements, if any, are there for getting a pair to bond and keeping a pair together? In cockatoos, such togetherness could last for decades and it does not seem unreasonable to ask what attractions and motivations might make such unions work.

Emotions in birds

To address such complex questions of attraction and motivations, a starting point might be to investigate what is known or has been surmised about the existence of emotions in birds. Basic emotions in birds, indeed also in mammals, have been well studied. According to Niko Tinbergen, emotions are tied to motivational systems present in all animals and basic to survival: hunger, aggression, fear and sex or, as Tinbergen put it more bluntly, the four fs: feed, flee, fight and fornicate (Tinbergen 1953).

These four basic tenets of emotions can be demonstrated and tested because each is regulated by hormones and basic physical signals. In fear and aggression, adrenalin and also corticosterone are involved, whether it is 'flee' or 'fight', because the basic motivator may be fear. Often testosterone is also involved, as in aggression and mating. Aggression is a controversial area (but a topic of continuing fascination) and is usually discussed in the context of defence and competition. To my knowledge, only one writer, Konrad Lorenz, has linked aggression with bonding (Lorenz 1964), a most baffling and controversial idea.

Lorenz was one of three scientists (the others were N. Tinbergen and K. von Frisch) who were awarded a Nobel prize for animal behaviour in 1976. Lorenz first became famous for his work with greylag geese, *Anser anser*, and his popular book translated as *King Solomon's Ring* (1952), named so in translation because of the legendary 'Seal of Solomon', a ring that allegedly gave King Solomon (King of Israel 970–931 BC) the power to speak to animals. Lorenz earned his scientific stripes for his work on imprinting in geese and ducks but he also wrote copiously on aggression.

In a relatively little-known paper, called 'Ritualized Fighting', published as a chapter in a book edited by Carthy and Ebling (1964), Lorenz makes an unusual claim. For him, there existed no doubt that there was a link between ritualised aggression and social bonds in birds. Although he admitted that we neither know 'whether all bond behaviour has arisen out of aggression, nor whether ritualised redirection of aggression is its only origin'. However, he claims that both were true for ducks and geese. In other words, ritualised fighting had a flipside and could be turned into appeasement, and vice versa. He explains this by having observed ritualised fights in swans and geese ending in 'triumph ceremonies'– a loud squawking ritual of several swans or geese, not unlike the choruses in Australian magpies and kookaburras, at the end of a successful eviction of an intruder or a predator. He called such triumph ceremonies redirected aggression and concluded that 'the bond of lifelong individual friendship keeping together wild geese and determining, by its immense strength, the whole structure of their society, is demonstrably based on the so-called triumph ceremony' (Lorenz 1964).

One could equally argue that triumph ceremonies arise after overcoming fear of losing it all and the triumph is a release of the stress that the group suffered. Another possibility, as has also been argued, is that the chorus is a bonding exercise when life is neither threatened nor stressful (Fig. 8.1). We do know that testosterone is one hormone that is activated both in attack and in sexual interactions.

Attack, as has been found, may also be a mechanism that can reduce stress. These contrasts (fear and triumph, affiliation and anger) may work in different combinations and may depend on the action of hormones and how each is deployed in different situations. The role of serotonin, usually thought to engender a sense of pleasure and

Fig. 8.1 Kookaburra family sitting together for an afternoon chorus. There had been no apparent threat. It just seemed as if the kookaburras were enjoying a family gathering. Possibly some such choruses, when not performed at the loudest range, are an expression of group affiliative sentiments and these may have nothing to do with fear, threats or aggression.

wellbeing, tends to be examined far less often. However, many of these observations by themselves imply or are still tied to the concept that bird behaviour is automatised, instinctual or, if manipulated, conditioned. In studying the evolution of these four basic traits, it was largely presumed that no processes were involved other than those biologically available via hormone manipulation. Descartes would also have been satisfied with such description of animal behaviour.

One might find Lorenz's assumption of the link between triumph ceremony and aggression a little far-fetched, but it raises important questions about closely bonded families and pairs. We rightly call such bonds affiliative, and Dunbar based his social brain hypothesis on the assumption for a greater need of social communication in bonded groups. This is an important suggestion, but it also may invite a romanticised view of living in families or groups. Not all instances of communication are expressions of affiliative needs. On the contrary, it can and has been argued that it is not 'love' but the daily struggle to survive in a group that fosters greater demands on the brain. To get a share of resources and be able to reproduce at some stage might require the learning of a set of strategies in potential conflict situations.

Many have argued that group/partner living is not always blissful at all and proponents of such ideas claim, not without justification, that conspecifics often have little choice other than to stay together. They may constantly compete with one another for limited resources and so continually need to challenge their cognitive ability through a form of a cognitive arms race (Barrett and Henzi 2005; Byrne and Bates 2010). This basic premise, commonly termed Machiavellian intelligence (Byrne and Whiten 1989), relies on the notion that most animals are unwilling collaborators, forced to live in groups to minimise the risks of predation and infanticide (in primates) from conspecifics (van Schaik and Kappeler 1997). This group living then allegedly required the adoption of behaviour, such as grooming and negotiation, to allow individuals to coexist, and to more easily find potential mates (Barrett and Henzi 2005). Yet, competition for food and for mates remains and gives rise to manipulation, deceit, as well as sub-alliances that may play each other off, or splinter off to form competing groups. In white-winged choughs, *Corcorax melanorhamphos*, for instance, one group may destroy the nests of another group, a behaviour called sabotage (Heinsohn 1988), and one group may even try to steal youngsters from another in order to make their group stronger and their territory more easily defendable (Heinsohn 1991). Even within groups, the mutual support that cooperative breeders are supposed to provide via helpers may not, in reality, always work in constructive ways: juvenile helpers may only pretend to help and gulp down the food they have found themselves (Kaplan 2015).

Group conflicts and competition in relatively stable groups have been confirmed in many species but the opposite case has not been made as well or as often, namely that positive observable behaviour, such as preening, may lead to robust reconciliation (Strier et al. 2002; Silk et al. 2004). Maintaining group cohesion while improving individual reproductive success may be at the heart of the social intelligence hypotheses but it is certainly hard-won.

Negative and positive emotions and the action of hormones

Fear is one of the fundamental emotions in all animals. In birds, there is a centre found on both sides of the brain that is designed to respond to such emotions, called the amygdala. Activating the amygdala does two things: increases adrenalin and raises the vigilance levels, as well as enable information as memory formation of the specific event that induced the fear response. Memory formation of this kind is crucial to survival. Agnvall and colleagues (2015) tested the relationship of fear (of humans) by conducting experiments for a number of physiological and behavioural traits in junglefowl (*Gallus gallus*), the primary wild ancestor of the domestic chicken in the family of Phasianidae, at home in India, Sri Lanka and South East Asia. They found that in fowl with low fear, base metabolic rates were higher, feeding efficiency was greater, plasma levels of serotonin were higher and exploratory behaviour was greater compared to birds with high levels of fear.

The absence of fear has a number of measurable health benefits and presumably makes room for positive emotions. They can act just as much as motivators as fear certainly can. The role of prolactin, neurotransmitters such as serotonin and dopamine are rarely mentioned in relation to a bird's actions and emotions. Serotonin (5-hydroxytryptamine) is a monoamine neurotransmitter that controls mood and certain functions in the brain. In humans, low levels of serotonin have been associated with depression and normal levels have an impact on sleep. Other actual biological functions, while complex and multifaceted, have been shown to include modulating memory, learning, cognition generally and even sexual appetite. Dopamine (3,4-dihydroxyphenethylamine), another neurotransmitter, partly with its own network, is commonly described as the 'reward' neurotransmitter while serotonin is often thought of as alleviating stress and promoting relaxation. It may be said that dopamine plays important roles in executive functions, motor control, motivation, arousal, reinforcement and reward. In prairie voles it has been found that the dopamine system even plays a key role in partner preferences and maintenance (Wang et al. 1999), providing a window into the underlying neuroendocrine system that may explain key elements in social attachment.

These functions have been identified in humans, monkeys and prairie voles but far less so in birds. There are some studies available in birds to suggest that hormones and neurotransmitters may also contribute substantially to executive functions and emotions. Sasaki and colleagues (2006), for instance, showed that singing in zebra finch males is associated with increased dopamine levels in Area X, an important nucleus in the song control system of birds (as shown in Chapter 2, Fig. 2.1). Dopamine levels are significantly higher with directed singing relative to undirected singing, while Feduccia and Duvauchelle (2008) showed that auditory stimulation alone (listening to directed song by a conspecific) releases dopamine and serotonin in the brain of the listening bird.

Research on emotions and the function of hormones in birds has moved beyond the Tinbergen/Lorenz model. The four fs of Tinbergen are all right-hemisphere functions. What does the left hemisphere do? The left hemisphere has a role inhibiting and controlling the negative emotions evoked in the right hemisphere (Fig. 8.2).

Emotions and the brain hemispheres

Here we have the insights of neuroscience and very specific findings about the human brain and the bird brain. While there are obvious differences between the two, these are so obvious, in fact, that the differences prevented comparative studies for a long time. Differences in size is one obvious discrepancy, another is that the bird brain's visual appearance is different from the human brain: birds do not have the convoluted area of the cortex which was once incorrectly believed to be the pre-condition for thought. The main difference is that the bird brain is not layered, as in the mammalian cortex. It has collections of cells, nuclei, but no layers; and the human brain has a convoluted surface while that of birds is smooth. As we now know, there are also very important similarities in the structure and function of human and bird brains.

Both human and bird brains (and for that matter, brains of all vertebrates) are structured into two halves, with some cross-links between the halves. These are called hemispheres. In humans and in birds there are important similarities in the architecture and the functions, despite the evolutionary distance between them. These halves may have similar but not identical functions – a very efficient

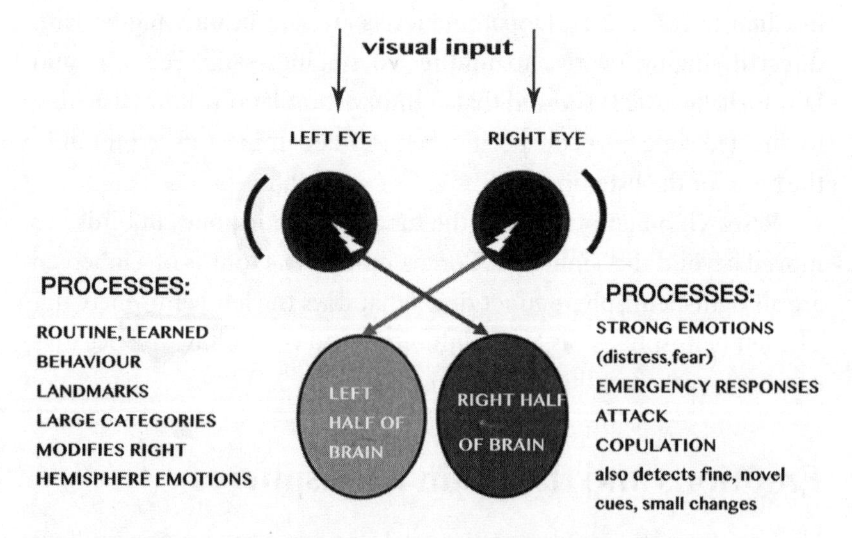

Fig. 8.2 Hemispheric specialisations in the bird brain for dealing with the natural world, with the social environment and with emotions (Rogers 2012).

arrangement that not only avoids duplications but enables the brain to perform many different and nuanced tasks. If certain tasks are largely performed by the left hemisphere and others consistently by the right hemisphere, we speak of lateralised brains, meaning the division of tasks is stable at the population level for that species (Rogers 2012).

Such evidence was accumulated in experiments testing birds with laterally placed eyes, by determining which eye is used in a specific task, or by covering one or the other eye with a patch and testing the difference in performance between seeing with the left or the right eye. The input from the left eye in all vertebrates with eyes positioned laterally goes to the right hemisphere and input from the right eye goes to the left hemisphere. In birds, these connections have been characterised in a simplified way here in Figure 8.2. The right hemisphere of the bird brain (and the human brain) has substantial capacity to deal with and modify emotions, especially negative emotions.

The right hemisphere is largely responsible for detecting fine details; it 'raises the alarm' when there is danger and it is generally capable of strong and instant action. Hence the left eye is used for 85 per cent of the time prior to an escape (Koboroff et al. 2008). As in other vertebrates, fear and escape are controlled by the right hemisphere (Lippolis et al. 2005). Human faces, as has been tested in chickens, are also processed in the right hemisphere (Salva et al. 2007). Martinho and colleagues (2015) showed asymmetry of the pigeon visual system, meaning that information acquired with the left eye is more readily available to control visually guided behaviour by the other eye. Both human and bird brains have a visuospatial bias towards the left eye/right hemisphere (Diekamp et al. 2005; Tommasi and Vallortigara, 2004; Rogers et al. 2013). The auditory system has not been investigated as often but it too shows hemispheric specialisations (Kaplan 2017b).

One of the capacities for which the right hemisphere is specialised is the discrimination of fine details, the ability to recognise conspecific individuals, mates and partners. While the right hemisphere is also responsible for strong negative emotions, it also regulates positive emotions and attachments. The left hemisphere, by contrast, largely takes care of routine functions and learned behaviour. It processes geographical markers and helps the bird recognise where it is by identifying landmarks. Classes of objects and organisms, however, are only processed as categories and thus the left hemisphere cannot distinguish between individuals or finer points. This important task is entirely managed by the right hemisphere (Vallortigara and Andrew 1994).

Another very important function of the left hemisphere is to modulate the strong emotions processed by the right hemisphere. Anger, aggression, or fear registered in the right hemisphere can be partly inhibited by the left hemisphere. For instance, the left hemisphere is also activated and can help in suppressing fear and panic via the connections across the two hemispheres, enabling the bird to make decisions based on experience, not on fear (Fig. 8.2).

The similarities between mammalian and bird brains should not be overdrawn, of course. In the human brain the link between the two halves is called the corpus callosum, a very strong link that does not fully develop until well into adulthood (the mid-20s) (Pujol et al. 1993). Interhemispheric transfers of visual information have been tested in children and it was found that for this visual function alone it takes at least eight years to fully develop (Meissner et al. 2017). Pujol and colleagues called the corpus callosum part of the highest order/latest maturing neural network of the human brain.

Birds do not have a corpus callosum, but they do have projections that transfer the information and much of that transfer speed and method is very task-specific. Some information may travel very swiftly between the two halves of the brain but, as Martinho and colleagues found in imprinting tasks in ducklings, visual information gathered with one eye was laterally isolated for at least three hours after exposure, a confirmation of the much earlier work by Gabriel Horn and Pat Bateson (Martinho et al. 2018). They concluded that there may be two exclusive streams and stores of visual information in the avian brain.

Alternative explanations

One of the obvious but rarely made alternative explanations is that birds with particular skill sets or problem-solving abilities may choose partners with similar cognitive abilities. Plumage brightness and health or clever dance steps may be no more than further verification of the existence of these specific skill sets. For instance, Cole and colleagues (2012) captured more than four hundred great tits and gave them novel problem-solving tasks, then released them back into the wild and the birds were then watched in their foraging and breeding performance. Their results showed that females among the problem-solvers produced larger clutches than non-solvers and that they also needed to spend less time foraging. These differences could not be accounted for by better breeding timing or better habitat but occurred because they were more efficient in using their environment. Presumably, such better outcomes also suggest that both parents shared similar skills and cognitive abilities. This is not a new idea. Boogert and colleagues (2008) found a strong positive correlation between the ability of male zebra finches to learn a new foraging task and their song complexity, the latter being a feature of considerable importance in female mate-choice.

Keagy and colleagues (2009) have argued for years that the cognitive dimension in sexual selection was not fully appreciated. They tested satin bowerbird males in a series of cognitive tasks and then followed their mating success and found an important link between female mate-choice/male mating success and cognitive ability (Keagy et al. 2009). Of course, this also means that females who do the choosing must have a way of detecting and discriminating between special skill sets and cognitive abilities of potential mates. There have been very few papers concentrating on this important part of the process of mate selection. An older study by Leitner and Catchpole (2002) investigated precisely this: they examined female canaries and found that those females that responded and discriminated more between male songs of different quality interestingly also had a larger song control nucleus (HVC) in the brain (shown in Fig. 2.1, Chapter 2) than those females that were less discerning (Leitner and Catchpole 2002). I alluded to this point in Chapter 3, arguing there that females really have to have brain power commensurate with or better than the males in order to make an informed choice.

Notably, mate-choice research in bonded pairs also tends not to dwell on possible involvement of emotions. This may have been an important oversight particularly in the Australian avian species with complex cognition that also share strong social, personal bonds. Somehow, when it comes to mate-choice and sexual activity in animals generally and birds particularly, the idea of cognitive decisions seems far removed from the assumed impulsiveness of love and sex or the often presumed individual emotional indifference to the individuality of a partner.

Yet the links between cognition and emotions have long been made in human psychology, such as the much-discussed theory put forward by Maslow, now known as Maslow's hierarchy of needs (1943, 1954). According to his theory, humans have a number of needs that have to be met, and they are in some hierarchical order. First, metabolic requirements for survival, such as food and other physiological needs, have to be met before prospective other investments can emerge. Then there is a need for safety, a need of belonging in social species, and finally, love and status. Cognitive processes are involved in the highest categories. It should be quite possible, in social species, to apply Maslow's hierarchy of needs to birds.

Many researchers now agree that in most examples of mate-choice, many other criteria may come into play. A paper by Tobias, Montgomery and Lyon (2012) that I particularly liked tried to theoretically overcome the limitations of having to explain everything in terms of sexual dimorphism, female choice and male competition. Tobias and colleagues argued that there are three processes at work simultaneously, namely natural selection, sexual and social selection. A fourth category perhaps ought to be cognitive selection, as has already been mentioned. Their main model can also accommodate several seemingly dissimilar factors as West-Eberhard (2014) first noted in 1983, arguing that social competition for non-sexual resources often involves the same sorts of traits produced by sexual selection. Hence it is possible that in early researchers' eagerness to demonstrate traits belonging to sexual selection actually missed the mark, misinterpreting and wrongly categorising elements of natural selection (such as health) as part of sexual selection.

By bringing in the social dimension, the authors opened the way to question the motivators for partner choice. For instance, one could argue that individual birds, while growing up, start forming a number of positive images observed in male and female parental behaviour influencing their own selection criteria for partner choice later. Certain features or traits, be this in general demeanour or in expressed responses, in a father, mother or another adult relative, may create a guide for a new generation as to what might or might not be desirable traits in a partner. It is at such moments of decision-making that cognitive abilities may play a role and go well beyond the view that birds merely go for the 'best in looks' or 'biggest'. Interestingly, female zebra finches prefer male songs that are closest to the song of their own fathers (Miller 1979; Lauay et al. 2004).

There have always been large-scale system approaches to somehow explain variations in behaviour and how they impact group and mating behaviour. Game theory, for instance, has been with us for nearly a century now, first published by John von Neumann in 1928 and later translated by Tucker and Luce in 1959, and purports to mathematically model strategies for competitive situations in which the outcome of a situation depends on the choices made by one participant which, in turn, depend on the actions of others. Game theory found its way into many fields, including biology, where it is known as evolutionary game theory (Maynard-Smith and Price 1973). In the application of game theory to animals, one of its basic tenets is that each social group will have a mix of behavioural traits.

In a sense, it is still with us (Newton 2018) because there remains the fascination with how individuals in groups move together or against each other, given the presence of certain environmental factors (in birds: predator load, or food availability). For instance, if a 'donor' has an item of interest, there are four basic possible scenarios but only one of four benefits both parties (Fig. 8.3).

Of course, one can explain interactions between participants in ways other than only strategic and/or competitive. Quality, nature and outcome of interactions, may depend on personalities and these may be able to explain certain outcomes. One claim is that reactive individuals tend to be more fearful whereas proactive individuals tend to be

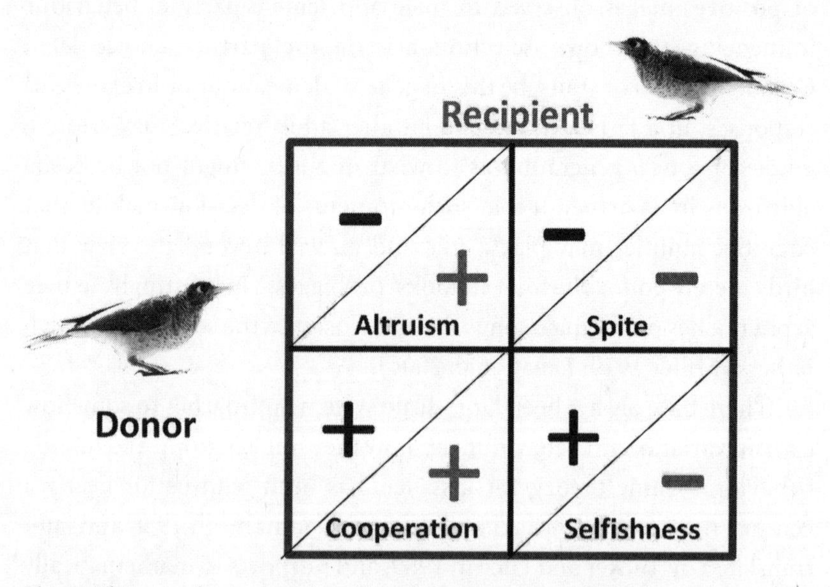

Fig. 8.3 The game theory model predicts the consequences of one altruistic individual and the possible response it might encounter. The model omits indifference and status issues in this simplified model (adapted from Pearson Scott Foresman – donated to Wikimedia article 'Game Theory', Wikimedia).

bolder and more aggressive. Proactive individuals are said to dominate in stable environments; however, because proactive individuals are allegedly insensitive to environmental change, they do poorly in fluctuating environments (Dingemanse et al. 2004). Coping styles have been studied in some detail in great tits (Drent et al. 2003) and in a range of vertebrates from fishes to primates.

Personalities and strategies aside, current studies suggest that the quality of social ties (bonds and communication) is associated with very similar levels of brain power as those described in great apes. This has been confirmed of parrots, cockatoos, a variety of corvid species, Australian magpies and a range of other songbirds, both captive and free-living (Rogers and Kaplan 2004; Shultz and Dunbar 2007). In other words, the cognitive distance between some birds and great apes may not be as large as once thought. Great apes have grown large brains and so have some birds, relative to body weight (Olkowicz et al. 2016). In either case, relevant experiments have shown that such brains functionally translate into abilities in problem-solving and other complex cognitive tasks, as was mentioned in Chapter 2 (fruit-box experiments with chimpanzees and keas, Miyata, et al. 2011). Using the same fruit-box, Whiten and colleagues (1996) showed in children and primates that foraging tasks requiring some problem-solving could also be achieved by imitative learning. Goffin cockatoos, a relative of the Australian sulphur-crested cockatoo, have also been tested on the fruit-box, again with positive results (Auersperg et al. 2013b). If cognitive abilities have increased in some birds and mammals, does this mean that emotional abilities have also increased in such species, and are these the same species that form long bonds?

Traits in partner choice

To my knowledge, there is very little actual evidence that birds may choose each other for similar reasons as humans do. Or, perhaps it is more correct to say that we have not as yet looked to test the possibilities of assortative matings, that is, mating that is based on similarities between individuals.

Attempts have been made to arrive at some measurable compatibility in bird pairs by testing and assessing personality types. This has been tested extensively in cockatiels at the instigation of breeders. Breeders noticed that many pairs, enforced or not, were simply not producing offspring or, if they bred at all, did not succeed in producing viable offspring (Yamamoto et al. 1989). Pre-breeding aggression was noted between enforced pairs. In 2010, Fox and Millam suggested the use of ratings to measure temperament in cockatiels. Such measures have been quite widespread in domesticated animals. Personality tests are used in horses and in dogs, especially in those dogs that are singled out for specialised training, such as guide dogs, in the military or in rescue. In cockatiels, these fall under three major rubrics, as Table 8.1 shows: agreeableness, boldness and affiliativeness.

It is no longer uncommon to link personality traits with sexual selection even in birds (Schuett et al. 2010) and, as Robert Plutchik

AGREEABLE
( ) Aggressive – Causes harm or potential harm, high frequency of aggressive behaviours.
( ) Gentle – Responds to others in an easy-going, kind, considerate manner. Is not rough or threatening.
( ) Submissive – Appeasing or acquiescing to others. Gives in readily to conspecifics.
( ) Tolerant – Permits other animals to make contact or interact in close proximity.
BOLD
( ) Daring – Is not restrained or tentative. Not timid, shy, or coy.
( ) Confident – Behaves in a positive, assured manner.
( ) Curious – Readily explores new situations, seeks out or investigates novel situations.
( ) Fearful – Retreats readily from others or from outside disturbances or novel objects, shows fearful behaviors.
( ) Insecure – Hesitates to act alone. Seeks reassurance from others.
AFFILIATIVE
( ) Sociable – Appears to like the company of others.
( ) Warm – Seeks or elicits bodily closeness, touching, grooming. (Schuett et al. 2010)

Table 8.1 Cockatiel personality inventory. Scales for the three personality factors.

rightly said in his essay 'The Nature of Emotions' (2009): 'Personality is usually taught as if it had little or nothing to do with emotions, words such as gloomy, resentful, anxious and calm can describe personality traits as well as emotional states.' Indeed, the lines are very blurred here between emotions and personality. Surprisingly, 'personality' has also been tested in zebra finch pairs, showing that pairs that are well matched according to personality trait indices have greater reproductive success (Schuett et al. 2011a, b). Mismatched pairs, as was shown in Gouldian finches, *Erythrura gouldiae*, maintained elevated stress hormone levels over several weeks, which also delayed egg laying (Griffith et al. 2011). Both results demonstrate that pairs can be matched and 'feel' comfortable with each other, or stressed if mismatched. Recent data from Steller's jays, *Cyanocitta stelleri*, a corvid that lives largely in the Rocky Mountains, has revealed that shared traits of exploratory and risk-taking behaviour make partners more compatible than others in several ways: they nest earlier and have better fledging rates than pairs scoring lower in similarity of such traits (Gabriel and Black 2012). In great tits, *Parus major*, it was also found that pairs with similar personalities have the highest long-term reproductive success (Both et al. 2005).

A study of zebra finches that avoided any reference to personality but ended up agreeing on the greater success of behaviourally 'compatible' pairs consisted of a series of rather cleverly devised behavioural experiments (Ihle et al. 2015). First, the experimenters allowed a large group of bachelor male and female zebra finches to form pairs, then placed them in a large aviary with a new crop of bachelor males and females and observed whether there was any difference in behaviour in pairs that had previously formed of their own volition and those that the experimenters had assigned to each other. The foremost and convincing result was that almost all pairs that had formed voluntarily stayed together (over 90 per cent) despite the option of finding new partners, while many of the assigned pairs fell apart. The second finding concerned their relative breeding success and, here too, the difference between self-selected and assigned couples was stark and surprising. Self-selected pairs, compared to arranged ones, had higher reproductive success overall which included a rather staggering 38 per cent lower rate of offspring mortality (Ihle et al. 2015). Crino and colleagues (2017) have recently confirmed in their study of zebra finches that stress reactivity and other factors can also have a detrimental effect on boldness and exploration (Crino et al. 2017).

Carere and Locurto have thus rightly argued that personality traits in animals can no longer be dismissed out of hand since they may account for the variability between individual animals and they may interact with cognition (Carere and Locurto 2011). One could even say that compatibility might well be a pre-condition for reproductive success and may also contribute to the longevity of the pair bond. This does not answer the question as to whether such similarities lead to greater mutual attractiveness in the first place or whether it is pot luck when birds happen to later discover how much they have in common.

What we mean by 'compatibility' may also not be the same things that birds look for in each other, of course, and what we see and believe may be based on human experiences. There may be much still to discover as to what makes a partner 'attractive' or what the motivations may be for pairing up with one and not another. Other researchers have felt that we need to also consider some biological and robustly testable criteria, such as circulating hormone levels, specifically testosterone, and to assess whether the partner cycles match. McGlothlin and colleagues (2004) found that if the male had substantially higher testosterone levels than the female, the pair was mismatched, with negative effects (delays) on egg laying and incubation. The researchers aptly titled their paper: 'Elevated testosterone reduces choosiness'. Hirschenhauser (2012) tested pairs of domestic ducks, *Anser domesticus*, and greylag geese, and she found that some stable partnerships actually did match while others did not.

In terms of mate-choice, such matters as personality cannot usually be decided in one meeting. In the bowerbird mating system, some key features as to how 'artistic' the male is, whether he's a good dancer or 'architect' may be resolved relatively quickly because the male does not take part in raising offspring, but in birds that bond in pairs and may stay together for a good many years, matters of personality, temperament and emotional investment, as it seems to be increasingly agreed, cannot be ignored (Sih and Bell 2008).

The personality tests for cockatiels showed that, despite the fact that the categories devised were borrowed from human behaviour, they apparently work to advantage when the intention is to produce viable offspring for the pet market. Such inventories are rarely tested over long periods of time, however. One wonders whether the pairs that were matched according to the scores received on a personality test would last over the distance of a lifetime if the birds were in their natural habitat or had had the ability to choose themselves.

Emotional 'intelligence' – an oxymoron?

A relatively recent concept has crept into the debate and that is the concept of emotional intelligence. It came to the fore perhaps first and most strongly in the new management culture. It proposed a model based on the competencies that enable a person to demonstrate intelligent use of their emotions in managing themselves and working with others to be effective at work. Daniel Goleman's 1995 book, simply called *Emotional Intelligence*, has become rather firmly entrenched in the business community. By 2001, Goleman's message had been enlarged and had become more dramatic in tone, calling the new edition *Primal leadership: Unleashing the power of emotional intelligence*. Tests have been devised, called the Emotional Competence Inventory (ECI).

However, for scientists, this is a mishmash that does not readily fit biological facts and presents contrasts that are likely to be contradictory in terms of brain function. As stated, emotions, negative ones at least, are largely controlled by the right brain hemisphere, while the left hemisphere may curb intense emotions to enable the animal to act appropriately (Rogers 2012; Rogers et al. 2013). Putting the two items together certainly makes it unclear how such a proposal translates into neurological function.

Researchers in psychology have asked about the importance of what is termed emotional intelligence in a different way for decades. They wanted to know what the relationship is between cognition and emotions (Allman et al. 2001) but the assumptions following from this line of enquiry have so far led mainly to the discovery of spindle cells in the brain, proclaimed to be unique to humans and great apes (Nimchinski et al. 1999), and these were apparently responsible for making a fast translation of emotions to cognition and vice versa possible. However, in the meantime, spindle cells have also been discovered in cetaceans (dolphins, whales), and while it has become accepted that cetaceans have very complex brains and are very smart (Marino et al. 2007), it is not entirely clear whether one type of cell could be solely responsible for 'the emotional brain'.

The traditional view was that emotions are irrational and human beings, at first only males, were considered rational. The problem is that rationality and cognition are not the same. Cognition is the entire package of having acquired knowledge and life experiences via sensory input, imitation, social or perceptual guidance or in direct learning. Importantly, such life experiences need to be laid down as memory to inform a new and present context or even apply past experience in such a way that the accumulated cognitive skill leads to new insights and problem-solving. As Richard Lazarus had argued from the 1960s onwards (Lazarus 1982), cognitive processes precede emotional ones, establishing a clear link between cognition and emotions well before neuroscience could confirm the brain processes involved. He argued that cognitive processes generate, influence, and shape the emotional response in every species that reacts with emotion.

Cognition is not an antecedent of emotions but for any species, no matter how limited its cognitive abilities may be, any events or encounters in the environment undergo some evaluative process. In some species, including a number of bird species, humans and other mammals, complex cognitive appraisal of the significance of events or encounters in relation to that individual's wellbeing may occur. Such appraisal, as Lazarus (1982) argued, does not imply anything about deliberate reflection, rationality, or awareness. Indeed, he is right in so far as we group these categories nowadays under 'theory of mind' (Spence et al. 2017).

Very little appraisal may have to go into deciding whether to flee from a lethal snake in striking distance if past experience has already taught birds that one needs to get away. However, fleeing may then also not require strong emotions, such as fear, because the individual already knows what to do about this danger. Fear can actually delay action and while it may be important to trigger such an emotion as a warning system, removal of fear based on knowledge contributes to survival. Other situations may require detailed appraisal, and partner choice would certainly fall within the ambit of complex encounters. Thus, cognition and emotions are often no longer regarded as separate subsystems but as dynamic interactions. Apart from reflex actions already provided as part of a genetic template, cognitive mediation is a necessary condition for emotions to be activated.

The idea of emotional intelligence partly assumes such a link between emotion and intelligence. Generally, the definition of emotional intelligence relied on Wechsler's definition of intelligence of the 1950s: 'Intelligence is the aggregate or global capacity of the individual to act purposefully, to think rationally, and to deal effectively with *his* [sic] environment.' One notes that this broad definition can easily be used for animals with as much or as little evidence as is generally proclaimed for humans.

There had also been a notion of social intelligence, but this never quite took off in human psychology because it was deemed to lack definitional clarity. Eventually, the problem of accounting for a variety of social behaviours was overcome by a new set of theories. Salovey and Mayer first used the term 'emotional intelligence' in 1990. They defined it as a form of social intelligence that involves the ability to monitor one's own and others' feelings and emotions, to discriminate among them, and to use this information to guide one's thinking and actions. To quote these researchers directly, emotional intelligence is a set of skills 'that may contribute to the accurate appraisal and expression of emotion in oneself and in others, their effective regulation, and the use of feelings to motivate, plan, and achieve in one's life' (Salovey and Mayer 1990).

As a theoretical approach, this was far more fruitful because it was delineated well enough from general intelligence without contradicting its definition. Moreover, it is a definition that can also be applied to animals. Even two of the three pillars of Wechsler's definition of general intelligence can be tested in animals and birds – 'acting purposefully' (i.e. intentional behaviour) and 'dealing effectively with the environment'. Salovey and Mayer also provide a detailed diagram of the different aspects of managing emotions and that is useful because identifiable units of behaviour can also be measured (Fig. 8.4). The

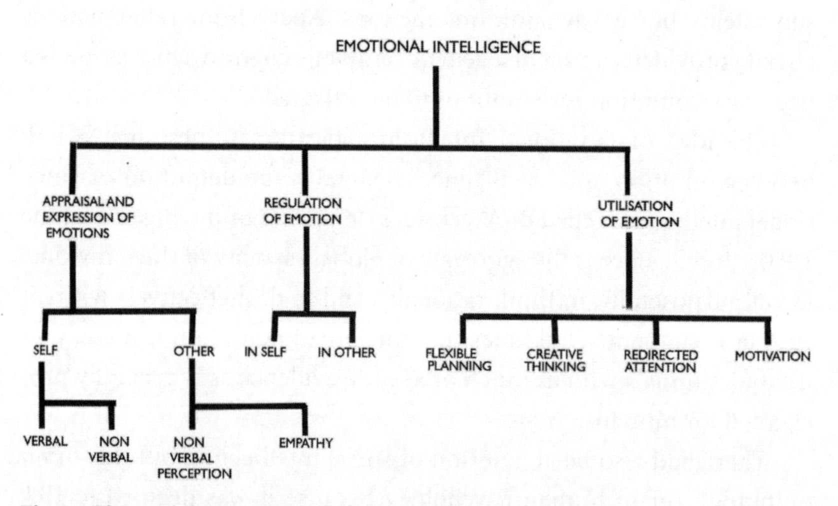

Fig. 8.4 The modular approach to management of emotions, referred to in humans as emotional intelligence (EI). Some of the subcategories may also become testable in birds and other vertebrates (based on Salovey and Mayer 1990).

modular approach to what emotional intelligence may entail has been outlined in the following manner.

The left two branches of Fig. 8.4, appraisal and regulation, can be either subconscious or intended in humans and possibly the same could apply to birds. Self-appraisal would be difficult to test in birds (pre-supposing self-awareness and usually studied in theory of mind type of questions), but non-verbal perception and even empathy can be tested in birds, although few have tried to do so. I am aware of just one study on birds that comes close to testing 'empathy' and this was consoling a victim in a post-conflict context (Fraser and Bugnyar 2010, 2011). In primate society, post-conflict behaviour is most often expressed in allogrooming. In birds, it was not even known to exist.

In a very detailed study of human behaviour (Schutte et al. 2001) it was found that high scorers in emotional intelligence also scored highly in empathy and social skills. Moreover, such individuals were more cooperative, more affectionate, and expressed greater marital satisfaction. Note that affection towards, and cooperation with, a partner feature very much in emotional intelligence (EI) and these two areas are certainly of interest in long-bonded bird partnerships. Cooperation in social relations, as used on human studies, is considered to consist of several attributes such as readiness to be helpful, to communicate and to enhance mutual power, meaning that the partners act as a team in mutual protection and support. And there is plenty of anecdotal evidence to support the notion that 'mutual protection and support' can be observed in bonded pairs from the smallest to the largest species.

One evolutionary/functional argument suggests that there is no point in evolving complex emotions unless these serve critical functions. A contrary view argues that emotions are relatively automatic, involuntary, are typically rapid responses that help organisms regulate, maintain, and overcome fear responses to suddenly imposed stimuli, as in response to fire, predators and so on, all instances in which Tinbergen's four fs fit perfectly.

One way to get a measure of levels of attachment between long-bonded partners is to design experiments that rely on such bonds. For instance, studies that investigate fear of novel objects (neophobia) can be set up in pairs or for individuals. We undertook a series of experiments with zebra finches in our laboratory and eventually used only paired birds in the study. When we wanted to test them individually (regardless of the planned behavioural study) we used a novel environment – a large aviary set up for monitoring their behaviour. With very rare exceptions, individuals would freeze and sit nearest to the small door through which they had entered the cage. They would not explore, fly, feed or even engage in personal preening behaviour. It made no difference whether these were young or old birds, had been in pair bonds for a relatively short period of time or had been a successful breeding pair over some years. We abandoned the idea of testing the birds individually very quickly. We then first introduced randomly selected birds, males and females in equal numbers, from two different aviaries, i.e. they had seen and heard each other but were not socially bonded or pairs. The same behaviour occurred; now both birds were freezing and remaining in the spot where they were first introduced to the new aviary. Again, this attempt had to be aborted. However, we then proceeded and deliberately chose only birds that we had recorded as having bonded into pairs and had at least a record of one nesting attempt (all birds were naïve, i.e. had not been taken to or seen the new aviary). We introduced such pairs to the same test arena. It was a large and enriched aviary with tree branches, hiding spots, good food in various locations and a variety of structures, with many of which they were already familiar.

Their behaviour changed entirely when introduced as a pair. One or the other bird would fly off and explore the entire aviary, feed and drink and use the aviary to advantage (the human observers were not visible to the birds). The other would follow but first inspections of some areas tended to be joint activities. All our tests from then on were only conducted with bonded pairs and only then were we able to study the actual topic of lateralisation when viewing potential predators (Rogers et al. 2018).

How much more difficult is it to experiment with the intention of conjuring up an emotion such as jealousy, and thereby wanting to provide evidence of a strong bond? It has been done in primates and most recently also in dogs. When Maninger and colleagues (2017) studied monogamous coppery titi monkeys (*Plecturocebus cupreus*) of the Amazon region for expressions of jealousy by purposely introducing a stranger male to be placed next to the paired female, they found that the male partner experienced stress and restlessness. His plasma testosterone and cortisol levels increased dramatically during the experiment (Maninger et al. 2017). Whether higher stress levels mean 'jealousy' is another matter. Jealousy, regarded as a complex negative emotion, had apparently been invoked in dogs in a number of experiments using similar techniques of bestowing attention or food on another dog and then recording the responses of the observing dog (Harris and Prouvost 2014). Cook and colleagues (2018) wanted to invoke the same type of emotion using a fake rival dog and had another one watch while spoiling that dog. They also took measurements of the amygdala and found highly increased levels of cortisol, the stress hormone in mammals, during the experiment when the observing dog became aggressive. The problem is that the same behaviour may be observed in guarding food resources and in this sense the term 'jealousy' would probably make less sense. Moreover, we already have a term that can be applied in such situations called 'mate-guarding' when applied to birds.

States of mind may be easier to assess than specific emotions in birds, although this required quite a bit of originality in experimental design. Melissa Bateson and her team (Matheson et al. 2008) tested whether environmental factors influence decision-making and choices in starlings. While this was not directly concerned with mate-choice, the implications for pair bonding are quite obvious. She divided groups of starlings into two groups: one housed in a depressingly bare, dark and uninspiring aviary with basic food and water supplies, the other in light and enriched aviaries also offering varied food. After some time in either environment, the starlings learned to remove lids from two different bowls – one had a white lid and always a favourite food, dark lid meant no food. It took the birds no time at all to make this discrimination and choose the white lid. However, then, cleverly, the researchers added a third lidded bowl to the other two which, in colour, was exactly mid-value between the white and the dark grey lid. The starlings had no prior experience with this mid-grey lid and it was literally up to them to decide whether it was worth the effort of checking for a food reward. Obviously, it was possible to interpret the lid either way: the grey as a darkening of the white lid could be signalling some food availability or, if relating to the dark lid, as not containing any food at all. The astonishing finding was that birds from the enriched cages more often than not flipped the grey lid while those held in bare cages flipped those grey lids significantly less often or not at all. Those in large and enriched cages were more 'optimistic', as shown by opening more grey lids than were the others, now termed 'pessimistic' (Matheson et al. 2008). If environmental factors have such powerful effects on food searching strategies in a bird one might well imagine that there may be 'depressed' or 'optimistic' individuals that might also behave differently in social bonds depending on their frame of mind.

We also know that birds are very effective in communicating their own emotions and, just as humans (de Gelder et al. 2014), may do so in facial expressions and body language. Birds have extensive body language and signals, including the face, by virtue of their ability to move feathers into various positions, as mentioned before, and many of these visual emotional expressions can have regulatory functions in close bonds (see details in Kaplan 2015). Tawny frogmouths also bond for life but, as non-songbirds, they do not have a wide range of vocal signals and, as crepuscular and nocturnal hunters, there are no plumage differences between the sexes. Body signals, however, are particularly varied and subtle, from feather raising in threat situations to expressions of mating intentions (Kaplan 2018b). In mating intention, the male's posture changes, his plumage gets fluffed on his lower abdomen and feathers are widely extended on his head (Fig. 8.5). The male also uses a direct stare, fixating the female and his pupils dilate to make his intention to mate very clear. A direct stare as a signal to invite sexual interaction in animals, to my knowledge, has so far only been reported in gorillas (Mazur 2015). Direct stares in primates are known as threat signals but both sexual advances and threats are governed by processes involving testosterone.

Fig. 8.5 Very rare image of a tawny frogmouth male displaying his mating intention. Note the feathers on the belly being extended outwards like a frock. Note also the direct stare and his dilated pupils as an invitation to mate. It was still daylight and the pupils would normally be quite constricted. Shortly after this image was taken, he mated. Tawny frogmouth pairs bond for life (Kaplan 2018b).

In competition, so the literature on emotional intelligence argues, communication is poor, suspicion and hostility may be part of daily interactions, while coercion, threats and deception can be part of the competitive relationship. The emphasis in the relationship focuses on dissimilar interests and such dissimilarities may be no greater than in cooperative couples that simply do not perceive such differences as divisive.

Very deeply embedded in the thinking of modern human society is the idea that competition is desirable and will lead to the very best outcomes and even raise the quality of the competitors over time. The downsides tend to be often overlooked, such as rivalry, a multitude of cheating strategies, fights, injuries or injurious tactics, which lead to stress, loss of health and even shorter lifespans. Most competitions in game form are at least contained in social rules to which all participants have to agree. Humans may be combative, territorial and predatory and it takes all manner of regulation to keep these characteristics in check.

There is a very nice but rare study against the model of competition which found that very competitive male fruit flies suffer bad consequences for their behaviour. Females rejected such competitive males. As a result, the males ended up not acquiring a mate and such behaviour even negatively affected their lifespan by shortening it (Lize et al. 2014).

9

The boring business of monogamy

There are two ways of looking at monogamy: one is in terms of reproduction and one in terms of the relationship itself. In birds, the former has been investigated in some detail. The surprising result that species classified as monogamous turn out to have extra-marital affairs and produce offspring in which the male partner is not the father has prompted the change to regard all monogamous avian species as 'socially monogamous'. Even some of the genetic studies have created uncertainties because it has been found that, in the same species, there may be pairs that are monogamous among certain clusters of pairs and promiscuous in others. This has been documented very well in noisy miners, once thought to be very promiscuous, but a study by Poldmaa and colleagues (1995) showed that they were monogamous. In another, more recent study conducted in another geographical area, noisy miners were once again found to have extra-pair matings (Barati et al. 2017).

The other option is to approach exclusive pair bonding from the point of view of a long-lasting social bond. When humans get married, the assumption behind their act is a promise of monogamy and permanency, at least in most societies and religions ('till death do us part'). In birds, as has been shown, rituals preceding pair bonding and mating may serve a similar function. A study on human mate-choice found overwhelmingly that choice of long-term partners fell under a 'likes-attract' rubric, participants showing a clear preference for partners who were similar to themselves across a number of key characteristics (Buston and Emlen, 2003). In essence, these results are not too different from the personality-matching exercise undertaken in manipulating breeding pair arrangements in cockatiels or zebra finches.

Familiarity and prosocial behaviour

The thought that 'likes' attract can also be read as 'familiarity' and these thoughts have led to a 'mate familiarity hypothesis' predicting that pair members become increasingly compatible with time, meaning that they will behave or respond similarly during daily challenges. However, this prediction about familiarity is usually assumed to start with courtship, mating and breeding.

Increasingly, we find that in birds, familiarity may well begin before sexual maturity of either partner. Significantly, this has so far been verified in the one group of birds of special interest here, namely the socially monogamous species that are pair-bonding for life. These may be very important findings, suggesting that such species may go through an adolescent training school of acquiring one-to-one experience in prosocial behaviour similar to the way human adolescents do.

Being familiar may indicate quite a number of things, ranging from relaxed friendliness to intimacy or at least a lack of cautious formality. Chapter 4 talked about 'childhood sweethearts' among cockatoos but, while these observations have been made quite often, they have not been followed up systematically. I was therefore overjoyed when I found a study by Teitelbaum et al. (2017), the first of its kind to my knowledge, that has addressed the concerns raised here.

The researchers have provided the first systematic investigation of pre-breeding association patterns of long-term monogamous pairs. They examined entire life histories based on tracking data of migratory whooping cranes, *Grus americana*. They had tagged a multitude of birds before sexual maturity and then analysed 58 breeding pairs of the ones that had been tagged. They made the astonishing discovery that more than 60 per cent of the 58 breeding pairs had started associating at least twelve months before first breeding, while 27 breeding pairs (sixteen per cent) had started associating with their future partner over two years before first breeding. These associations happened before either one of the future partners had reached sexual maturity. The researchers suggested that there are potential benefits for pre-breeding relationships by providing support in competitive contexts and increasing partner familiarity. An earlier study had found that barnacle geese, *Branta leucopsis*, breeding in the Arctic Circle, preferentially paired up with partners they had known from early on (Choudhury and Black 1994).

Familiarity has an immediately apparent advantage. It is the least stressful way of relating to another without the stresses of breeding and raising offspring. The other is an important finding: the association between pairs-to-be is not directly linked to sex and reproduction! This not part of Tinbergen's four fs, this is something else and something we did not really know about. It is tempting to formulate a new prediction that long-term bonds may be preceded by and anchored in this pre-mature pair bond based on mutual choice; one could call it a pre-sexual prosociality hypothesis suggesting that those pairs with such juvenile history of bonding will also be more successful in parenting and in producing surviving offspring.

Close associations are very likely to foster prosocial behaviour. Indeed, a pre-sexual bond may become a training ground for learning mutual responsiveness between the pair partners and perhaps even lead to voluntary sharing and mutual support. This development of prosocial behaviour has been studied extensively in humans from childhood to adolescence, and developmental changes have been noted in prosocial behaviour in the human brain using simple experiments of costly and non-costly exchanges of gifts (Do et al. 2019). Increasingly, neuroimaging has been used to trace the development of such traits as reciprocity (van den Bos et al. 2010). Similar comparative studies have also begun to be conducted in birds.

Self-control

There have been two major developments that have changed perceptions about a bird's freedom to act. One is the role of experience, the other the role of social learning. Both involve memory and we know now that birds can form strong memories of past events and can acquire new knowledge, and thus change their behaviour, by social learning. These questions have been studied extensively and a large literature exists on social learning. However, the question of emotions in such learning processes has only begun to be addressed very recently.

More specifically, it has been asked whether birds have developed any executive functions in the brain to inhibit or delay specific spontaneous responses on the basis of learning. This refers not just to inhibiting strong emotions by the left hemisphere, but something more cognitive; for instance, when birds have learned that sometimes waiting to respond carries greater rewards than acting. Such learning might be acquired in these pre-breeding associations in which partner responsiveness may shape deliberate behavioural decisions.

Self-control is one of the obvious executive functions in which spontaneous and strong emotional impulses in the right hemisphere can be inhibited by the left hemisphere and, presumably, such instances of self-control are often based on learning. For instance, having had an experience when it was ultimately more advantageous to wait than to act might lead to self-control even when a new situation in a different context presents itself.

We do not know and, so far, have not been able to test whether cockatoos or particularly clever native perching birds, such as Torresian crows, Australian ravens or magpies and possibly an unexpectedly high number of other land birds, have a special form of self-control, called in psychology 'delayed gratification'. No doubt there would be many surprises in how much better birds may do in these situations.

The simplest example of deferred gratification is to reject something placed before you because you already know that something better may turn up. This has been tested in children, primates (Beran and Evans 2009) and in corvids such as carrion crows and common ravens, *Corvus corax* (Hillemann et al. 2014). Children aged four or five do not do much better than birds or primates in such tasks. In all cases, the subjects were trained to know that the food they were offered in the first instance might not be the last food offered and that the second lot of offerings could contain treats that were far more attractive, provided they did not touch the first. Hence, the individuals had to exercise self-restraint if they wanted the better option. There were apparent time limits on such self-control: beyond ten minutes waiting time, the tested birds caved in and most acquired the first, lesser choice. In terms of cognitive ability, self-restraint was clearly a top-down executive function (Dufour et al. 2012).

A fascinating study by Auersperg and colleagues (2013a) tested exactly that in Goffin cockatoos, also called Tanimbar cockatoos because of their distribution on the Tanimbar Islands archipelago in Indonesia, and they are of interest as a species because of their close relatedness to the sulphur-crested cockatoo, corella and the galah. The researcher devised a way of testing quality and quantities of food for an exchange test. By using at first a quality preference test (desirable foods) then a quantity preference test, they were able to confirm the birds' ability to discriminate between different quantities of the same food. The birds were then trained to return an inedible object into the experimenter's hands to receive a reward from the other hand and, in subsequent tests, subjects could exchange an intact initial food item for an expected one of different quality or quantity. All subjects readily exchanged one for a preferred item. While these tests are quite lengthy because an experiment like this needs many trials, the end result was that cockatoos exchanged significantly more often than ravens tested in a similar set of tasks.

These telling results from a chain of tests on delayed gratification were able to show conclusively that Goffin cockatoos possess high levels of impulse control. The birds were able to wait for gains in quality and, to some extent, quantity.

Kayabayi and colleagues (2016) chose a much simpler task called motor self-regulation, which underlies impulse control. They intentionally applied the same experiment that Maclean et al. (2014) had used earlier to test primates and now used the same method to test birds in order to establish whether birds also possess motor self-regulation. Kayabayi and colleagues chose three corvid species, the common raven, jackdaw (*Corvus monedula*) and the New Caledonian crow (*Corvus moneduloides*). The common raven is at home in Eurasia and North America, jackdaws are found in Europe and the New Caledonian crow is at home exclusively in New Caledonia, an island nation north-east of Australia.

The way they tested motor self-regulation required a simple, elegant experimental design which did not introduce choices for the birds. First they placed an opaque open-ended cylinder within the test aviary and then placed a treat inside this cylinder while a bird was watching, then the experimenter removed his/her arm and the observing individual bird was released into the test cage containing the cylinder with the food item. All tested birds were able to solve the problem (retrieving the hidden food item) and do so in the very first instance without hesitation or training. In the second round of tests, the experimenters replaced the opaque cylinder with another identical cylinder in length and diameter (also open at each end). However, this perspex cylinder was entirely transparent. Again, the treat was placed into the centre of the cylinder while a bird was watching. The food item could now be seen, not just at the time before it was placed in the cylinder but during the entire process. The question that this raised was: would the birds only have eyes for the treat and try to get it in the shortest, most direct way in the centre of the cylinder, i.e. through the glass (impulsive-direct stimulus response) by pecking, for instance or, counter-intuitively, would they go to one of the ends and retrieve the treat as they had done without hesitation from the opaque cylinder. Again, a bird was released into the test cage immediately after the treat had been placed and the experimenter's presence removed. Ravens immediately went to one of the open ends of the cylinder, showed no hesitation and made no mistakes in the retrieval of the treat at all. Jackdaws tested the plexiglass once or twice but otherwise retrieved the treats without trial-pecking at the plexiglass, while New Caledonian crows, known worldwide for their exceptional tool use, made a few mistakes but still had over 90 per cent of successful responses.

As Table 9.1 below shows, the results on the avian performance slotted in neatly among the results obtained for the same task used to test great apes, despite substantial differences in overall brain volume.

These new discoveries have placed birds in a different light and league. Only two decades ago, it would have been unthinkable to suggest

Species (Great apes and Corvids)	**Cylinder Task completed (in %)**	**Brain (endocranial) vol (in cm³)**
Chimpanzee	100	368.4
Raven	**100**	**14.5**
Orangutan	99.1	377.4
Jackdaw	**97.0**	**5.2**
Bonobo	95.0	341.3
New Caledonian crow	**92.0**	**7.3**

Table 9.1 Motor-inhibition task results for both corvid and great apes.
First column: percentage of successful retrievals of the treat; second column: overall brain volume. Bold type: results on performance by corvids (Kayabayi et al. 2016); regular type: test results on performance by great apes (MacLean et al. 2014).

that the cognitive abilities of great apes could be compared with those of birds! After all, as the brain volumes in Table 9.1 show, bird brains are very small compared to those of great apes. We now know, however, that it is not just a matter of overall brain size but of the brain's capacity for storing information. Modern technology allows us to use memory sticks that can fit several books, and much more, comfortably into the smallest spaces. Conceptually, this perhaps makes it easier to accept that memory storage capacity can be measured not in physical size but in bytes. In the brain, it depends on the number of neurons, how densely packed they are, and how complex and functional the connections are between them. Even some very small songbirds may perform better in cognitive tasks than could ever have been suspected (Kaplan 2018c). Fortunately, because the zebra finch has featured so prominently in research, any findings on zebra finches tend to be included in research on birds that are almost exclusively northern hemisphere species. Kayabayi et al. (2016) who tested not just corvids but a range of various well-known high-latitude songbirds also showed that in such a motor-control task, a low-latitude species such as the zebra finch punches well above its weight while the large-brained neotropic orange-winged amazon (*Amazona amazonica*) performed exceptionally poorly even though its brain volume is almost identical to that of the New Caledonian crow (Fig. 9.1).

On the basis of performance in the three species of ravens, my prediction would be that the galah or the sulphur-crested cockatoo would be among the top performers, as would be the Australian magpie, all highly capable of problem-solving. Galahs and sulphur-crested cockatoos have among the largest bird brains relative to body weight and all tests so far conducted with a very close relative of both species, Goffin cockatoo, would make this a strong possibility. And there may be a good many more, including some Australian parrots.

At the very least it would seem premature, if not just exaggeration, to declare the European corvids as the brightest birds in the world, as has been said (Turner 2016). This simply cannot be claimed without

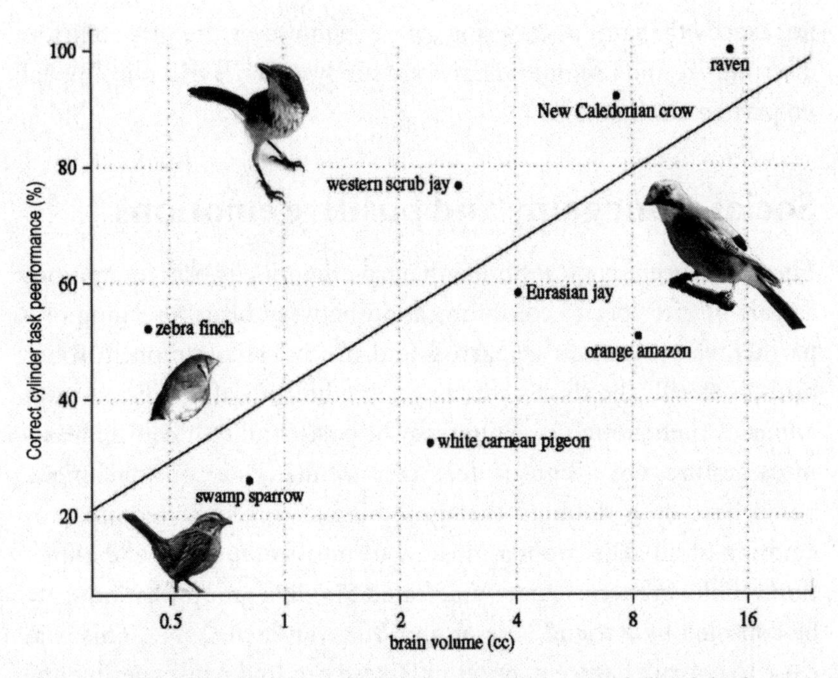

Fig. 9.1 Cylinder trials. The Y-axis shows in how many per cent of all trials birds succeeded in retrieving the treat from one or the other side of the transparent cylinder. The X-axis indicates brain volume. The swamp sparrow (*Melospiza georgiana*) performed particularly poorly, managing to get just over 20 per cent of retrievals, the white carneau pigeon (derived from *Columba livia*) did not perform much better, given that is has far more brain volume. Note that the only Australian bird listed, the zebra finch, performed nearly as well as the Eurasian jay, *Garrulus glandarius*. The common raven and the chimpanzee were the only animals with a 100 per cent retrieval rate, although the New Caledonian crow (*Corvus moneduloides*) and the Californian or western scrub jay (*Aphelocoma californica*) did well (adapted from Kayabayi et al. 2016).

data on more than half the world's population of birds, especially those of ancient lineages in the southern hemisphere and the tropics. This is why the research on a species such as the Goffin cockatoo (southern hemisphere, long-lived and with its origin of evolution in East Gondwana) is so very important.

For an argument of emotions, it is a start to have some tests that show discrimination in quality. The tests, usually done with food, are not exactly the same as choosing a partner, however, the very ability to discriminate and become selective are surely qualities that may impact on partner choice.

Social monogamy and positive emotions

There have been very few studies that have described positive emotions as part of interspecies communication between birds. Preening of a partner, very common in parrots and much less common in songbirds, is usually the closest we can get to admitting affiliations. As was argued earlier, though, preening may be post-conflict and an appeasement gesture, not a sign of deep commitment, love or attachment. Some have even doubted that grooming or preening requires any emotion at all. The problem is how to measure it and make affiliation visible. In raven society, a defeated bird in a group was shown to be consoled by a friend (Fraser and Bugnyar 2010, 2011). This is as close to empathy as we may get unless we can find new experimental designs.

It has so far rarely been investigated how Australian birds decide on choosing partners if the obvious signs of displays, of plumage differences or other sexual differences, are minimal or missing. Equally, it is worth noting that the literature concerned with the 'battle of the sexes', on mate-choice and displays mainly, is enormous while the literature on monogamy is sparse (Black 1996).

Admittedly, monogamy may hold little excitement. All that smooching and self-enclosed satisfaction of a happy couple may even get a little tedious. Lots of that goes on among cockatoos (Fig. 9.2). It's not half as much fun as watching a good fight.

Facetiousness aside, there are some obvious benefits in socially monogamous pair bonds. Coordination of activities can converge to a near-perfect fit as is shown in magpie lark duetting. Hall and Magrath (2007) rightly saw this as a sign of the pair's experience and a durable bond. Such increased experience and familiarity with a mate may also

Fig. 9.2 Sulphur-crested cockatoo pairs express a range of affectionate gestures, such as closely leaning into each other and pseudo- or symbolic allopreening, as above, with heads angled towards each other, or whole-body cuddling next to each other (photo courtesy of Nick Gibson Photography).

improve breeding performance, and as Black (1996) explained, there are energy savings to be made on a daily basis. Remaining with the old partner reduces the time and energy of searching for and sampling a new mate, and may give the pair the advantage of an early start to breeding. But those reasons do not make a compelling argument for long-term pair bonds, they are merely stating that an alternative could be worse.

Partner affection and mutual attention

The idea of affection, of individual integrity involving mutual support and defence of two individual birds of whatever sex and, heaven forbid, sexuality, are still topics treated with relative discomfort or simply not dealt with. True, it is difficult to quantify affection other than by signals that we recognise and have often deemed to be signs of affection, such as mutual preening (Fig. 9.2). But even such acts tend to be objectified at times by pointing out that preening reduces parasites. While this may be so, some aspects of affection may well become measurable in biological ways. One study tried to do this by hormone measurements in the great tit. Pairs with similar baseline corticosterone levels and higher reproductive success were also more likely to remain together after the breeding season. The authors of this study (Ouyang et al. 2014) suggested that pair bond longevity may be related to both hormonal (endocrine) similarity as well as reproductive success.

It is probably unavoidable that all such studies are reductionist, in the sense that they may only represent a small, albeit important, aspect of what a bond actually means in a bird's life history and the quantity and quality of offspring. We have a substantial body of literature to show that paired and single-parent parents will defend their offspring vigorously, either by mobbing, by bluffing or by elaborate subterfuge displays, such as feigning injury of the adult bird. Does the same repertoire apply to the partner? Would partners defend each other, or is there such a thing as consoling a partner when things have not gone so well? There are plenty of examples of such behaviour among mammals, in elephants, wolf packs or a pride of lions, and even in pods of humpback whales and dolphins, as well as in great apes and capuchin monkeys. In birds, we have only one definitive example, namely studies showing that common ravens may console a member of the group when they have lost an in-group conflict, as already mentioned (Fraser and Bugnyar 2010).

As argued before (Chapter 6), sexual plumage dimorphism for reproductive incentives may largely have been an adaptation in higher latitudes or altitude – made for birds in a hurry. This is not a new thought and of relatively little consequence since sexual dimorphism can also be expressed vocally. That sexual selection even requires such signals may be overstating the case. There is also the case of hidden sexual dimorphism, meaning that some dimorphism may exist, but it is hidden from human eyes, and may or may not be important in mate-choice.

Previous chapters have described some pre-bonding and mating rituals, but their most important aspect has so far not been mentioned. While male displays for mating in any shape or form are self-advertisements for the individual male, elaborate pair courtship displays signal the exact opposite. The former may be to get a female to accept a suitor, even if for the short-term only, while the latter is to forge a bond. Their courtship signals harmonising a union between two birds and it may involve extraordinary feats of physical exertion.

White-bellied sea-eagles, *Haliaeetus leucogaste*, similar to American bald eagles, have probably the most spine-chilling courtship aerial display, in which they often cartwheel mid-air. The two birds fly very high and close together, then one sea-eagle flips over with outstretched legs and talons facing upwards into the sky. It is in free fall and at that point the second bird folds its wings and dives down vertically to catch up, outstretches its talons to catch the talons of the other. Then both start cartwheeling, using their wings a little but still hurtling down at break-neck speed. Unless they time this absolutely correctly to the split-second, both birds would crash into the ground and die. It takes extraordinary coordination to release the talons just in time to remain clear of the ground.

Other pairs may be less daring but equally coordinated, performing choreographed dances, as do cranes (Takeda and Kutsuka 2018) and brolgas, *Grus rubicundus*, and these may be very graceful and gentle. Others perform 'walks' together. Emperor penguins even walk with purpose and, as mentioned, a large group of flamingos meet as singletons and then go on a walk together, a rhythmically highly coordinated affair, accentuated by regular staccato movements of the head to left, right, left, alternating in an almost comical way. And, of course, as already described, there is the well-known and often filmed 'walk on water' performance by several species of grebes. Their water dance is usually preceded by an elaborate series of choreographed movements by both birds at the same time while both male and female grebe swim next to each other, performing movements that are mirrored in the partner. In all these cases, the rituals are expressions of harmonising in a specific way. There is no doubt that cooperation can win out over competition.

Monomorphism or unisex, almost?

We have a tendency to categorise the world into male and female organisms. When a child is born, it is the first question we ask: 'Is it a boy or a girl?' And we do so even in societies in which neither religion, nor custom make this of any real consequence, economic or social, and in the face of growing knowledge that gender assignments have their ambiguities and difficulties both at birth and even later, at least in the human species. The absolute and unmistakable divide between the sexes can be blurred by external morphological features. There are genetic and chromosomal aspects, then gender can be assigned by internal morphological features, suppressed or heightened by hormones and determined by phenotype. It has happened, and not too rarely either, that the wrong gender was assigned at birth (ambivalent genitalia) and that such a decision led to major problems when that individual reached puberty, and even to suicide when the individual concerned felt trapped in the 'wrong' body. It seems that we feel entirely confused when we cannot tell to which sex a person belongs. Our language also reflects a deep sense of division of the world into male and female and, although there are some languages that do not differentiate between male and female, in most, it is almost impossible to talk about something or somebody without expressing a gender divide.

Robyn Burgess

A rare and beautiful moment of unselfconscious and carefree daily life among galah partners. Raised crest and wings spread indicate a playful mood. The drinking galah, left, has a confident posture after taking a sip.

Gisela Kaplan

A spangled drongo back hit by sunlight, revealing the refraction of light on the structural colour of the wings.

Gisela Kaplan

The same bird from the front, revealing colour patterns on its chest, not visible on days of overcast skies.

Gisela Kaplan

A white-headed pigeon reveals its subtle turquoise markings on the wings (also structural colour).

Bobbi Marchini

New Holland honeyeater (*Phylidonyris novaehollandia*). The adult on the left (white eyes) is interacting with the juvenile on the right (grey eyes).

Bobbi Marchini

A pair of black-necked storks (*Ephippiorhynchus asiaticus*). The female (left) has very conspicuous yellow eyes, while the iris of the male (right) is brown.

Gisela Kaplan

Blue-faced honeyeaters. Left: juvenile (green/iridescent eye patch). Right: the same bird two years later. The patch has changed colour to a bright blue, indicating sexual maturity. Juveniles grow for another year and, as can be seen, are noticeably larger and have a longer beak.

Gisela Kaplan

A juvenile male Alexandra's or princess parrot (*Polytelis alexandrae*), one of the few truly nomadic parrot species in Australia. The subtle pastel colours become stronger as he assumes adult plumage – especially a light blue patch on top of the head that will mark him as a male. These parrots are very fast learners and excellent mimics.

Gisela Kaplan

A pair of king parrots (*Ephippiorhynchus asiaticus*), which are among the few Australian parrots that are strongly sexually dimorphic in plumage: male on left, female on right.

Gisela Kaplan

Sex identification may nevertheless be difficult. Here, the same bird is photographed a few months apart. On the left, it appears to be female; on the right, red feathers coming through below the beak and on the chest indicate that the king parrot juvenile is turning into an adult male.

Gisela Kaplan

A pair of affectionate red-tailed black cockatoos leaning their heads towards each other. There is a sense of total equality in the partnership.

Gisela Kaplan

A pair of quietly efficient pied currawong parents – indistinguishable from each other.

Bobbi Marchini

Mutual preening in devoted long-bonded pairs of little corellas is a regular occurrence.

Gisela Kaplan

A red-tailed black cockatoo male watching the author's every move from high above, roosting at least ten metres up in an exposed patch of tree. Red-tailed black cockatoos, like some other cockatoo species, are extremely suspicious of human presence and will usually flee at the slightest movement even long distances away.

Bobbi Marchini

Rare shot of the exact moment during their courtship flight when the female whistling kite (*Haliastur sphenurus*) flies in close proximity to the male. In fact, she moves just a few inches above the male, holding this formation briefly. Presumably, because of updrafts, this is a difficult manoeuvre; he has to desist from flipping over and possibly meeting talons. They then fly next to each other and eventually separate.

Gisela Kaplan

A brolga pair preening, mirroring their actions. Is it synchrony or contagion?

Rainbow bee-eaters preparing a nest burrow.

Arriving with their catch, a bee-eater pair tends to consume it on a permanent roosting spot where they regularly congregate.

Australian raven family: male (left), female (middle) and juvenile (brown eyes, right). Wherever the youngster flies, the parents will follow and will roost in close proximity. Raven offspring are probably the most carefully supervised youngsters among birds and they very rarely come to any harm.

Gisela Kaplan

Rainbow lorikeets are known to travel and roost in large family groups and tend to be cantankerous, but pairs stick closely together and peacefully share resources.

Gisela Kaplan

A pair of wild galahs with young daughter. Galah youngsters are lucky – they have a social group, personal friends, creche supervisors and their considerate parents.

Gisela Kaplan

Eastern rosella. Left: hatchling (two days post-hatching, naked and blind). Right: a few weeks later (the same bird), feathers are growing in individual sheaths that eventually break and reveal the beautifully coloured feathers of this parrot.

Gisela Kaplan

Another supremely altricial species – the kookaburra. On the left, two siblings, hatched probably two days apart, are barely able to sit. Blind and naked, the youngest is probably just two days old. They cannot thermoregulate but their tree nest hole protects them from wind and rain. The right image shows the same two birds a week later – the first-hatched is just about to open its eyes and the first layer of pin feathers is well developed, but not so in the second-hatched.

Gisela Kaplan

This nest was picked up off the ground, probably knocked down by a cat. One bird survived and kept on sitting in the nest – it was hand-raised in that nest and then grew into a beautiful eastern spinebill (as a juvenile still missing the characteristic adult black marking across the front).

Gisela Kaplan

A little eagle nestling. Birds of prey can afford to have snow-white offspring. Without enemies, standing out in the nest does not have the same immediate and deadly consequences as in smaller songbirds. This is a well-fed, healthy (single) offspring – note that the crop below the neck is entirely full.

Alternatively, countless examples have also shown that in humans, ambiguity of maleness and femaleness may add to rather than subtract from sexual attraction, a fact cleverly explored and exploited by many artists and popstars such as Annie Lennox, Yves Saint Laurent and others (Kaplan and Rogers 1987).

In birds, we transfer our need to categorise the sexes and tend to look more often for differences than for similarities, even though differences may be falsely thought of as sexual dimorphism serving sexual selection. As already noted, climate, altitude, migration and other social variables may lead to and/or reinforce sexual dimorphism. It is just as important to ask why evolution favoured the abolition of strong sex differences in so many bird species, be these doves (see Fig. 4.6) or spangled drongos (Fig. 9.3).

Fig. 9.3 A pair of spangled drongos roosting together. They also do their hawk-flying and general foraging together as well as sharing their parental care. To the human eye, they are certainly very similar and the term 'unisex' would be quite appropriate here.

Moreover, in some species, both females and males have ornaments referred to as elaborate monomorphism (Tarvin and Murphy 2012). Monomorphism refers to sameness or essentially similar type in appearance and even in song between males and females. The term applies here only to the adult form and does not suggest that the same form is retained throughout the various stages of development, as was made clear in discussing juvenile plumage and eye colour in Chapter 7. A good example of such monomorphism or unisex is the bee-eater. There may be slight differences in plumage brightness, but the variations may have to do with climate conditions and other factors rather than with biologically selected differences. The only difference that may be a little more consistent in bee-eaters is the adult ornament, a single elongated bristle that protrudes from the tail feathers and may be slightly longer in males.

In cases of extreme differences, as in eclectus parrots, the striking female red plumage may have nothing to do with sexual selection and everything to do with resources, in this case nesting holes that females may and do fight over with each other. Females may spend months in such a nest hole prior to nesting in order to safeguard its ownership (Heinsohn et al. 2005).

For those species that look alike but have UV reflectance, we have coined the expression hidden dimorphism that, while true, may simply reinforce the belief that these signals are the key to partner choice. However, at no point is it argued here that males and females are so much the same that they don't recognise the sexes. The question is rather why differences have disappeared or have never developed in so many Australian species and why human research focuses on the relatively few species that show stark differences.

To our eyes at least, many bird pairs look not just similar, they look like peas in a pod, utterly identical (Figs. 9.3, 9.4). In the adult populations of white-winged choughs, apostlebirds, ravens, crows, currawongs, butcherbirds, many pigeons and doves for instance (as in Fig. 4.6), any differences in physical appearance between male and

Fig. 9.4 Is it a male or a female? There is no way to tell for the human onlooker. Left: This currawong had been orphaned after a wing injury and was hand-raised. I called him Benny. Five years later, 'he' returned, easily identifiable because of the slightly abnormal position of his right wing, and made a nest and lay eggs and was revealed to be a female. Right: The grey butcherbird males and females are identical in build, plumage and song. Both sing, although Gayle Johnson found that male butcherbirds have a special breeding song that, apparently, is unique to the male (Johnson 2003).

female appear to be entirely absent. If we do not have some perceivable differences in body size, eye, beak or leg colour to help us in the identification, we, as human onlookers, have little hope of identifying the sex of a bird correctly.

One may search for more differences in future, as some are eager to do, as if to uphold the old female/male dichotomies, possibly reflecting engrained human biases, but this should not stop us from examining monomorphism as a possibly very important dimension in bird evolution, deserving of at least as much attention. The evidence of a large number of Australian species that do not have stark differences in plumage, song or otherwise need to be accounted for in evolution.

In other words, unisex can be viewed in several different ways. Perhaps there was little or no longer any evolutionary pressure on looking different, or it might have been selected to reduce competition and fighting between males or females.

Alternatively, giving up differences may have been another major step in the direction of cooperation fostered by eliminating criteria that might trigger competition. Overt competition is largely absent in so many Australian species and it would be important to understand more fully why this may have occurred and what the implications may be. One of the questions is whether the overt absence of difference means that mate-choice is based on different criteria and whether the notion of cooperative behaviour is tied to similarity rather than difference.

Added to this, females and males may jointly incubate eggs and feed the youngsters in turn, so it is perhaps not surprising that equality is also often expressed vocally, in behaviour and in plumage.

Indeed, Australian species often seem rather egalitarian, to borrow a socio-political term. Although one needs to add that monomorphism may not always mean equality. Especially in groups, a very strict hierarchy may be established. Yet there is often no difference in the song between male and female, and no marked difference in plumage or size, brooding and feeding of youngsters or defending them. Many pair-bonded species brood, nest, feed and protect their offspring equally or, even if some role division is apparent, share the overall workload in raising offspring. In tawny frogmouths, as I described elsewhere in detail (Kaplan 2018b), the pair has a strict roster system even during incubation.

Equality means that the partners ought to be equal in crucial ways. This may include similar efficiency in foraging and responsiveness to danger but it can also mean that the partners may bring near equal stocks of knowledge and experience to their bond.

Causes or consequences of 'equality'

Unisex in appearance does not mean equality. Looking alike does not mean sharing nor does unisex of necessity refer to an expectation or behaviour of empathy. An individual may not necessarily feel motivated to support or help another just because they look similar to themselves, although research in humans has shown that prosocial and helping behaviour is likely to be stronger and more readily expressed towards someone who is similar to the individual called upon to help (Hogg and Turner 1985). To individuals to whom we attribute qualities similar to our own, there tends to be a more spontaneous chance of active supportive intervention and participation, called prosocial behaviour (Sharrock et al. 1990).

Prosocial behaviour in animals has generally been treated as a rubbery and possibly unscientific category but it has now been confirmed to exist (Cronin 2012). If there had been discussion of the idea of thinking of another in a supportive way, it has generally been expressed in the most Machiavellian way possible: because genes are selfish, the only way altruism can work on any level is by helping individuals to eventually reap benefits from that act for oneself and one's own genetic line. Reciprocal altruism means if I invest in you with any kindness or help, I will put you in the position where you will have to repay this and help me (Hattori et al. 2005). In American English, there is an expression, 'I owe you' referring to a favour being done to someone who then acknowledges a debt to be repaid to that person. Helping behaviour and altruism thus have had a relatively bad run because it seemed a wishy-washy concept that could not easily be proven or has been treated as if motivated entirely by selfishness and competition (Roberts 1998).

However, humans getting married used to, and many still do, promise to the marriage partner to 'love and cherish, in sickness and in health'. Mutual support is built into the contract and so is affection. Could the same be claimed for long-bonding bird couples? Environmental endocrinology, even if reductionist, might elucidate here that helping behaviour is perhaps not a wishy-washy psychological category but one related to hormone management and registration in the right hemisphere of the brain. The function of hormones in birds has been investigated for a long time and, increasingly, there is interest beyond testosterone and corticosterone, the stress hormone, and how it responds to environmental conditions. The specific hormone that has had relatively little attention by comparison (Angelier et al. 2016) is prolactin. It occurs in all vertebrates, including humans and birds, and has many varied and important regulatory functions.

In humans, prolactin is related to sex and reproduction. Secreted from the pituitary gland in response to eating, mating, ovulation and nursing (i.e. producing milk in females) it also plays an essential role in metabolism, regulation of the immune system and pancreatic development. Gratto-Trevor and colleagues (1990) chose two species of shorebirds with very different social systems to see whether prolactin had any role to play in incubation (Fig. 9.5). One was the semipalmated sandpiper, *Calidris pusilla*, a socially monogamous species with long-term partnerships in which both partners incubate the eggs equally, the other the red-necked phalarope, *Phalaropus Isobatus*, a polyandrous species in which only the male does the incubation. Both

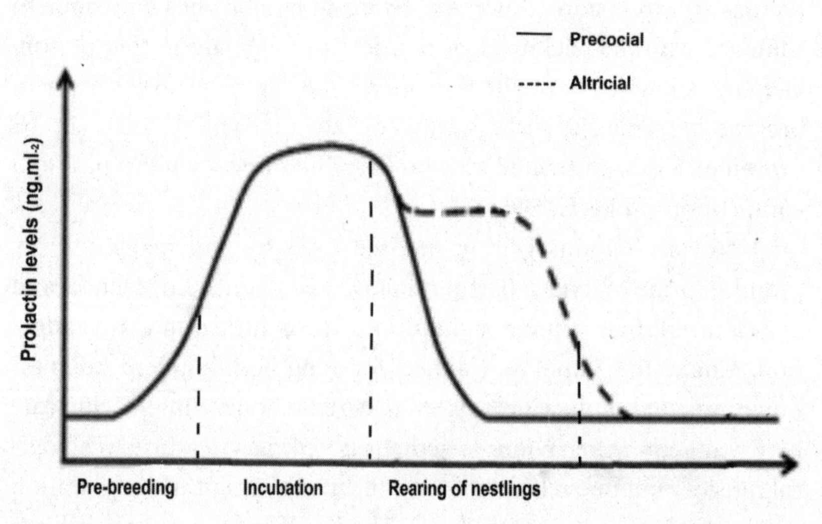

Fig. 9.5 The rise of prolactin in the blood over the pre-breeding period to the end of the rearing of nestlings. (Simplified and redrawn from Angelier et al. 2016.)

species breed in the subarctic and in relative proximity to each other. They found that high prolactin levels are correlated with consistent incubation behaviour. Importantly, in sandpipers the prolactin levels were the same in males and females. In the phalaropes, only the males had high prolactin counts, confirming that this is indeed correlated to incubation since only the male incubates the eggs (Fig. 9.5). The role of prolactin in breeding behaviour has been confirmed in a wide variety of birds, both in precocial and in altricial species as well as in mammals.

Having established the link between prolactin and incubation, Schoech and colleagues (1996) went further by studying cooperatively breeding scrub jays in Florida and also measuring prolactin levels. This study, and that is why it is described here, provides the first clear evidence of a strong correlative link between circulating prolactin levels and allo-parental care, i.e. between prolactin and helping behaviour from individual non-breeding birds that are not the parents of the brood.

In non-breeding birds within the same breeding family, prolactin levels increased even before the non-breeders started helping and doing their part in feeding the new clutch. Hence, there is an adaptive physiological mechanism in place that promotes helping behaviour. We do not have studies that have examined Australian cooperative species in this regard but since prolactin plays a role in seasonal adjustments, there is every reason to suspect that increases in prolactin in non-breeding helpers would also be found. Mays et al. (1991), who found similar results in the role of prolactin in cooperatively hunting Harris hawks, confirmed that the existence of a physiological mechanism facilitated helping behaviour.

Perhaps social monogamy is not all that boring. First, affectionate partners constantly refresh their bonds, usually on a daily basis by cuddles, allopreening moments and by moments of foraging closely together. In some species, regular sex appears to be part of the bond, as is close vocal and non-vocal communication. The partners live together and rely completely on each other. Second, monogamy and cooperation are correlated, at least over evolutionary time: the former developing traits that can be co-opted for the latter. Dillard and Westneat (2016) even pointed out that monogamy may be an important causal factor in the evolution of altruism, thus these are important traits that opened up entirely new possibilities in bonding partners.

10

Parenthood, spoilt offspring and life-history rewards

Imitation, mimicry and mirror neurons

Only for the last decade has it been conceivable to probe the minds of birds for their prosocial and affective behaviour. One unlikely route was via the discovery of mirror neurons and their importance for mimicry and imitation. Mimicry refers to the copying of sounds, shapes and colours while the term imitation tends to be used to describe the copying of body movements most often observed in great apes and humans. Much of what is termed mimicry is not relevant here because the mimicry of the colour or shape of, for example, a noxious beetle by a totally harmless beetle, is an adaptation and genetically fixed. Mimicry in birds refers generally to vocal mimicry while imitation, also called motor imitation, can be a yawn or a scratching, an arm movement or body posture, and even walking with a certain gait or limp imitated from another performing such movements or actions. Vocal mimicry in birds has been discussed frequently because some birds mimic other birds, and even mammals and inanimate objects in the wild. For instance, lyrebirds, magpies, butcherbirds, bowerbirds, some honeyeaters, pipits, orioles, cockatoos and spangled drongos are known to mimic, but there may be more. Additionally, the mimicry of parrots in captivity has made mimicry a very well known but inadequately explained phenomenon. Motor imitation has at times been thought to be impossible to be performed by birds (more on this later). Mimicry has always been a problem for ethologists because, despite concerted efforts and many experiments, definitive functions that worked across a broad range of species could not be established convincingly (Kelley et al. 2008; Wickler and Haubert 2013).

This seemed to confirm the popular view that apes 'ape' and parrots 'parrot', meaning that, by and large, the motor imitation in primates including humans and the vocal mimicry in birds were ultimately 'mindless' exercises, without meaning to or for the species.

Two separate research endeavours began to change all that. One occurred by utilisation of human language in order to communicate with primates and birds in specialised laboratories. One of the researchers, Irene Pepperberg, had an African grey parrot, *Psittacus erithacus*, called Alex. She not only taught her African grey parrot to produce human words, but deliberately put commands and questions into brief but correct English sentences, provided the words for specific objects and concepts and then asked him questions about them (Pepperberg 2009). Alex used about 100 words and correctly replied to questions asked. He was even able to express desires. Some gorillas, orang-utans, chimpanzees and bonobos were trained in sign language and could reply in sign language and to commands (Brakke and Savage-Rumbaugh 1995). The very fact that primates and parrots could do cognitively similar things certainly helped to change our perspective about their comprehension of the human world (Rogers and Kaplan 2004), but this research did not answer the question about what motor imitation in primates and humans and vocal mimicry in birds signified, if anything.

Between 1992 and 2008, several crucial discoveries were made in neuroscience that turned out to be seminal for the idea that animals have the capacity for feeling with and for another. That also has ramifications for pair bonding.

The discovery was that of so-called mirror neurons in the brain, first in primates (Di Pellegrino et al. 1992), then in birds (Prather 2008) and eventually in humans (Keysers and Gazzola 2010; Ferrari and Rizzolati 2014). Mirror neurons are so called because they activate when a sound or movement is not performed by an individual but observed or listened to, and because they commit to memory auditory or visual information that maintains total fidelity of the item seen or heard. The representation of the sound listened to or watched is stored in memory in such a way that the individual can practise against this representation. Motor imitation or imitation movement, once thought of as immaterial funny clowning, then raised the question of whether being able to identify and memorise another individual's movements or facial expressions so closely, and have the brain function to sustain such imitations, could be regarded as the first step of learning. It was a major breakthrough because these findings confirmed the presence of brain mechanisms capable of dealing with the acquisition of movement and vocal information from others by juveniles and adults alike.

Importantly, the mirror neurons in birds belong to a population of neurons that is not replaced, as other neurons in the song system are, but is stable throughout song development. Prather and colleagues (2008) showed convincingly that one bird listening to another's vocalisations activates neurons that would also fire had the bird sung the same passages itself. Crucially, the songbird brain has a way of committing this perfect copy of the original sound to memory against which it can practise what was heard and so match its own song to one it has heard. It is this stability that enables the juveniles to learn.

If somebody else's movements and vocalisations can be copied in full, the pattern of activity is already incorporated in the brain of the learner and can be accessed by that learner. I use the word 'learner' deliberately. We now know that imitation and mimicry are the very first and crucially important stages in learning. They are not mindless. Mimicry has a role to play in vocal acquisitions of songbirds and, as discussed elsewhere, in the development of vocalisations in magpies (Kaplan 2017a).

Being able to 'keep a copy' of the original sound may well lead to better responsiveness to environmental factors and threats.

On the road to empathy

Some researchers have argued that mirror neurons, by implication, do a lot more than just mimic. Behavioural mimicry has been related to being capable of creating affiliation which may confer significant evolutionary advantages on the mimicker. In unexpected ways, mimicry may be regarded as perspective-taking of another and this is an accepted aspect of empathy (Lakin et al. 2003), thus providing a possible bridge to another's mind. If an avian or primate brain is able to approximate the movements of someone else with its own movements, perhaps it can also detect other concrete or abstract states of mind (Gallese 2001, 2007) and, at a stretch when applied to birds, even the intentions of others (Iacoboni et al. 2005). The ability for keen observational powers has survival value. Even three-day-old chickens can discriminate between familiar and stranger conspecifics (Vallortigara 1992) and such ability is essential for their survival. However, such social recognition and the attraction towards a potential mate are not the same thing, of course. If attraction is founded on similarity, one objection could be that this would seem to demand some form of self-recognition. Self-recognition is difficult if not impossible to test, though there have been attempts made in this direction.

One way to show it is to let birds look into a mirror and ascertain whether the bird recognises the image in the mirror as one of the itself. A series of experiments was conducted by Prior et al. (2008), testing the Eurasian magpie (*Pica pica*) for evidence of self-recognition. In those experiments, before the bird is presented with a large mirror, a coloured dot is affixed to an area on the belly of the bird where it will not be detected by the bird without the mirror. Any attempt to remove it from its own body rather than peck at it in the mirror is regarded as evidence that the animal being tested is aware that the dot was affixed to its own body and not to another bird.

However, it cannot be assumed that animals necessarily recognise themselves in the mirror. From our local yellow-breasted robin, and by observing some babblers vigorously attacking the external rear-vision mirror of the car, it becomes evident that the ability for self-recognition in a mirror is not universally shared in birds and mammals. In fact, a large number of birds have been tested, including budgerigars, zebra finches and a few 'heavy-weights' – species which we know already have substantial cognitive abilities such as keas, African grey parrots, New Caledonian crows, jackdaws and others, and in all cases, excepting the Eurasian magpies, the experiments did not return results that showed that these species recognise that the image in the mirror is of themselves (Derégnaucourt and Bovet 2016). And even more recently, keas and Goffin cockatoos, already known to be amongst the birds with the largest brains and impressive cognitive abilities, have failed the mirror self-recognition test. It cannot be assumed that, be it a drongo or a cockatoo, any individual bird can look at his or her partner and conclude that he/she looks 'like me'. This would be absurd, especially if there is (so far) no evidence that such a concept as 'me' actually exists in birds. Moreover, the entire issue of self-recognition as a sign of cognition has been seriously questioned when it was discovered that a fish, the cleaner wrasse, *Labroides dimidiatus*, is capable of self-recognition using the mirror test (Kohda et al. 2019).

Mimicking may not develop or presuppose a concept of 'me' or of accessing the state of mind of another, but does offer a route to empathy as a pre-reflective, automatic mechanism of mirroring the action or vocal behaviour of another. In the literature on human development, it has been found that empathy is not just a desirable social attribute or a praiseworthy moral position, but biologically of great importance for any social co-existence. Stern and Cassidy (2017) summarised the effects of low levels of empathy at different stages of development. In children, low empathy is associated with poor peer relationships, hostility, and bullying; in adolescence, it manifests as aggression and antisocial behaviour and, in adults, low empathy is linked to domestic violence, child abuse and general violence.

Terminologies such as 'empathy' are loaded concepts, however. As Daniel Batson (2009) reminded us, in an attempt to answer two basic questions about empathy, there are at least eight different ways empathy can be defined. The two questions are: how can one know what another person/primate/bird is thinking? And what leads one individual to respond with care to a suffering other? The number of categories belonging to the first question are complex, internal processes and have usually been discussed under theory of mind in primates (Frith and Frith 2005). This has not been tested in birds and would therefore be idle speculation. The second question is relevant here because it involves behaviour such as adopting the posture or matching the neural responses of an observed other, or having a state of distress evoked by witnessing another's distress.

Finally, empathy assumes a close link with the other's physical existence. I move as you do and therefore I 'know' you better. In social psychology, a discipline not really designed for considering animals, some tenets sound surprisingly similar to examining relationships between long-bonded birds, and become even more plausible from the standpoint of social neuroscience (Decety and Ickes 2009). One is called the theory of social-cognitive transference, and it proposes that mental representations of attachment figures strongly influence how we judge others (Laurita et al. 2019). This may also be true in birds, even if individual participants are not aware of the influence other attachment figures might have had. One paper had the telling title 'I like you but I don't know why' (Günaydin et al. 2012).

Imitation also serves a social function, and it seems to be generally agreed that social mimicry is a powerful tool in bonding and binding people together, functioning as a social glue, often referred to in the literature as prosocial behaviour (Stel et al. 2008). Such social or movement mimicry is also more than 'social glue' – in humans it has been shown to lead to more pronounced expressions of empathy, fuelled by a belief or feeling of the onlooker (the one being mimicked) that the state of mind and feelings of the other, mimicking individual, are accessible because the 'other' has already been classified as a candidate that is 'like me'. A very compelling study was conducted by De Coster and colleagues in 2013 in which experiments combined mimicry and emotional identification with another person. They produced evidence that, indeed, there is an underlying cognitive core mechanism that links shared representations in the sensory and motor domains. This gets us tantalisingly close to arguing that such cognitive core mechanisms might well also be present in some birds, at least in those with identifiable lifelong bonds and exceptional cognitive abilities. It seems that such species may well fulfil all the preconditions in the sensory and motor domains (i.e. those that engage in mimicry of another, especially in body movement imitations) to be capable of empathy and mutual affection.

Another aspect of mimicry as described in human psychology is called interactional synchrony, and what is called social contagion effect. This means that within a group, convergence of behaviour can occur purely because one person within the group may have displayed that behaviour and others tuned in (Chartrand and Lakin 2013). Contagion behaviour has been well known and described in animals, again chiefly in primates. The best known is the contagion of the yawn – when one animal yawns, another might well also start yawning. This has been shown in chimpanzees (Campbell and De Waal 2011), in gelada baboons (Palagi et al. 2009) and even in domestic dogs (Romero et al. 2013).

To my knowledge, this has not been tested in birds. However, sulphur-crested cockatoos show obvious signs of behavioural contagion with their head-bobbing. If someone head-bobs to another human and the bird observes the action, the cockatoo will also produce some very exaggerated head-bobbing behaviour that does not occur when people just pass him. It takes little to trigger this behaviour.

Then there is the category of emotional contagion, used widely in the study of humans. There are at least a few studies that have tackled this topic, and some anecdotal evidence of its potential existence in birds. One anecdotal and horrible event was the death of two charming, beautiful pastel pink/blue/grey and very active princess parrots, *Polytelis alexandrae*, of inland Australia, one of the few parrots to engage in mobbing behaviour when a predator approaches. The pair was housed in a large aviary secured with chicken-wire and an internal layer of strong steel wire so the birds would not have their delicate feet injured when they chose to hang on the wire. I had spotted a goshawk, *Accipiter fasciatus*, on a house roof opposite us but was not overly concerned because the aviary had a roof and the wiring was solid. Seconds later, however, the goshawk launched an attack, throwing itself with enormous speed and power at the side of the aviary wall, killing the male parrot instantly. The female was nowhere near the edge of the aviary but had witnessed the attack. She dropped off the perch shortly after the male had fallen dead to the ground and she lay there, breathing heavily, and then died a few hours later, entirely physically uninjured. Her literally dropping off the perch can be interpreted simply as a direct consequence of the sound, vibration and impact of the large goshawk or it could also be regarded as a response to seeing her bonded partner thrown off the wire and lifeless on the floor. The former would simply be a direct expression of fear that put her in shock, the second option would be emotional contagion.

In common marmosets, *Callithrix jacchus*, a small South American primate and one of the few primates to pair-bond, we were able to fully document a case where one marmoset had an accident when jumping between branches was killed by the fall. The dead marmoset was removed as quickly as possible, but the partner remained and his cortisol levels, measured daily, rose dramatically (an almost four-fold increase) immediately after the incident and remained elevated for days (Kaplan et al. 2012).

In both cases, the onlooking partners were not injured themselves.

In the case of the marmoset, one might argue that the distress over days was merely caused by the absence of the partner, but the readings of cortisol levels were identical when the dead marmoset was present and when it was absent. In the case of the princess parrot, the sudden and noisy appearance of the goshawk could have been frightening enough to induce shock, but most shocks are survivable. I also documented the case of a free-living tawny frogmouth that never left the side of its partner after it had been hit and killed by a car. The surviving partner then suddenly died after a 'vigil' of four days, never moving from the partner's side, just quietly whimpering (Kaplan 2018b).

Positive emotional contagion has so far been tested in just two species, common ravens and keas, both of which happen to form lifelong pair bonds, are playful and cognitively among the top achievers in the bird world.

Osvath and Sima (2014) found some evidence of positive emotional contagion in common sub-adult ravens. In another study, conducted with New Zealand's keas, the experimenters used a very simple and effective design in order to test the absence or presence of emotional contagion. They played back vocalisations that keas use when involved in play and other positive interactions, called a warble, and also tested separately a number of other vocalisations and neutral sounds not related to social communication. When they played back a warble, and only then, the keas spontaneously began to engage in play behaviour but rarely following any other kea vocalisation played back to them (Schwing et al. 2017). This is a very good experimental design because it convincingly showed that the trigger was not based on social interaction with other keas but a sound whose memory was associated with play. Here is a good example of positive emotional contagion, suggesting that birds listen carefully to each other, have specific memories of good and bad experiences and can influence each other merely by expressing a specific behaviour. Since keas are very likely to be Gondwanan in origin and thus share the same stem ancestry as all the Australian cockatoos and parrots (Wright et al. 2008), we are offered some insight into the emotional dimensions of parrot life and get a glimpse of how influential one expressed behaviour can be on other individuals.

Social contagion is less controversial in birds but not much easier to test. The many studies we have on birds show a convergence of vocal behaviour in pairs and even in movements and behavioural repertoire. Dakin and Ryder (2018) recently took the plunge and tested wire-tailed manakin males, *Pipra filicauda*. This lek-breeding South American species is unusual because the displaying male is joined by a coalition of young males who then perform with him. They concluded that social contagion drives the dynamic network partnerships and thus promotes cooperation.

Synchrony

Australia has many cooperative species but in terms of synchrony, there is a wealth of material for the student of bird behaviour. Bird groups such as apostlebirds (Baldwin 1974), white-winged choughs or even grey-crowned babblers and others offer opportunity to study exceptional behavioural synchrony and to figure out how they continually synchronise their behaviour in the many different activities they undertake together. In bonded pairs, we may find many examples of synchronisation of behaviour. Synchronisation is, in fact, ubiquitous in vertebrates and requires little in terms of emotional investment, empathy or positive affect. For instance, in ungulates, a band or flock may move together and forage at the same time and often in the same direction. Many examples have been mentioned, be they vocal (in duetting) or visual choosing to do activities in unison. In affiliative bonds, synchronised behaviour has been measured and observed in many species. Breeding synchrony is widely practised, from wildebeest in large herds dropping their young within a day or two of each other, to colonial nesters hatching their broods simultaneously, and in either case creating such a glut of offspring that their overall survival chances are greatly improved. However, synchrony may suggest affiliative bonds. For instance, in wild bottlenose dolphins, *Tursiops aduncus*, a high level of pair-swimming synchronisation and breathing is regarded as high-level affiliation between the individuals (Duranton and Gaunet 2016; Sakai et al. 2010). The kind of synchrony of bonded bird pairs appears to be qualitatively very different, even if equally adaptive. Mariette and Griffith (2012) conducted a very nice study of zebra finches in the wild demonstrating their affiliative bond by synchronising foraging time, time of arrival and time spent near the nest. And in a study of galah pairs, an extensive repertoire of synchronising movements was identified, be this simultaneous parallel head-bobbing, simultaneous preening or, interestingly, mirror-image stretching of one wing when facing each other, i.e. one bird stretched the right wing and the other the left wing so that, to the onlooker, the wings of both birds seen together looked like a shield (Rogers and McCulloch 1981).

Many courtship rituals have been described in previous chapters, including single male performances by satin and regent bowerbirds, lyrebirds, Victoria's riflebird and others to attract a female, with the males then having no involvement in raising offspring. A number of examples were also given of courtship performances involving both male and female, such as those by brolgas, the little wattlebird and, perhaps the most complex one, of albatross species. In cockatoos, initially there may be lengthy periods of mutual preening. In galahs, the various symbolic actions of sham preenings, stretchings and mutual preenings clearly form part of a synchronising set of activities. Obviously, there are many styles and variations of the theme. Importantly, some of these rituals continue to be performed throughout their lives, such as mutual preenings and gift-giving as in grebes and kookaburras, while other segments of the courtship interaction serve as recognition devices, as in albatross, or merge into important daily activities that contribute to the ongoing success of a couple. In successful couples, the precision in duetting, for instance, tends to improve over the years, as in magpie larks and eastern whipbirds. Even general vocalisations may begin to converge, as in budgerigars. Such convergences in sound and synchrony in body movements may also signal to others that they are a couple.

Unless these activities have future survival value (defence of partner, parenting), and some activities do, the question is: what is the point to all this? I would argue that many of these pairing courtship dances are more than just an exercise in synchronising and symbolic promises for future reliance on the partner. The 'I do as you do' may be the result of emotional contagion in the other. It may be mimicry in the sense of empathy. It certainly is not a mindless or unemotional occasion. The long sessions of allopreening and close voluntary touching in long-bonded cockatoos may be an unusual adaptation brought about by the need for a very long partnership commitment when breeding; at least, as we know from studies of the function of serotonin, it is likely that such activities may feel good.

How brain pathways evolved to generate complex social behaviour, as Chakraborty and Jarvis (2015) rightly argued, remains an enigmatic but fundamental question in biology. Admittedly, it is a substantial speculative step to extrapolate from observable limited symbolism about partner compatibility to a meaningful commitment involving attachment. Clearly, though, some species have now been shown to have accumulated a set of qualities that, together, provide fertile ground for the expansion of cognitive, communicative and emotional abilities. Each of those qualities might initially have evolved separately for whatever compelling reason and the appropriate neural networks established but eventually, with possible cross-connections, could then have enabled a whole new set of abilities. Among such qualities is the capacity for complex vocal learning. In many songbirds, parrots and cockatoos, such abilities were not just confined to a specific developmental window, as in zebra finches (Slater et al.1988; Jones et al. 1996), but made the brain receptive to new inputs throughout life (Auersperg et al. 2013b).

Combined with increased capacity for cognitive flexibility it appears that this also led to an increase in the capacity to use and attend to non-vocal signals even including movement imitation (Heyes and Saggerson 2002; explained in detail in Kaplan 2015) and a pronounced need for substantial social contacts and ties. An interesting study of vocal learning in keas showed that without visual exposure to other keas, isolated keas barely learned or expressed any vocal behaviour (Wein et al. 2018). While the brain of many parrots including macaws and amazons, but especially cockatoos and keas, is known to have strong auditory–motor connections, and thus confer sophisticated audio-motor processing abilities, these are not enough without strong social confirmation. Children in isolation wither and so do most birds, especially parrots. All parrots have a noticeable tendency to form long-term social bonds. They do so with a special skill set: a powerful combination not just of communicative skills but of listening and watching skills that could expand into attentiveness, even empathy, attachment and the ability to alter behaviour in accordance with a partner's needs.

A recent article suggests that cockatoos are also capable of spontaneous and imitative body movements, studied in detail in just one sulphur-crested cockatoo called Snowball. The authors argued that parrots are unusual in that they share such traits with humans (Keehn et al. 2019). Perhaps this needs one correction. Rhythmicity in birds did not just start with cockatoos. As De Tommaso et al. (2019) discovered, even naïve three-day-old chicks spontaneously differentiate between rhythms (De Tommaso et al. 2019). This ability thus appears to have very ancient roots and may suggest that motion imitation, synchrony and other precisely timed pair events (such as dance) have antecedents and a long evolutionary history in birds, as indeed in humans.

Love affairs or not?

The word 'love' was advisedly not used before in connection with bird bonds. And here I have to first relate an observation in preparation for this book that still seems to hold true at the end of writing. The book started out with Tinbergen's four fs as the basic motivation system in birds. Research has since added more emotions to the avian repertoire.

I was surprised to find, though, that in almost all accounts birds have been readily credited with negative emotions (such as aggression) but with barely any positive ones. Strangely, admitting to negative emotions in birds carries less risk for the human researcher of being regarded as needlessly anthropomorphising and therefore distorting and overestimating the relevance and depth of existence of any of these potential mechanisms. Darwin (1904) mentions one positive emotion (happiness), no doubt observed in domestic dogs, and much later, Damasio (in his book *Descartes' Error*, 2006) added 'sympathy' in a list of new emotions that are arguably still negative (such as guilt or pride). Otherwise there are no positive emotions mentioned, let alone investigated. Schweiger et al. (2013) argued very similarly with respect to human emotions. Even in the human specialisations of psychophysiology and neurobiology, they argue, positive emotions have received far less attention than the investigation of negative affect. Anger, fear or sadness have been extensively studied but, in the positive spectrum, 'only pleasure has been considered frequently enough to be included in a meta-analysis' (Schweiger et al. 2013).

The word 'love' is never mentioned in the literature on pair bonding. In relation to animal relationships in general, I believe I have only read the word used by one author, Marc Bekoff (2010) but not before and not since. This is not very surprising since we really do not know what it is – is love an emotion, a state of being, a feeling or an obsession? Writing about love is as old as the written history of humans but it has largely been the province of literary narratives and poetry. Advice books on love have flourished in the last hundred years or so but they mainly consist of marriage guidance books or relationship guidance books. Whenever there is a book written about this topic it is bound to have a wide readership. Graham Chapman's recent book *The Five Love Languages* (2016) made it to the *New York Times* Bestseller List within weeks of publication. Significantly, the subtitle promised to inform the reader how to make relationships last. Chapman builds on our understanding of the forms of love, first described and handed down to us from the ancient Greeks, and these descriptions seem to hold as much currency today as two thousand years ago. There are as many as seven loves described but it seems that five of them have retained some agreed validity. These five are, still to this day, named by their Greek names: Eros (passionate love/sex), Philia (friendship), Storge (love for family/kinship), Pragma (enduring love) and Agape (the most abstract 'unconditional love' for God, country or one's children).

Perhaps we should ask the birds how they do it – for their success in keeping relationships together is likely to be much higher than that in human society – we need at least to think about this. We need to think why we are more willing to assess negative emotions than positive ones in animals, let alone birds, and whether this is a scientifically sustainable attitude. I can think of at least three of the 'Five Loves' that could apply to birds. They may not be applicable to all birds perhaps, but at least to some considerable number of species, such as Philia (friendship), Storge (kinship) and Pragma (enduring pair bonds). And while one may prevaricate about the meanings and the likelihood or unlikelihood of their applicability to birds, George Vaillant, Harvard Professor in Psychiatry, rightly pointed out (in relation to human behaviour) that the literature tends to 'miss the motivational tree for the forest' when it comes to love and relationships. In his view, it is attachment of one person to another which, he says, even in humans has nothing to do with consciousness (or self-awareness?) but everything to do with community (Vailliant 2011).

Translated into bird life, we are back (partly) to the social brain hypothesis but partly have transcended it because (perhaps) without attachments of some kind, the edifice of long-term bonds and the benefits such bonds obviously bring would collapse on itself like a house of cards.

Interestingly, in research, whether one reads about human, mammalian or avian bonds, the conclusions are very similar and usually consist of three important principles. Fletcher and colleagues (2015) argue that close bonds are a 'commitment device' to motivate pair bonding. Second, pair bonding facilitates preparedness for the major investment of raising offspring and third, it also fosters the evolution of further social intelligence and cooperation. The social intelligence hypothesis, as discussed in Chapter 2, posits that complex cognition and enlarged 'executive brains' evolved in response to challenges that are associated with social complexity.

The literature on social, cognitive and affective neuroscience in humans has discriminated between categories such as 'newly in love' and 'long-term romance' based on self-reporting by the couples. These couples have been examined and compared on the basis of brain activities and neurohormonal status.

The data show that in 'new love' particularly, the dopamine system is involved, and that system also modulates anxiety and pain (Acevedo et al. 2012). By contrast, long-term romantic love in humans recruits opioid- and serotonin-rich neural regions not found in 'new love'. Eventually, one set of hormonal recruitments supplants the other, that is, the dopamine levels subside and neuro-opioid and serotonin levels increase. Dopamine has its own network in the brain, called dopaminergic projections, which synthesises and releases the neurotransmitter dopamine and, broadly speaking, is called the reward system. Trying to tease out the role of the opioid receptors and serotonin gets complicated because of their interactive role. They also work to stabilise the immune system and have an effect on sleep.

In humans, it may take two years 'for an enduring attachment bond to be fully established' (Hazan and Zeifman 1994). This is a surprising finding and one wonders whether bond formation in birds, even if such bonding occurs by slightly different means, may also take some time to get fully established.

From an evolutionary point of view, there is compelling evidence for the development of strong bonds. Opie and colleagues (2013) used 230 primate species to show that there is a strong relationship between

Fig. 10.1 Pair of red-tailed black cockatoos. It is not breeding time and yet these birds show a great deal of affection towards each other. Their pair and parenting commitments are one of the longest among tree-breeding birds worldwide.

the evolution of social monogamy and parental care but not in the way one might have thought. They found that parental care followed rather than preceded the appearance of monogamy. Such a conclusion makes a good deal of sense, bearing in mind that the same activation of neurohormones in the brain is at work for established bonds as well as for parental care (Opie et al. 2019).

Unexpectedly, one ends up with a formulation that turns former assumptions around – in some cases, it is not the impetus for reproduction that makes them pair-bond but pair bonding that makes them reproduce. Given that sequence, pair bonding is the lynchpin for further evolutionary developments in the life histories and cognition of birds. Since modern songbirds, cockatoos and parrots evolved in Australia, Australian native birds are an ideal model to exemplify this.

The subtle and complicated coordination of hormones and their variously fine-tuned levels of activation in the brain to elicit certain behaviour or moods, including attachment behaviour, has been well documented for reproduction, and here the four fs that Tinbergen identified apply. However, for biological parents to stay together and ensure the successful upbringing of their offspring, a good deal more has to happen than just evolving a drive to reproduce. Many animals walk away once the eggs are fertilised and deposited. The 'extra' behaviour needed for bonding and parental care is usually referred to as the phylogenetically ancient attachment system, which can be found in mammals and birds. In mammals, it has been thought that lactation is partly responsible for a strong bond between infant and mother and, as was already stated, few mammalian species form pairs and jointly raise their offspring. Hence, 'bonds' in mammals are generally discussed as mother–infant bonds while, in bird bonds, it is precisely so very unusual that adults form close bonds which had been considered essential for survival only as mother–infant bonds (the mammalian perspective).

Birds, of course, do not lactate, hence the physical closeness may not arise from physical proximity via the feeding method but on a biologically based behavioural system geared to the hatchlings' expression of hunger or distress (Hazan and Zeifman 1994; Laurita et al. 2019). As discussed in Chapter 8, high prolactin levels also play a role in parental behaviour in birds, and are at the same high level in males and females when both incubate and rear their brood (Gratto-Trevor et al. 1990).

Social monogamy is therefore a preadaptation before extended 'altriciality' of offspring was possible.

Helplessness as an advantage: altriciality, emotions and the brain

Altriciality refers to the system of allowing new life to hatch or be born very prematurely so that the new offspring can be fed and cared for outside the egg or the womb. Biologically, it is a very high-risk strategy but also one that maximises growth potential of the organism because the new organism is not spatially constrained and may have evolved over long periods of time (Fig. 10.2).

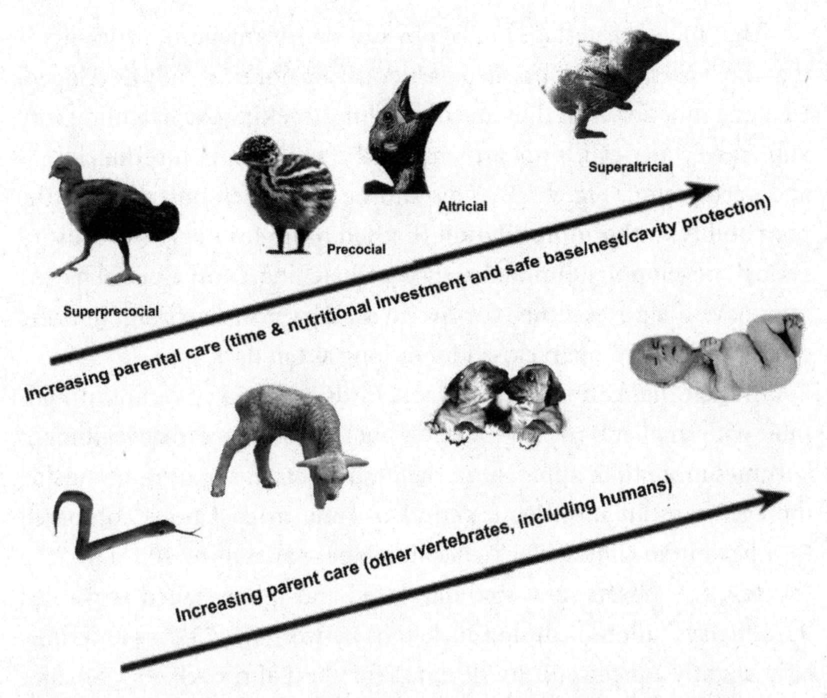

Fig. 10.2 From precocial to altricial models of reproduction. Upper line (left): Superprecocial refers to species that are fully developed and get no parental help, are fully feathered and self-feeding (shown here is a young brush turkey). Precocial refers to those species that hatch fully feathered and are self-feeding but get parental support for safety and guidance to food sources, as most waterbirds do (shown above is a young emu). Altricial refers to the vast majority of passerine birds that hatch in an utterly helpless state. Parental care tends to extend beyond the fledging period (nestling shown here is an apostlebird). Superaltricial refers to entirely underdeveloped hatchlings that are naked, blind and often cannot hear. Opening of the eyes can take up to ten days (shown here: a kookaburra nestling, two days old). In other vertebrates, a similar gradation of dependence on parental care can be shown. In snakes, live young are independent from day one, be they hatched or live births. Semiprecocial as ungulates which can stand on their feet within hours of birth, their bodies are fully covered by fur but, unlike birds, they derive their main nourishment from the mother's milk (lamb shown here). Canines are more typically altricial. They grow up in a den which they usually can leave only after six weeks post-birth and are entirely dependent on the parents for feeding and safety (ridgeback pups shown here). Superaltricial here are humans, naked with none of the senses well-developed. The dependence on adult care is the longest among all mammals and extends to well after sexual maturity (all photos taken by the author; face of human baby purposely distorted to safeguard anonymity).

The single greatest and most obvious disadvantage of altriciality is that the senses, and the brain in particular, are not even fully developed, let alone functional, at the time of hatching, making the hatchling very vulnerable. Altricial birds are among the most immature hatchlings and vertebrates (Fig. 10.2). This can be easily demonstrated in the poor ability of thermoregulation (limited or no feathers) and sensory (visual) development immediately post-hatching. Most altricial hatchlings have their eyes closed for two to six days post-hatching. In some species, the eyes remain closed for as long as ten days.

In their incubation periods, large birds and cockatoos are comparable with smaller birds (21–32 days) but the difference in development becomes more than apparent in the nestling state. Maturation outside the egg takes an inordinate period of time in cockatoos compared to other birds. Glossy black cockatoos may take up to 105 days (the shortest ever observed was 60 days), red and yellow-tailed cockatoos 90–100 days, sulphur-crested cockatoos between 66–73 days and similarly slightly longer (up to 79 days) for the palm cockatoo. Smaller cockatoos, such as the galah, need a little less time but even for these offspring they still have seven weeks of being tied to the nest hole before they are ready to fledge (Murphy et al. 2003). Australian ravens, another large land bird, take 40–45 days from hatching to fledging, while magpies have the more usual incubation period of twenty days plus four weeks in the nest (Kaplan 2019a).

Without wishing to divert too far into the breeding cycles, these examples may suffice to demonstrate how far development has been drawn out, presumably to maximise physical and cognitive development in some species. This is a very fragile system because it requires low stress and substantial nutritional input over a long period of time to maintain the telomeres intact (see next page). The fact that palm cockatoos lay only one egg, and most black cockatoos and the sulphur-crested cockatoos lay usually one to two eggs and often only every second year, shows how reproduction is pushed to the very slow lane compared to other birds.

Determining lifespan: telomeres and altriciality

There is another element to altriciality that is very much worth noting here. In 2012, Heidinger and colleagues published a very important paper on the biological predictability of longevity for species and even for an individual of a species. They examined telomeres in detail and chose zebra finches for an investigation on the predictability of life expectancy. Telomeres (Fig. 10.3) are the end caps of a chromosome, four for each chromosome. Telomeres have several functions – one is to protect chromosomes, found in cell nuclei, from sticking together. They also have a protective role of the chromosomes during cell divisions via a special enzyme called telomerase. Without telomeres, important DNA would be lost every time a cell divides. If the cells are in good condition and not compromised, the telomeres lengthen. There seems no disagreement that the shorter the telomeres, the shorter the lifespan, and the longer they are, the higher the rate of survival (Haussmann et al. 2005 ; Tricola et al. 2018), but there is some disagreement as to why and when telomeres shorten. In the aging process, cell deterioration is thought to be expressed by telomeres getting shorter

Fig. 10.3 One chromosome is shown and the end caps (marked 'T') are the telomeres.

but a detailed study found, by contrast, that early negative experiences weigh in heavily and shorten telomeres, affecting lifespan, while telomeres stabilise in adulthood (Hall et al. 2004). If their study is more representative than the aging argument, this has immediate implications for raising highly altricial offspring, because the damage can be done at the dependent age. Obviously, the better the provisioning of offspring and the lower the stress, the less likely the offspring are to suffer telomere-length loss. Developmental stress is an important topic and suggests that parenting and pair bonds provide the social glue that can prevent premature telomere loss (Boonekamp et al. 2014). In this way, one can see the very dynamic interaction between environment, evolution and individual species' life history playing out at biochemical level. There can be substantial variations in telomere length even between individuals of the same species and, as Heidinger et al. (2012) agreed with previous research, these can be predictive of longevity.

The variability also indicates that, to some extent, living birds are in some way capable of determining their life history.

There is a further point to be made and this concerns reproduction. Heidinger et al. (2012) argued that, metabolically, reproduction is a particularly expensive activity and could lead to a loss of telomere length as well as to their attrition unless the organism has the physiological capability of activating telomere restoration processes. In other words, it would be of substantial advantage for a bird to lay few and small eggs, compared to the typical large number of eggs of high-latitude songbirds that may actually have to re-nest several times due to predator activity. Very large birds, such as the cockatoos, have very long lifespans, do not usually re-nest and lay few eggs. Their telomeres should be in good order.

To come back to the study by Heidinger and colleagues (2012), the slow rate of reproduction in cockatoos hints at a trade-off with life expectancy. By lowering the physiological cost of reproduction, presumably the female can up-regulate antioxidant defences and/or activate telomere restoration processes to the required extent.

Long telomeres not only minimise adverse effects in the short-term but may increase the lifespan of the breeding female. At the same time, the nestling is developing slowly over a three-month period in the nest and continues on a maturational process for another five to six years, a time to gain experience under guidance, form memories and develop a brain that is extraordinarily large.

Weighing up the evidence

The question in this final chapter is how to arrive at a clearer picture in light of all the information so far gleaned. Australian species have all types of reproductive systems and these have been introduced and discussed in some detail. Previous chapters have also shown that birds may form very close bonds. How they are constituted, and what, from an evolutionary point of view, drove some species to form alliances that can be emotionally and cognitively sophisticated and complex? Why are such bonds valuable – not in a moral or aesthetic sense, but in a biological sense?

Post-Cartesian thinking has viewed organisms as active agents and the environment as a kind of objective background, a stage prop in front of which the actors perform. An environment was understood to be able to impose constraints on survival of the organisms acting within it but Järvilehto (2009) reminded us that the environment is far from static, nor is it inert with respect to the organism. The environment may exert pressures that lead to adaptations of the organisms living in it, and it provides opportunities and risks. Comparing shorebirds with land birds is inviting one to compare their habitats; that is, to compare a multitude of landscapes with water surfaces. Forest environments and open woodlands are said to be complex environments that require a variety of foraging skills and memory for places where food might be found and when fruit ripen.

There appears to be a correlation between the complexity of the environmental niche and greater brain volume relative to body weight (Sayol et al. 2017). If the latter is true, one would expect that complex environments, such as open and closed forests, or variable environments, such as those influenced by droughts, create a context in which both male and female would need to excel in certain abilities. For instance, they would need an excellent sense of geography and memory of timing for food availability. Thus specific cognitive ability in both sexes might have been selected for as part of natural selection.

As to the variety of foraging skills, one needs to look at the typical range of plants that grow in rainforests. Hardwood trees often become fully mature only around 90–100 years of age. If they happen to be fruiting trees, they produce nothing edible at all for a long time and then often only sporadically. Blackbutt (*E. pilularis*) do not mature until they are over 100 years old and develop nest holes usually after 165–200 years of growth (Ngugi et al. 2015). Many fruits that are produced, some of them on tough vines, tend to be well defended and difficult to reach, with sharp or even poisonous thorns, or they may be hard-shelled or too big or they get produced at irregular intervals. Then there is the problem of predators that can be exacerbated in forests because such an environment allows them to melt into the green foliage and encourages ambush hunting. Parrots and cockatoos are forest species in origin, even if some species are now living in semi-arid environments, suggesting that their environments were traditionally, and in a sense often still are, complex foraging niches. Quite often we associate lush forests with the idea of being an easy food basket and, in a sense, that may be true, but the food sources are hidden or spread far and wide, and the knowledge to find them may make extraordinary demands on memory and innovativeness.

Hormonal adaptations

Another set of data now available for birds concerns the multitude of hormones and neurotransmitters in the brain. These too can be measured, and increasingly, researchers have looked at the oxytocin and dopamine systems and at specific brain agents such as serotonin and others that have positive effects on the organism. Surprisingly, research on such systems in terms of emotions and management of emotions is rather recent even in human behaviour. Hormones can make us compulsive, dependent, can be manipulated if things go wrong, but they also effectively control emotions that stand in the way of survival such as fear and generally ensure a balanced perception of the challenges around us. They provide the mechanisms by which one of the strongest bonds in nature, that between a mammalian mother and offspring, can endure. Since birds do not lactate the bonds between birds and offspring were thought to be merely genetically pre-programmed triggers brought about by behaviours from the nestlings, such as open beaks and/or specific calls, for instance. No doubt, such triggers exist and are initially very important. However, such triggers may not be enough in prolonged parenting when the need for feeding offspring has well passed and offspring continue to stay with their natal group.

To argue that hormones are set in place to regulate reproduction does not explain why relationships between parenting partners last beyond the fledging and the departure of offspring. Job done and the relationship could fall apart. But they do not, because the pair has its own resources of 'emotional intelligence', additional resources that evolved at the hormonal level as well as at the cognitive level. The actions of neuropeptides and activations of specific neurotransmitters can engender a feeling of wellbeing, even upbeat moods and positivity. In both primates and birds, simple behavioural mechanisms such as allopreening (preening someone else) and roosting closely together (Fig.10.1) are linked to oxytocin. Allopreening has often been argued as having as its main function the protection against ectoparasites. However, a convincing case has been made that, ultimately, this argument cannot hold because, if it were true, one would expect allopreening to be evenly spread across species, be they avian or mammalian. However, relatively few birds engage in allopreening and hence other functions had to be explored (Kenny et al. 2017).

As was described earlier, comparison of levels of hormones, including testosterone, showed that when levels of hormones between the two partners are similar, they are overall more successful in rearing young. Hence 'convergence' is not just a superficial visual impression but is deeply embedded in the biology capable of being malleable and responsive to input and/or changed conditions. For instance, testosterone levels have been shown to co-vary in stable partnerships of birds and reproductive success is greater when corticosterone levels are similar between partners (Hirschenhauser 2012).

The question here is whether such hormonal co-variations were similar to begin with (the partners are compatible) or a result of the bonding, and whether there is any evidence for a possible crossover that makes one bird adopt a similar hormonal profile as that of its partner. One very clever experiment asked this question in relation to corticosterone levels in birds. The authors (Noguera et al. 2017) used the yellow-legged gull, *Larus michahellis*, a long-lived social seabird, and implanted higher levels of corticosterone in some of the gull chicks. While the artificial raising of the stress hormone led to faster anti-predator responses, it put the implanted birds at a great disadvantage: they grew more slowly than unaffected chicks, retained a smaller size, had poor quality plumage and cell damage. In other words, stress is bad for any organism, as early research into the welfare of laboratory rats had already amply demonstrated. The brains of rats in stressful and non-enriched environments were 5.7 per cent smaller than those within enriched and stimulating environments and this was so just within one month of testing. The deprived juvenile rats had fewer neural connections and brain size remained smaller into adulthood and their lifespan was also shorter (Krech and Rosenzweig 1962; Diamond et al. 1972).

However, the significance of the yellow-legged gull study by Noguera and colleagues also lay in the surprise finding that the chicks that did not have artificially implanted high stress levels were also affected whilst growing up with high stress siblings. Their corticosterone levels were elevated as well, even though they had normal baseline stress levels at the start of the experiment. Stress often translates into the expression of powerful emotions and the findings are a reminder that hormone-induced moods can be adopted by close siblings or, for that matter, by adult partners. The entire hormonal system is highly responsive to environmental events and can assist in the survival of organisms but once prolonged it is uniquely harmful. Conversely, the hormonal system is also equipped to engender feelings of wellbeing and calm, induce and even enhance attachment and belonging. Such hormone systems and their activation in the brain are at the very core of maintaining adult relationships and buttressing long-term commitment to raising demanding offspring.

Early friendships

The argument was made that sexual dimorphism may not feature highly in Australian birds bonding. So how do they get together and choose each other? Not a small issue given that many partner for life. And here comes an interesting observation whose momentous importance has largely been overlooked. Thinking of the social flocks of galahs and corellas (socially monogamous long-bonded birds) it is clear that they contain several age groups. Breeding pairs, bachelors and juveniles can all be found in the one flock. In other words, juveniles have the opportunity for same-age company while they are adolescents and learn to socialise within their own age group. They can form firm friendships or bonds well before sexual maturity and they often do, and not just among cockatoos. Adolescent friendships have barely been mentioned or considered in birds (although there is a vast literature on social learning and social intelligence in primates).

It's important to note here that in adolescent friendships, bonding is de-coupled from reproduction. The young immature friendship pair has time to get to know each other and 'tune into' each other's movements, habits and vocalisations. Apart from some shore and sea birds, this seems to be particularly relevant to cockatoos although one might need to look very carefully and in detail at songbirds socialising as juveniles. Notably, in groups with early friendships, one also notes that sexual maturity may be delayed, and that in a number of species, it seems that females may reach sexual maturity a year or two earlier than males while in some species it may be the other way around.

Vocal convergence or 'tuning in' may take different and measurable forms. In vocalisations, especially in duetting, precision and speed of similar vocal output by the pair is one measure. Then there is the convergence of song with the predictive value for reproductive success and for the pair remaining together.

Fig. 10.4 This eastern rosella chick was saved from its nest after a severe hailstorm. The female had stayed on the nest and had died shielding her hatchlings. Of the four newly hatched chicks only one could be saved. It is one day old. Its head is no more than the size of a fingernail and it is able to hold up its long and pencil-sized neck just for seconds in order to accept food. The nose tube is pronounced (and later disappears), the dark bulge (a dark purply blue) is the area of the eye. The yellow beak is like soft leather and so malleable that it bends readily while the bird's head is resting. Apart from a few downy wisps on the head and neck the bird is entirely naked and pink-skinned.

The brain and altriciality

The common expression that the brain is the most 'expensive' organ to develop is well established but may be misleading. The 'expense' is one of nutritional requirement because neurons use up ten times more energy than the cells of the body (Yu et al. 2014). We know from humans and mammals that energy consumption in the brain accounts for over 20 per cent of total oxygen metabolism (Watts et al. 2018) and neurons consume 75–80 per cent of energy produced in the brain (Hyder et al. 2013). Because of the many restorative functions that need to be performed for maintenance of a healthy brain, such as attending to synaptic energy depletion and the requirement for an elevated metabolic rate in neurons, the brain tends to get priority for maintenance over other functions. The nutritional value of food determines how much can be diverted into the growth of the brain (Watts et al. 2018).

Altricial nestlings are nothing like the fluffy chicks of chickens, ducks, emus and brush turkeys. Their complete blindness and fragile build make it obvious that chicks of parrots, cockatoos and many songbirds need substantial care. Altricial species chicks can afford to be slow in their development because they have parents that have committed to looking after them for a considerable time.

Slow development also means time for the brain to grow and in a range of birds this signals the ability to acquire greater brain power than is possible in the developmentally contracted timetable of precocial birds. In fact, the length of development outside the egg, or womb in mammals, is correlated with relative brain size. Iwaniuk and Nelson (2003) found significant differences in as many as eighteen orders of birds showing that length of parental care was strongly correlated with brain size or, as Chiappa et al. (2018) importantly suggested, the length of the altricial period is associated with evolutionary changes in the cognitive system. Conversely, migratory species for which the developmental period is usually short are said to have significantly smaller brains than resident birds, and this would further confirm that length of altricial period matters in brain development (Sol et al. 2010).

Indeed, more than half a century ago, Sutter (1951) had already noticed that, during a lifespan, the brain of nest-bound (nidicolous) vertebrates expands eight to ten times its initial post-hatch/post-birth size; while those that develop quickly/spend less time in their natal environment (nidifugous), can expect brain growth to be just 1.5 to 2.5 times the initial size. For such substantial growth rates of the brain to occur, the brain needs not just nutrients but every bit of growth also requires relevant supportive tissue (Seybold and Rahmann 1985).

Garcia-Peña and colleagues (2013) asked also whether the mating system itself has anything to do with brain development and ultimate size, and although this study was conducted using shorebirds, the results are noteworthy. They found that precocial species indeed have smaller brains and so have polyandrous species but neither promiscuity nor polygyny seem to affect brain size (Garcia-Peña et al. 2013). Reliably, monogamy offers the best outcome.

However, stretching development out as far as possible is a risky business and a great drain on the adults. It is perhaps not surprising then that such extremes of dependence have not been tried and sustained in too many orders and that is reflected in the kinds of bonds and commitments of adults as a prerequisite to make such a system work. Only in cetaceans (dolphins), elephants and primates (great apes in particular) do we find highly complex and cognitive abilities, deep affection and/or strong cooperative alliances and long-lasting bonds, though in cetaceans and elephants these are not pair bonds but matriarchal sister, aunt and cousin bonds (Rehkämper et al. 1991). Even smaller is the number of orders in which the responsibility for raising young rests almost entirely and exclusively on pairs and here, humans and birds are the only orders remaining. While the combination of large brains and long immaturity may be considered a high-risk strategy, the evolutionary outcome tells a different story: birds have evolved into one of the most numerous orders, and humans into one of the most populous species, forever growing in numbers.

The profound discovery of cognition in animals across some vertebrates, including birds, has now also allowed us to ask whether cognitive abilities and large brains are pivotal in partner choice, and enduring attachment.

Put all the elements together – permanent pair bond formation, long time of dependency of offspring (long enough to acquire plenty of skills, problem-solving abilities and a certain resilience to risk and danger). Add to this close, even empathetic social interactions and a highly evolved brain to deal with complex environments – and it can be seen how such a constellation might strengthen survival. Attachment thus seems an ingenious social response to reactive internal processes (such as fear increasing stress) that can become self-destructive. Remarkably, as has been shown, some avian species have maximised their resilience in the face of stress by forming firm attachments and effectively maintaining these in secure bonds – very similar to the way many human bonds work.

The book has hopefully shown that there is a tradition in Australian birds of sticking together and triumphing over adversity because of affection, cooperation and enduring social monogamies, rewarding the pairs with surviving offspring, extraordinarily long lifespans and large brains.

Epilogue

This book has been about bonding, sex and mate-choice in Australian birds and has drawn on wider evolutionary changes that led to cooperation and bonds based on criteria that may be as varied as they are in human society. Overall, it has been argued that the most successful, longest-lived and most intelligent of Australian land birds have succeeded by reducing the competitive differences between the sexes, by becoming more similar to each other in plumage and song, by removing elements of coercion that are certainly present in avian species with an intact penis and by forming cooperative units. These units may consist of pairs, small family groups with helpers and even larger groups.

It was further argued that such specific constellations led to a substantial increase in brain power and decision-making capacity. It was argued that individuality, such a highly prized quality in human society, occurs also in avian species. It is ultimately only possible when an organism has grown beyond a biological framework, so often described in animals as almost automatic, genetically pre-determined or sexually imprinted behaviour.

However, the really important facet in the life histories of the most exceptional birds is how, and for how long and how well they raise their offspring. For many years, we have been misled into thinking that genes are the overriding predictive factor for life histories (Kaplan and Rogers 2004). We know now that environmental factors can have a dramatic effect on organisms and even change the architecture and capacity of the brain, the availability of appropriate responses and can alter life expectancies.

This book has proposed that life in bonds is not all about reproduction but about cooperation, mutual support and about intelligent choices and commitments, in the context of which the social brain finds perhaps one of its most advanced expressions.

We have been misled, in the spirit of capitalism, that competition is the driving force of evolution and the most worthwhile of goals in human society because it is meant to achieve the best possible outcomes. Yet there is evidence that cooperation yields the greatest rewards by fostering more stress-resistant populations capable of assessing threats and dangers more readily, by an ever-increasing capacity for problem-solving and making intelligent choices (Cauchard et al. 2013). There is also evidence of quiet self-involved play being related to creativity and even original thought.

In the wider world, it can be shown that cooperation can become inter-group and lead to more stable and ultimately successful groups (Robinson and Barker 2017). As a final comment, one might well cite the case of two different life strategies that were also highlighted in one of David Attenborough's documentaries: the life of wood ants, *Formica lugubris*, which were studied in the Jura Mountains in Switzerland. One group of wood ants had hundreds of queens that did not compete and were able to set up new territories, and the original single colony grew to interconnected colonies over 100 kilometres long. The other group consisted of genetically the same wood ants, but their strategy was to compete. After years of observation, their group remained the same size, with no expansion and no gains but the deaths of tens of thousands of individuals by many warlike excursions when any group of the colony went out to expand into the territory of another. Procter and colleagues (2016) tested whether the successful and peaceful expansion of one group of wood ants was possible because of high relatedness between the socially connected and low relatedness in unconnected nests. They found no difference in inter-nest genetic relatedness between the two types of wood ant strategies and concluded that neighbouring pairs of connected nests show a social and cooperative distinction, but no genetic distinction (Procter et al. 2016). Such colonies have been called super-organisms and they, as does the ancient Australian bird life, tell us something about possible evolutionary choices.

Also, the book showed that as parental supervision became longer and parental investment in hatchling and post-fledging care increased in duration and attention, birds' brains had time to mature under the guard of protective adults, to learn and also to deal with stresses more effectively than in those species without long learning periods. Furthermore, as Kramer and Russel (2015) argued, monogamy as a system of reproduction, at least in hominids, may have been the ancestral form from which cooperative models arose. Perhaps it was also so in modern birds. It seems to be the recipe that leads to brains with higher functional capacity and cognition. The social context in which this can happen appears best when parental care is extended well beyond fledging and the bond of the pair itself has strength and commitment.

Finally, the book has taken the risky step of deliberately comparing the ability of humans and birds to form bonds and pursuing some of the arguments that are usually made in human psychology and human neuroscience to test whether emotional bonds and strong attachments would even be biologically conceivable.

Latest research has given more than enough hints to suggest that in some species (humans, great apes and some birds) the cognitive brain had grown in conjunction with the 'emotional brain'. The latter is a short form for explaining the presences of powerful hormones that regulate stress and induce positive emotions, such as oxytocin (Tops et al. 2014) and these are well developed in birds. Importantly, a considerable literature has now shown that oxytocin also modulates various aspects of social behaviours such as empathy, trust, in-group preference and memory of socially relevant cues in humans, in primates (Crockford et al. 2013) and in birds. The role of oxytocin has been argued in two ways: the prosocial argument is that oxytocin mainly enhances affiliative prosocial behaviours, often identified as attachment in human psychology, or that oxytocin improves social performance by reducing stress (Shamay-Tsoory and Abu-Akel 2016). No matter which line of argument one follows, both arrive at the view that more oxytocin leads to more cooperative behaviour, to strengthened bonds, and thus possibly to longer lifespans.

As we were once surprised that chimpanzees could use tools and stunned by a gorilla's ability to grieve for a kitten, it is now time to further investigate and concede that the class of birds may not just have vocal learning in common with humans but, in some highly evolved species, also the emotional ability for selective and enduring attachment to others. We usually call it love, but it is rather 'pragma', based on attachment and commitment, and making possible empathy and even the controversial 'altruism'.

We have long believed that all that humans do is unique and there is this very thick dividing line between us and other animals. The insights of the past decades have shown with overwhelming clarity, however, that there are antecedents to or convergences with most human behaviours in animals.

Glossary

Adaptation – evolutionary process involving genetic change to fit a particular environmental niche. An adaptation can be physiological, behavioural, or even structural. It is a trait that confers a selective advantage (see also: selective advantage).

Aggression – a behaviour in response to a threat or can refer to premature and insistent defence and intolerance of other species (a dysfunctional act usually harmful to perpetrator and victim alike)

Agnostids – early forms of invertebrate characterised by an external skeleton, a segmented body, and paired jointed appendages believed to have developed first in the Cambrian Period

Agonistic behaviour – the term is used in ethology to identify all fighting behaviour (ritualised or not) for which a clear function can be established (i.e. nest defence, mate-guarding, fighting for breeding rights etc), as opposed to aggression

Agonistic display – fighting behaviour (e.g. for territory or females) that has become ritualised and tends to avoid clashes that cause injury or death

Allogrooming – the act of grooming someone else (a close 'other') of the same species – an important activity in bonding

Altricial/altriciality – altricial is usually contrasted with precocial (see also: precocial). Altricial young hatch in a physical state of immaturity fully dependent on parental care; at hatching, altricial birds are often naked and blind and eye opening may take from two to ten days after hatching. Feathering (of down or plumage) may take from a week to three weeks. Flight feathers develop last, as a precondition for fledging (see below). The majority of birds are altricial.

Androgen-based pheromones – secreted sexual chemical signals, that act as attractants – widespread in mammals and insects for sexual attractions

Antipredator vigilance – monitoring of threats related to predators or to territorial takeovers

Apoptosis – cell death

Associative learning – learning taking place as a result of forming an association between two stimuli or between a specific stimulus and an observed particular outcome

Assortative mating – non-random mating in which animals select their mates according to a shared trait. Individuals select mates on the basis of phenotypic similarity to themselves.

Attenuation – of sound refers to the gradual loss of amplitude and even frequencies over distance

Auditory – pertaining to the sense of hearing

Avoidance behaviour – a wide range of strategies that are either innate or learned (or modified by experience) designed to get out of harm's way and escape danger, ranging from freezing to alarm or distress calling, to flying away or hiding

Brain plasticity – ability of the brain to remain receptive to learning throughout life and be capable of remembering what has been learned, for instance, the ability to learn new song or sounds as adults

Brood parasite – cuckoos, for instance, usurp the services of other avian species to raise the cuckoo's young, at the expense of the young of that species. Cuckoo chicks often eliminate hatchlings of the host parents.

Cambrian period – 543–485 million years ago

Carinate and ratite birds – distinction made between birds that can fly, carinate birds, and those that are flightless (ratite). Anatomically, the distinction is obvious: flighted birds have keeled breastbones for the attachment of flight muscles. Flightless birds have flat breastbones (no keel for attachment of muscles).

Cerebral hemispheres – the two symmetrical parts of the forebrain

Cetaceans – order of completely aquatic placental mammals comprising whales and dolphins. Humans, birds and cetaceans belong to the exceptional orders that have in common that they can learn their vocalisations.

Chromatic – relates to colour (e.g. chromatic vision means the ability to see colour)

Cloaca – (also called the vent) is the opening to a bird's digestive, reproductive and urinary tracts

Cognition – higher mental processes enabling an organism to solve problems, form concepts and associations and use innovation to overcome difficulties

Cognitive bias – birds, and animals in general, may develop a negative or positive bias towards objects and in exploration depending on past experience

Conspecific – another individual of the same species, could be a stranger, a mate or family member (as opposed to heterospecific; see entry)

Contagion behaviour – copying of the behaviour of other individuals, so that the behaviour spreads throughout a group or population

Cooperative behaviour – raising and feeding of nestlings by group members in addition to parental care. In the wider understanding of cooperative behaviour sentinel duties for the group and other shared group tasks such as minding a crèche also belong in the catalogue of cooperative behaviour displayed in many Australian avian species.

Corpus callosum – wide, thick nerve tract consisting of a bundle of fibres that connects the two hemispheres of the brain (only found in placental mammals)

Corticosterone – the main stress hormone in birds. It is released from the adrenal cortex into the blood stream

Crepuscular feeders – birds that feed in twilight of dawn and dusk

Cretaceous – last period of the Mesozoic era, extending from about 144 million years ago (the end of the Jurassic period) to 65 million years ago (the time of mass extinction)

Crystallised song – a song that is learned by a songbird as a juvenile and then fixed into a permanent form before reaching sexual maturity. For instance, zebra finch juvenile males are tutored, often by their father, to learn their song that they then sing for the rest of their lives during the breeding season.

Delayed gratification – resisting the temptation to take a smaller reward when a larger reward is expected to come later

Diester – see: esters

Dopamine – a neurotransmitter in the brain. It is synthesised and released by one neuron and then released into the synapse between that neuron and another neuron. Thus, it acts as a signal to stimulate the second neurone to fire (i.e. it activates the second neuron).

East Gondwana – part of the supercontinent that eventually separated and drifted north, turning in an anti-clockwise manner (by as much as 180°) to become Australia as we know it today

Ectoparasites – organisms that feed on other organisms by invading the outside of their bodies and may specialise in particular regions of the body, i.e. feathers, hair, orifices, sebaceous glands, nares

Esters – a class of diverse chemical compounds that occur in a wide variety of organisms (plants and animals): monoesters contain one functional ester group, and diesters, two functional groups.

Birds may switch from monoester to diester preening wax during courtship

Ethology – the formal study of animal behaviour

Fear – for ecologists, fear represents what animals probably experience when facing threats by predators and conspecifics. In humans, fear is typically viewed as the conscious feeling that arises when a person is threatened. More generally, fear can be viewed as a state that links threatening stimuli to a set of responses to such threats, including physiological and behavioural changes.

Gloger's rule – named after the zoologist Constantin WL Gloger (1803–1863), stating that birds in climates with high relative humidity are darker than conspecifics in climates with low relative humidity

Heterospecific – an individual of another species

Higher Vocal Centre (HVC) – songbirds have specific nuclei in the brain designed for reception and production of song. The High Vocal Centre, (HVC) is the most important nucleus. Non-songbirds do not have a high vocal centre.

Hippocampus – area in the centre of the cerebral cortex, important especially for learning and spatial memory

Hypothalamic neuropeptide – called GnIH, which acts directly on the pituitary to inhibit luteinizing hormone (LH) and follicle-stimulating hormone (FSH) release, both of which act on the gonads

Innate – innate behaviour refers to behaviour that is genetically encoded and requires little to no learning. Reflexes are innate.

Interhemispheric transfer – transfer of information from one hemisphere to the other. In birds, this can be manifested as learning using one eye being transferred as memory available when the other eye is used. Such a transfer does not always occur.

Landscape of fear – Expression coined by ecologists to indicate that the risk posed by predators can vary both in time and in space in the habitat of an animal

Lateralisation – structural and/or functional differences between the left and right sides of the brain

Life-history traits – crucial data concerning life and death, e.g. age of sexual maturity and mating, clutch size, number of clutches per season, survival rate, overall developmental patterns and life expectancy

Lock and key hypothesis – the penis has to fit the size of female anal region

Longevity – total lifespan

Machiavellian intelligence – an important but derogatory term in cognitive science referring to the ability of an animal to make deals, make or break alliances and rules, be purposely misleading, engage in trickery and deception

Major histocompatibility complex (MHC) – a set of proteins on the cell surface, essential for the immune system to recognise foreign molecules

Mate familiarity hypothesis – partner familiarity and long-term monogamy, which may account for increased reproductive success of older birds

Metabolism – the chemical and physical processes continuously going on in living organisms and cells, consisting of anabolism and catabolism, organic and chemical processes inside of organisms that are necessary to maintain life, or how quickly you burn calories or fat

Miocene – geological epoch from 23 to five million years ago

Mirror neurons – specific neurons discovered in the bird brain (and in mammals and humans) enabling the individual to learn by listening or watching. The neurons fire when listening to another bird's song in the same manner as if the bird had sung the same passage itself.

Monoamine neurotransmitters – a summary term for specific neurotransmitters which are monoamines, such as dopamine, noradrenaline, adrenaline and serotonin

Monogamy – male and female birds make a total social commitment to staying together and rearing their young. It is the most common mating system in birds and relatively uncommon in other classes of animals, including even mammals.

Monogamy/social monogamy – being bonded to only one partner. The word 'social' has been added because sexual activity may involve extra-marital activity and result in offspring that are raised by the bonded pair.

Motor self-regulation – requires the user to override motor impulses instigated by important perceptual stimuli, and so represents a fundamental inhibitory skill

Moult – shedding of feathers and even skin to be replaced by new ones

Natural selection – a process that partially explains evolution. According to Darwin, the better adapted individuals are more likely to survive and reproduce (see also: sexual selection).

Neocortex – the neocortex forms the greatest part of the mammalian brain and has six layers. The prefrontal cortex is located at the very front of the cortex. Birds do not have a neocortex.

Neophobia – fear of anything new

Neurogenesis – generating new neurons in the brain; adult neurogenesis is largely confined to birds and cold-blooded species. This is rare in mammals.

Neurons – nerve cells

Neurotransmitter – any chemical substance released at the end of a nerve axon and into the synapse that aids the transfer of the electrical impulse to the next neuron, a muscle fibre, or some other structure

Nidiculous – staying in a nest and depending on adult care until mature. Sometimes used interchangeably with 'altricial'.

Nidifugous – opposite to nidiculous: fleeing nest shortly after hatching, meaning the organism is advanced enough in development to feed itself

Olfactory – pertaining to the sense of smell

Opsin – a protein that is released in the eye by the action of light

Oscines – songbird. A distinction is made between true oscines and sub-oscines. Pittas belong to the latter – the definition depends on the number of muscles servicing the syrinx.

Oxymoron – self-contradicting word or group of words

Oxytocin – a hormone and a neurotransmitter that is associated with empathy, trust, sexual activity and relationship-building. Oxytocin is normally produced in the posterior lobe of the hypothalamus and released by the posterior pituitary. It is released during social bonding.

Parallax – movement of the head so that the position of an object can be appraised from different positions and depth can be determined

Passerines – perching birds; a vast group of birds (over half of all species) defined by their feet as species that roost in trees. All songbirds and suboscines make up this group.

Phallus – penis

Phenotype – physical appearance and behaviour of a species, particular traits that are the result of both environmental and genetic factors

Pheromone – a chemical excreted by one animal and affecting the behaviour or physiology of another member of its species

Phylogeny – the study of the evolutionary relationship between species

Plastic song – song that is malleable and then either sets into a fixed pattern (crystallised song: see above) or remains plastic for the rest of a bird's life (based on improvisation or a large memory, or both)

Pleistocene – glacial and post-glacial period ranges from 2.5 million years ago to 11,700 years ago – the period when modern Aboriginal peoples arrived in Australia

Polyandry – female animal with more than one male mate

Polygamy – pattern of mating in which an animal has more than one mate

Polygyny – a male animal has more than one female mate

Polymorphic genes – different DNA sequences at the same locus of the genome in the population and that may cause differences between individuals in the same population/species. Hence, multiple forms of a single gene exist in a species.

Precocial – birds that are feathered and able to move about and even forage a few days after hatching

Pre-emptive vigilance – vigilance to detect signs of predator activity or signs that neighbours are threatening before they actually launch their attacks

Prolactin – hormone produced by the lactotroph cells of the pituitary gland, usually associated with breast lactation in human females and mammals generally but is also present in birds

Ratites – group of birds, largely flightless, to which ostriches, emus, rheas and kiwis belong

Sahul – was the name of the continent when modern Australia consisted of a single Pleistocene-era continent which connected Australia with New Guinea and Tasmania. The name 'Sahull' or 'Sahoel' first appeared on seventeenth-century Dutch maps.

Scaling rule – (in metabolism) the smaller the organism, the larger the surface area in relation to body size, and hence the rate of metabolism is higher in smaller birds than in larger ones

Sebaceous gland – specialised microscopic glands in the skin secreting oily or waxy materials

Selective advantage – via natural selection, traits are selected for that have a stronger chance of an organism's survival than had been the case in this species before

Serotonin – in the brain it is a neurotransmitter, also known as 5-hydroxytryptamine (5-HT). Also present in the bowel, and blood platelets.

Sexual dimorphism – a consistent difference and distinctiveness between males and females in certain behavioural, physical or physiological features traits. In species of male/male competition, the male may have a bright and colourful plumage to attract a female. Males tend to mate with many females and do not help in raising their young, but not always. Size difference between male and female is also a sexually dimorphic trait. In some species, females are smaller, in others (most birds of prey) the male is smaller.

Sexual selection – an additional finding by Charles Darwin that organisms thrived and speciated not just by the powers of natural selection, but males and females chose each other (or females chose males) according to certain criteria of health, plumage, experience and a variety of other characteristics that may remain yet to be found

Social brain hypothesis – argues that human intelligence did not evolve primarily as a means to solve ecological problems, but rather as a means of surviving and reproducing in large and complex social groups

Social vigilance – Monitoring of threats related to conspecifics

Songbird – a bird possessing at least four pairs of syringeal muscles. All songbirds belong to the group of passerine birds.

Sperm competition – the competitive process between spermatozoa of two or more different males to fertilise the same egg during sexual reproduction. Competition can occur when females have multiple potential mating partners.

Sunda – is the shelf of modern South East Asia at a time when sea levels were about 130 metres lower than they are today, exposing more islands than are known today and also merging landmasses known as islands today that were once merged with the landmass of South East Asia, such as Borneo

Syrinx – the syrinx, located in the chest at the bronchial bifurcation, performs the tasks that the larynx performs in humans, namely producing sound. It has membranes over which the exhaled air is moved, vibrating them. The muscles surrounding the syrinx provide the mechanical means to move the membrane to produce different sounds.

Telomeres – caps at each end of a chromosome to protect chromosome

Tetrachromatic – the provision of four independent channels (cone cells) in the eye to process colour

Thermoregulation – process that ensures that the core body temperature remains the same

Threat – any cue that signals a potential attack

Trilobites – now extinct, one of the earliest known arthropods that flourished for 300 million years and fell victim to the Permian Extinction events around 252 million years ago. Trilobites left plenty of fossil records because, just as agnostids (see above), they had an external skeleton.

Uropygial gland – also called oil gland or preen gland. Varies in size and function between species and may be used for feather maintenance, waterproofing, protection against parasites as well as in courtship (see also: sebaceous glands).

UVS – ultraviolet sensitivity

Vigilance – monitoring of potential or actual threats using different sensory modes (e.g. visual, auditory). Typically, vigilance involves the cessation of ongoing activities to monitor the surroundings for danger. This monitoring can involve several behavioural patterns depending on the species, including movements of the head to bring different areas into visual focus, sniffing, and reorientation of the ears.

Vocal learning – the ability of some species and orders to learn new sounds and sequences beyond templates that may be innate

VS – violet sensitivity

Wallace Line – indicates a faunal boundary line separating the ecozones of Asia and Wallacea, a transitional zone between Asia and Australia

Wallacea – the group of islands between the South East Asian mainland (and including Borneo), Papua New Guinea to the east and the Australian continent to the south. This designation is not arbitrary. The Wallace line that defines Wallacea in the west was based on observations by Alfred Russell Wallace (1877).

Bird names mentioned or discussed in the book

Australian birds

(* indicates species introduced to Australia; Italics: Latin species name; bracket indicates family name, which may contain many species.)

Albert lyrebird, *Menura alberti*
Alexandra's or princess parrot, *Polytelis alexandrae*
Apostlebirds, *Struthidea cinereal*
Australian brush turkey, *Alectura lathami*
Australian bustard, *Ardeotis australis*
Australian king parrot, *Alisterus scapularis*
Australian koels, *Eudynamys (orientalis) cyanocephalu*
Australian magpie, *Gymnorhina tibicen*
Australian raven, *Corvus coronoides*
Blackbirds, *Turdus merula**
Black-faced cuckoo-shrike, *Coracina novaehollandiae*
Black-necked stork, *Ephippiorhynchus-asiaticus*
Black swan, *Cygnus atratus*
Blue-faced honeyeaters, *Entomyzon cyanotis*
Bourke's parrots, *Neopsephotus bourkii*

Brolga, *Grus rubicundus*
Brown goshawk, *Accipiter fasciatus*
Brown honeyeater, *Lichmera indistincta*
Brown thornbill, *Acanthiza pusilla*
Brush turkey, see Australian brush turkey
Budgerigar, *Melopsittacus undulatus*
Bulbuls, red-whiskered, *Pycnonotus jocosus**
Bush stone curlew, *Burhinus grallarius*
Butcherbirds (Cracticidae)
Chickens (Galliformes), see also Junglefowl
Chiming wedgebill, *Psophodes occidentalis*
Cockatiel, *Leptolophus (Nymphicus) hollandicus*
Cockatoos (Cacatuidae)
Comb-crested jacanas, *Irediparra gallinacea*
Corvids, see Ravens and Crows
Crimson rosella, *Platycercus elegans*
Cuckoo-shrikes (Campephagidae)
Currawongs, see pied currawong
Dollarbird, *Eurystomus orientalis*
Drongos, see spangled drongo
Ducks (Anatidae)
Eastern reef egret, *Ardea sacra*
Eastern rosella, *Platycercus eximius*
Eastern whipbirds, *Psophodes olivaceus*
Eclectus parrot, *Eclectus roratus*
Emu, *Dromaius novaehollandiae*
Fairy-wrens (Maluridae)
Fantails (Rhipiduridae)
Feral/common pigeons, *Columba livia**
Galah, *Cacatua roseicapilla*
Geese (Anatidae)
Goshawk, see brown goshawk
Gouldian finches, *Erythrura gouldiae*

Grasswrens (Amytornis)
Great bowerbird, *Chlamydera nuchalis*
Great crested grebe, *Podiceps cristatus*
Great frigate bird, *Fregata minor*
Grebes, see great crested grebe
Grey butcherbird, *Cracticus torquatus*
Grey fantail, *Rhipidura albscapa*
Ground Cuckoo-shrike, *Coracina maxima*
Helmeted friarbirds, *Philemon buceroides*
Honeyeaters (Meliphagidae)
House sparrows, *Passer domesticus**
Indian or common myna, *Acridotheres tristis**
Jacky winter, *Microeca fascinans*
Kookaburra, see Laughing kookaburra
Laughing kookaburra, *Dacelo novaeguineae*
Letter-winged kite, *Elanus scriptus*
Little corella, *Cacatua sanguinea*
Little eagle, *Hieraaetus morphnoides*
Little wattlebird, *Anthichaera chrysoptera*
Lotus bird, see comb-crested jacana
Lyrebirds (Menuridae)
Magpie lark, *Grallina cyanoleuca*
Malleefowl, *Leipoa ocellata*
Mangrove honeyeater, *Lichenostomus fasciogularis*
Musk duck, *Biziura lobate*
Myna, see Indian myna
New Holland honeyeater, *Phylidonyris novaehollandiae*
Noisy miner, *Manorina melanocephala*
Osprey, *Pandion halia*etus
Owlet nightjars, *Aegotheles cristatus*
Palm cockatoo, *Probosciger aterrimus*
Pardalotes (Pardalotidae)
Parrots (Psittacidae)

Peaceful doves, *Geopelia striata*
Pheasant coucal, *Centropus phasianinus*
Pied butcherbird, *Cracticus nigrogularis*
Pied currawong, *Strepera graculina*
Pink cockatoo (also Major Mitchell Cockatoo), *Lophochroa leadbeateri*
Purple-crowned fairy-wren, *Malurus coronatus*
Rainbow bee-eater, *Merops ornatus*
Ravens and crows (Corvidae)
Red-backed fairy-wren, *Malurus melanocephalus*
Red-browed firetail (finch), *Neochmia temporalis*
Red-rumped parrot, *Psephotus haematonotus*
Red-tailed black cockatoo, *Calyptorhynchus banksii*
Red wattlebirds, *Anthochaera carunculate*
Regent bowerbird, *Sericulus chrysocephalus*
Rosellas, genus Platycercus (Psittaculidae)
Rufous whistler, *Pachycephala rufiventris*
Satin bowerbird, *Ptilonorgynchua violacens*
Scaly-breasted lorikeets, *Trichoglossus chlorolepidotus*
Scarlet robin, *Petroica boodang*
Shining flycatcher, *Myiagra alecto*
Shrikes (Laniidae)
Silvereye, *Zosterops lateralis*
Singing honeyeater, *Lichenostomus virescens*
Southern cassowary, *Casuarius casuarius*
Spangled drongo, *Dicrurus bracteatus*
Spotted nightjar, *Eurostopodus argus*
Spotted pardalote, *Pardalotus punctatus*
Star finch, *Neochmia ruficauda*
Starlings, *Sturnus vulgaris**
Striated pardalote, *Pardalotus striatus*
Sulphur-crested cockatoo, *Cacatua galerita*
Superb fairy-wren, *Malurus cyaneus*

Superb lyrebird, *Menura novaehollandiae*
Superb parrot, *Polytelis swainsonii*
Swallows (Hirundininae ssp)
Tawny frogmouth, *Podargus strigoides*
Thick-billed grasswren, *Amytornis modestus*
Topknot pigeon, *Lopholaimus antarcticus*
Torresian crow, *Corvus orru*
Varied honeyeater, *Lichenostomus versicolor*
Varied sittella, *Daphoenositta chrysoptera*
Victoria's riflebird, *Ptiloris victoriae*
Welcome swallow, *Hirundo neoxena*
Whistlers, Pachycephalidae (Mangrove golden, golden, grey, olive, rufous)
Whistling kite, *Haliastur sphenurus*
White-bellied sea-eagle, *Haliaeetus leucogaste*
White-breasted woodswallow, *Artamus leucorynchus*
White-headed pigeon, *Columba leucomela*
White-winged chough, *Corcorax melanorhamphos*
Wedge-tailed eagle, *Aquila audax*
Wompoo fruit-dove, *Ptilinopus superbus*
Zebra finch, *Taeniopygia guttata*

Birds from other countries/continents

African grey parrot, *Psittacus erithacus*
Baltimore oriole, *Icterus galbula*
Blackbirds (Icteridae)
Black-throated blue warblers, *Dendroica caerulescens*
Blue and yellow macaw, *Ara ararauna*
Blue tit, *Cyanistes caeruleus*
Bobolink, *Dolichonyx oryzivorus*
Capercaillie, *Tetrao urogallus*
Carrion crow, *Corvus corone corone*

Cattle egret, *Bubulcus ibis*
Common raven, *Corvus corax*
Dark-eyed juncos, *Junco hyemalis*
Domestic ducks, *Anser domesticus*
Eurasian jay, *Garrulus glandarius*
Eurasian magpie, *Pica pica*
Fiery-throated hummingbird, *Panterpe insignis*
Flightless cormorant, *Phalacrocorax harrisi*
Galapagos albatross, *Phoebastria irrorate*
Goffin cockatoo, *Cacatua goffiniana*
Great skuas, *Catharacta skua*
Great spotted cuckoo, *Clamator glandarius*
Great tit, *Parus major*
Greater vasa parrot, *Coracopsis vasa*
Green-backed flycatcher, *Ficedula elisae*
Greylag geese, *Anser anser*
Hummingbirds (Trochilidae)
Jackdaw, *Corvus monedula*
Japanese quail, *Coturnix japonica*
Kakapo, *Strigops habroptilus*
Kea, *Nestor notabilis*
Kiwi, *Apteryx australis*
Laysan albatross, *Phoebastria immutabilis*
Long-tailed manakin, *Chiroxipia linearis*
Moa (extinct), *Dinornis novaezealandiae*
Moluccan cockatoo, *Cacatua moluccensis*
New Caledonian crow, *Corvus moneduloides*
Nightingale, *Luscinia megarhynchos*
Orange-fronted parakeets, *Aratinga canicularis*
Orange-winged amazon, *Amazona amazonica*
Ostrich, *Struthio camelus*
Peach-faced lovebird, *Agapornis roseicollis*
Penduline tit, *Remiz pendulinus*

Ratite genus *Crypturellus* (Tinamidae)
Red-crowned crane, *Grus japonensis*
Red-lored parrot, *Amazona autumnalis*
Red-necked phalarope, *Phalaropus Isobatus*
Rheas (Rheidae)
Salmon-crested cockatoo, see Moluccan c.
Semipalmated sandpiper, *Calidris pusilla*
Snares penguin, *Eudyptes robustus*
Steller's jays, *Cyanocitta stelleri*
Swamp sparrow, *Melospiza georgiana*
Tawny-bellied seedeater, *Sporophila hypoxantha*
Tinamou (Tinamidae)
Umbrella cockatoo, see White cockatoo
Wandering albatross, *Diomedea exulans*
Western scrub jay, *Aphelocoma californica*
White-browed sparrow weavers, *Plocepasser mahali*
White carneau pigeon (derived from *Columba livia*)
White cockatoo, *Cacatua alba*
Whooping crane, *Grus americana*
Willow tits, *Poecile montanus*
Wire-tailed manakin males, *Pipra filicauda*
Yellow-headed parrot, *Amazona oratrix*
Yellow-legged gull, *Larus michahellis*

References

Acevedo, BP, Aron, A, Fisher, HE and Brown, LL (2012) Neural correlates of long-term intense romantic love. *Social Cognitive and Affective Neuroscience* 7 (2, 1), 145–159, https://doi.org/10.1093/scan/nsq092.

Adkins-Regan, E and Krakauer, A (2000) Removal of adult males from the rearing environment increases preferences for same-sex partners in the zebra finch. *Animal Behaviour* 60, 47–53.

Adler, T (1997) Animals' fancies: Why members of some species prefer their own sex. *Science News* 151 (1), 8–9.

Agnvall, B, Katajamaa, R, Altimiras, J and Jensen, P (2015) Is domestication driven by reduced fear of humans? Boldness, metabolism and serotonin levels in divergently selected red junglefowl (Gallus gallus). *Biology Letters* 11, 20150509. http://dx.doi.org/10.1098 rsbl. 2015.0509.

Ahumada, JA (2001) Comparison of the reproductive biology of two neotropical wrens in an unpredictable environment in north-eastern Colombia. *The Auk* 118, 191–210.

Allman, JM, Hakeem, A, Erwin, JM, Nimchinsky, E and Hof, P (2001) The anterior cingulate cortex: the evolution of an interface between emotion and cognition. *Annals of the New York Academy of Sciences* 935 (1), 107–117.

Andersson, S, Örnborg, J and Andersson, M (1998) Ultraviolet sexual dimorphism and assortative mating in blue tits. *Proceedings of the Royal Society of London B: Biological Sciences* 265, 445–450.

Angelier, F, Wingfield, JC, Tartu, S and Chastel, O (2016) Does prolactin mediate parental and life-history decisions in response to environmental conditions in birds? A review. *Hormones and Behavior* 77, 18–29.

Annette, G (2011) RFamide Peptides: Structure, Function, Mechanisms and Pharmaceutical Potential. *Pharmaceuticals* 4 (9), 1248–1280.

Arnold, KE and Owens, IPF (1998) Cooperative breeding in birds: a comparative test of the life history hypothesis. *Proceedings of the Royal Society of London B: Biological Sciences* 265, 739–745.

Auersperg, AMI, Laumer, IB and Bugnyar, T (2013a) Goffin cockatoos wait for qualitative and quantitative gains but prefer 'better' to 'more'. *Biology Letters* 9, 20121092.

Auersperg, AMI, Kacelnik, A and von Bayern, AM (2013b) Explorative learning and functional inferences on a five-step means-means-end problem in Goffin's cockatoos (Cacatua goffini). *PloS ONE*, 8 (7), p.e68979.

Auersperg, AMI, Borasinski, S, Laumer, I and Kacelnik, A (2017) Goffin's cockatoos make the same tool type from different materials. *Biology Letters* 12, 20160689. http://dx.doi.org/10.1098/ rsbl.2016.0689.

Austin, VI, Higgott, C, Viguier, A, Grundy, L, Russell, AF and Griffith, SC (2019) Song rate and duetting in the Chirruping Wedgebill (Psophodes cristatus): frequency, form and functions, *Emu*, 1–9.

Australian State of the Environment Committee (2016) *Australia State of the Environment 2016*. Independent Report to the Commonwealth Minister for the Environment and Energy. Australian Government, Canberra

Badyaev, AV (2006) Colorful Phenotypes of Colorless Genotypes: Toward a New Evolutionary Synthesis of Color Displays. In: G.R.Hill and K.J.McGraw (Eds.) *Bird Coloration. Vol. 2: Function and Evolution,* 349–379. Harvard College, MASS, USA.

Badyaev, AV and Ghalambor, CK (2001) Evolution of life histories along elevational gradients: trade-off between parental care and fecundity. *Ecology* 82 (10), 2948–2960.

Bagemihl, B (1999) *Biological Exuberance. Animal homosexuality and natural diversity.* Profile Books Ltd, London, UK.

Baglione V, Marcos JM, Canestrari D and Ekman, J (2002) Direct fitness benefits of group living in a complex cooperative society of carrion crows, Corvus corone corone. *Animal Behaviour* 64, 887–893.

Bailey, SF (1978) Latitudinal gradients in colors and patterns of passerine birds. *The Condor* 80 (4), 372–381.

Baldwin, M (1974) Studies of the apostle bird at Inverell part 1: General behaviour. *Sunbird: Journal of the Queensland Ornithological Society* 5 (4), p.77.

Balthazar, J and Taziaux, M (2009) The underestimated role of olfaction in avian reproduction? *Behavioral Brain Research* (2), 248–259. doi:10. 1016/ j.bbr.2008.08.036.

Banerjee, SB and Adkins-Regan, E (2014) Same-sex partner preference in adult male zebra finch offspring raised in the absence of maternal care. *Animal Behaviour* 92, 167(7).

References

Barati, A, Andrew, RL, Gorrell, JC and McDonald, PG (2017) Extra-pair paternity is not driven by inbreeding avoidance and does not affect provisioning rates in a co-operatively breeding bird, the noisy miner (Manorina melanocephala). *Behavioral Ecology* 29 (1), 244–252.

Barker, FK, Barrowclough, GF and Groth, JG (2002) A phylogenetic hypothesis for passerine birds: taxonomic and biogeographic implications of an analysis of nuclear DNA sequence data. *Proceedings of the Royal Society of London B: Biological Sciences*, 269 (1488), 295–308.

Barker, FK, Cibois, A, Schikler, PA, Feinstein, J and Cracraft, J (2004) Phylogeny and diversification of the largest avian radiation. *Proceedings of the National Academy of Sciences of the USA*, 101, 11040–11045.

Barrett, L and Henzi, P (2005) The social nature of primate cognition. *Proceedings of the Royal Society B: Biological Sciences*, 272 (1575), 1865-1875. doi:10.1098/rstb.2006.19

Barrett, L, Henzi, P and Rendall, D (2007) Social brains, simple minds: does social complexity really require cognitive complexity? *Philosophical Transactions of the Royal Society of London B: Biological Sciences*, 362 (1480), 561-575.

Bartsch, C, Weiss, M and Kipper, S (2015) Multiple song features are related to paternal effort in common nightingales. *BMC Evolutionary Biology*, 15 (1) 115. doi: 10.1186/s12862-015-0390-5.

Bateson, P (1982) Preferences for cousins in Japanese quail. *Nature* 295 (5846), 236–237.

Batson, D (2009) These things called Empathy: Eight Related but Distinct Phenomena. In: *The Social Neuroscience of Empathy*. (Eds J. Decety and W. Ickes; pp. 3–15). MIT Press, Cambridge, MA.

Battiston, MM, Wilson, DR, Graham, BA, Kovach, KA and Mennill, DJ (2015) Rufous-and-white wrens Thryophilus rufalbus do not exhibit a dear enemy effect towards conspecific or heterospecific competitors. *Current Zoology*, 61 (1), 23–33.

Beaumont, LJ, McAllan, I and Hughes, L (2006) A matter of timing: changes in the first date of arrival and last date of departure of Australian migratory birds. *Global Change Biology* 12 (7), 1339–1354.

Bekoff, M (2010) *The Emotional Lives of Animals*. New World Library, Novato, California.

Benichov, JI, Benezra, SE, Vallentin, D, Globerson, E, Long, MA and Tchernichovski, O (2016) The forebrain song system mediates predictive call timing in female and male zebra finches. *Current Biology* 26 (3), 309–318.

Bennett, ATD, Cuthill, IC, Partridge, JC and Maier, EJ (1996) Ultraviolet vision and mate-choice in zebra finches. *Nature* 380 (6573), 433.

Bennett, ATD and Théry, M (2007) Avian color vision and coloration: Multidisciplinary Evolutionary Biology. *The American Naturalist* 169, S1–S6.

Bennett, EL, Rosenzweig, MR and Diamond, MC (1969) Rat Brain: Effects of Environmental Enrichment on Wet and Dry Weights. *Science*, New Series, 163 (3869), 825–826.

Beran, MJ, and Evans, TA (2009) Delay of gratification by chimpanzees (Pan troglodytes) in working and waiting situations. *Behavioural Processes* 80, 177–181.

Beruldsen, G (2003) *Australian Birds, their Nests and Eggs.* Self-published. ISBN 0-646-42798-9.

Billabong Sanctuary (2019) Sulphur-crested cockatoo. https://www.billabongsanctuary com.au/sulphur-crested-cockatoo/

Birkhead, TR, Pellatt, J and Hunter, FM (1988) Extra-pair copulation and sperm competition in the zebra finch. *Nature* 334 (6177), 60–66.

Bischof, HJ (1994) Sexual imprinting as a two-stage process. *Causal Mechanisms of Behavioural Development: Festschrift for Jaap Kruuit.*pp.82–97.

Black, A and Gower, P (2017) *Grasswrens: Australian outback identities.* AXIOM, Stepney, South Australia.

Black, JM ed. (1996) *Partnerships in Birds: The Study of Monogamy.* Oxford University Press, UK.

Bloch NI (2015) Evolution of opsin expression in birds driven by sexual selection and habitat. *Proceedings of the Royal Society B: Biological Sciences* 282, 20142321. http://dx.doi.org/10.1098/rspb.2014.2321

Blueweiss, L, Fox, H, Kudzma, V, Nakashima, D, Peters, R and Sams, S (1978) Relationships between body size and some life history parameters. *Oecologi* 37 (2), 257–272.

Boag, PT (1987) Effects of nestling diet on growth and adult size of zebra finches (Poephila guttata). *The Auk*, 155–166.

Boekel, C (2016) Notes on the Status and Behaviour of the Purple-crowned Fairy-wren Malurus coronatus in the Victoria River Downs area, Northern Territory. *Australian Field Ornithology* 8 (3).

Bogale, BA, Aoyama, M and Sugita, S (2011a) Categorical learning between 'male' and 'female' photographic human faces in jungle crows (Corvus macrorhynchos). *Behavioural Processes* 86, 109–118. doi:10.1016/j. beproc.2010.10.002.

Boland, CRJ, Heinsohn, R and Cockburn, A (1997) Deception by helpers in co-operatively-breeding white-winged choughs and its experimental manipulation. *Behavioural Ecology and Sociobiology* 88, 295–302.

Boland, CRJ (1998) Helpers improve nest defence in cooperatively breeding white-winged choughs. *Emu* 98 (4), 320–324.

Boland, CRJ (2004) Breeding biology of rainbow bee-eaters (Merops ornatus): a migratory, colonial, cooperative bird. *The Auk* 121 (3), 811–823.

Boogert, NJ, Giraldeau, L-A and Lefebvre, L (2008) Song complexity correlates with learning ability in zebra finch males. *Animal Behaviour* 76, 1735–1741, doi:10.1016/j.anbehav. 2008.08.009.

References

Boonekamp JJ, Mulder GA, Salomons HM, Dijkstra C and Verhulst S. (2014) Nestling telomere shortening, but not telomere length, reflects developmental stress and predicts survival in wild birds. *Proceedings of the Royal Society B: Biological Sciences* 281: 20133287. http://dx.doi.org/10.1098/rspb.2013.3287.

Borgia, G (1995) Complex male display and female choice in the spotted bowerbird: specialised functions for different bower decorations. *Animal Behaviour* 49 (5), 1291–1301.

Both, C, Dingemanse, NJ, Drent, PJ and Tinbergen, JM (2005) Pairs of extreme avian personalities have highest reproductive success. *Journal of Animal Ecology* 74 (4), 667–674.

Bottjer, SW, Miesner, EA and Arnold, AP (1984) Forebrain lesions disrupt development but not maintenance of song in passerine birds. *Science* 224, 901–903.

Boucaud, IC, Mariette, MM, Villain, AS and Vignal, C (2016) Vocal negotiation over parental care? Acoustic communication at the nest predicts partners' incubation share. *Biological Journal of the Linnean Society* 117 (2), 322–336.

Boughman, JW (2002) How sensory drive can promote speciation. *Trends in Ecology and Evolution* 17(12), 571–577.

Bowmaker, JK, Heath, LA, Wilkie, SE and Hunt, DM (1997) Visual pigments and oil droplets from six classes of photoreceptor in the retinas of birds. *Vision Research* 37 (16), 2183–2194.

Brakke, KE and Savage-Rumbaugh, ES (1995) The development of language skills in bonobo and chimpanzee: I. Comprehension. *Language & Communication* 15 (2), 121–148.

Brennan, PLR, Birkhead, TR, Zyskowski, K, Waag, JVD and Prum, RO (2008) Independent evolutionary reductions of the phallus in basal birds. *Journal of Avian Biology* 39, 487–492.

Briskie, JV and Montgomerie, R (1997) Sexual selection and the intromittent organ of birds. *Journal of Avian Biology* 28, 73–86.

Briskie, JV and Montgomerie, R (2001) Efficient copulation and the evolutionary loss of the avian intromittent organ. *Journal of Avian Biology* 32, 184–187.

Brouwer, L, van de Pol, M, Aranzamendi, NH, Bain, G, Baldassarre, DT, Brooker, LC, Brooker, MG, Colombelli-Négrel, D, Enbody, E, Gielow, K and Hall, ML (2017) Multiple hypotheses explain variation in extra-pair paternity at different levels in a single bird family. *Molecular Ecology* 26 (23), 6717-6729.

Brown, ED and Farabaugh SM (1991) Song sharing in a group-living songbird, the Australian magpie, *Gymnorhina tibicen*, III: sex specificity and individual specificity of vocal parts in communal chorus and duet songs. *Behaviour* 118(3–4), 244–274. doi:10.1163/ 156853991 X00319.

Brown, JL (1969) Territorial behavior and population regulation in birds: a review and re-evaluation. *The Wilson Bulletin* 293–329.

Bugnyar T, Kijne, M and Kotrschal, K (2001) Food calling in ravens: are yells referential signals? *Animal Behaviour* 61:949–958. doi: 10.1006/anbe.2000.1668.

Burne, THJ and Rogers, LJ (1995) Odors, volatiles and approach-avoidance behavior of the domestic chick (*Gallus gallus domesticus*). *International Journal of Comparative Psychology* 8 (3), 99–114.

Burtt Jr, EH and Ichida, JM (2004) Gloger's rule, feather-degrading bacteria, and color variation among song sparrows. *The Condor* 106 (3), 681–686.

Burtt, EH, Schroeder, MR, Smith, LA, Sroka, JE and McGraw, KJ (2010) Colourful parrot feathers resist bacterial degradation. *Biology Letters, The Royal Society*, doi:10.1098/rsbl .2010.0716.

Buss, DM and Schmitt, DP (1993) Sexual strategies theory: an evolutionary perspective on human mating. *Psychological Review* 100 (2), 204-232.

Buston, PM and Emlen, ST (2003) Cognitive processes underlying human mate choice: The relationship between self-perception and mate preference in Western society. *Proceedings of the National Academy of Sciences* 100 (15), 8805–8810.

Byers, BE and Kroodsma, DE (2009) Female mate-choice and songbird song repertoires. *Animal Behaviour* 77, 13–22. doi:10.1016/j.anbehav.2008.10.003.

Byrne, RW and Bates, LA (2010) Primate social cognition: uniquely primate, uniquely social, or just unique? *Neuron* 65 (6), 815–830.

Byrne, R and Whiten, A (1989) Machiavellian intelligence: social expertise and the evolution of intellect in monkeys, apes, and humans. Oxford science publications, Oxford, UK.

Cadková, L (2015) Do they speak language? *Biosemiotics* 8, 9-27. doi: 10.1007/s12304-014-9225-9.

Campbell, MW and De Waal, FB (2011) Ingroup-outgroup bias in contagious yawning by chimpanzees supports link to empathy. *PloS one* 6(4), p.e18283.

Candolin, U (2003) The use of multiple cues in mate choice. *Biological Reviews* 78 (4), 575-595.

Canestrari, D, Bolopo, D, Turligs, TCJ, Röder, G, Marcos, JM and Baglione, V (2014) From parasitism to mutualism: unexpected interactions between a cuckoo and its host. *Science* 343, 1350–1352.

Cardillo, M (1999) Latitude and rates of diversification in birds and butterflies. *Proceedings of the Royal Society B: Biological Sciences* 266, 1221-1225.

Carere, C and Locurto, C (2011) Interaction between animal personality and animal cognition. *Current Zoology* 57 (4) 491–498.

Caro, SP and Balthazart, J (2010) Pheromones in birds: myth or reality? *Journal of Comparative Physiology A* 196 (10), 751–766.

Caro, SP, Balthazar, J and Bonadonna, F (2015) The perfume of reproduction in birds: Chemosignalling in avian social life. *Hormones and Behavior* 68, 25-42. Doi.org/10.1016/ j.yhbeh.2014.06.001

References

Carrick, R (1963) Ecological significance of territory in the Australian Magpie, Gymnorhina tibicen. *Proceedings of the XIII International Ornithology Congress* 74 and 753.

Cauchard, L, Boogert, NJ, Lefebvre, L, Dubois, F and Doligez, B (2013) Problem-solving performance is correlated with reproductive success in a wild bird population. *Animal Behaviour* 85, 19–26.

Chakraborty, M and Jarvis, ED (2015) Brain evolution by brain pathway duplication. *Philosophical Transactions of the Royal Society B: Biological Sciences* 370 (1684), 20150056.

Chambers, GK, Boon, WM, Buckley, TR and Hitchmough, RA (2001) Using molecular methods to understand the Gondwanan affinities of the New Zealand biota: three case studies. *Australian Journal of Botany* 49(3), 377–387.

Chapman, G (2015) *The Five Love Languages. The Secret to Love That Lasts.* Moody Publishers/Northfield Publishing.

Chartrand, TL and Lakin, JL (2013) The antecedents and consequences of human behavioral mimicry. *Annual Review of Psychology* 64, 285–308.

Chen, G, Xia, C, Dong, L, Lyu, N and Zhang, Y (2018) Delayed plumage maturation in green-backed flycatchers (Ficedula elisae): An evidence of female mimicry. *Ethology* doi: 10.1111/eth.12825

Chew, SJ, Vicario, DS and Nottebohm, F (1996) A large-capacity memory system that recognizes the calls and songs of individual birds. *Proceedings of the National Academy of Sciences*, 93(5), 1950–1955.

Chiappa, P, Singh, S and Pellicer, F (2018) The degree of altriciality and performance in a cognitive task show correlated evolution. *PloS One* 13 (10), p.e0205128.

Choudhury, S (1995) Divorce in birds: a review of the hypotheses. *Animal Behaviour* 50, 413–429.

Choudhury, S and Black, JM (1994) Barnacle geese preferentially pair with familiar associates from early life. *Animal Behaviour* 48, 81e88. https://doi.org/10.1006/anbe.1994.1213

Clark, GA (1979) Body weights of birds: a review. *Condor* 81, 193–202.

Clarke, MF (1997) A review of studies of the breeding biology of Australian birds from 1986-1995: biases and consequences. *Emu* 97, 283–289.

Clutton-Brock, T (1991) *The Evolution of Parental Care.* Princeton University Press; Princeton, NJ USA.

Cnotka J, Möhle, M and Rehkämper, G (2008) Navigational experience affects hippocampus size in homing pigeons. *Brain, Behavior and Evolution* 72 (3), 233–238.

Cockburn, A (1996) Why do so many Australian birds cooperate: social evolution in the Corvida? In *Frontiers of Population Ecology;* Eds RB Floyd, AW Sheppard and PJ De Barro (pp. 451–472). CSIRO Publishing, Melbourne.

Cockburn, A (2006) Prevalence of different modes of parental care in birds. *Proceedings of the Royal Society B: Biological Sciences* 273, 1375–1383. doi:10.1098/rspb.2005.3458.

Cockburn, A, Brouwer, L, Margraf, N, Osmond, HL and Van de Pol, M (2016) *Superb fairy-wrens: making the worst of a good job* (pp. 133-149). Cambridge University Press, Cambridge.

Cole, EF, Morand-Ferron, J, Hinks, AE and Quinn, JL (2012) Cognitive ability influences reproductive life history variation in the wild. *Current Biology* 22, 1808-1812.

Collis, K and Borgia, G (1993) The costs of male display and delayed plumage maturation in the Satin Bowerbird (Ptilonorynchus violaceus). *Ethology* 94, 59–71.

Cook, P, Prichard, A, Spivak, M and Berns, GS (2018) Jealousy in dogs? Evidence from brain imaging. *Animal Sentience* 117, 1–14.

Corfield, JR, Price, K, Iwaniuk, AN, Gutiérrez-Ibáñez, C, Birkhead, T and Wylie, DR (2015) Diversity in olfactory bulb size in birds reflects allometry, ecology, and phylogeny. *Frontiers in Neuroanatomy* 9, 102. doi: 10.3389/fnana.2015.00102.

Cornelius, JM, Perfito, N, Zann, R, Breuner, CW and Hahn, TP (2011) Physiological trade-offs in self-maintenance: plumage molt and stress physiology in Birds. *The Journal of Experimental Biology* 214, 2768-2777. doi:10.1242/ jeb.057174.

Coulson, JC (1966) The influence of the pair-bond and age on the breeding biology of the kittiwake gull, Rissa tridactyla. *The Journal of Animal Ecology,* 269–279.

Cracraft, J (2001) Avian evolution, Gondwana biogeography and the Cretaceous-Tertiary mass extinction event. *Proceedings of the Royal Society B: Biological Sciences* 268, 459–469. doi:10.1098/ rspb.2000.1368.

Cracraft, J, Barker, FK, Braun, M, Harshman, J, Dyke, GJ, Feinstein, J, Stanley, S, Cibois, A, Schikler, P, Beresford, P, García-Moreno, J, Sorenson, MD, Yuri, T and Mindell, DP (2004) Phylogenetic relationships among modern birds (Neornithes) – toward an avian tree of life. In *Assembling the Tree of Life*; (Eds J Cracraft and MJ Donoghue, pp. 468–489). Oxford University Press, New York.

Craig, AJFK and Hulley, PE (2004) Iris colour in passerine birds: why be bright-eyed? *South African Journal of Science* 100 (11–12), 584–588.

Crino, OL, Buchanan, KL, Trompf, L, Mainwaring, MC and Griffith, SC (2017) Stress reactivity, condition, and foraging behavior in zebra finches: effects on boldness, exploration, and sociality. *General and Comparative Endocrinology* 244, 101–107.

Crockford, C, Wittig, R, Langergraber, K, Ziegler, T, Zuberbühler, K and Deschner, T (2013) Urinary oxytocin and social bonding in related and unrelated wild chimpanzees. *Proceedings of the Royal Society: Biology* 280, 20122765.

Cronin, KA (2012) Prosocial behaviour in animals: the influence of social relationships, communication and rewards. *Animal Behaviour* 84 (5), 1085–1093.

Cronin, KA, Kurian, AV and Snowdon, CT (2005) Cooperative problem solving in a cooperatively breeding primate (Saguinus oedipus). *Animal Behaviour* 69 (1), 133–142.

Culina, A, Radersma, R and Sheldon, BC (2015) Trading up: the fitness consequences of divorce in monogamous birds. *Biological Reviews* 90 (4), 1015–1034.

Curtis, HS (1972) The Albert lyrebird in display. *Emu 72* (3), 81–84.

Custance, D, Whiten, A and Fredman, T (1999) Social learning of an artificial fruit task in capuchin monkeys (Cebus apella). *Journal of Comparative Psychology* 113(1), 13.

Dahlin, CR and Benedict, L (2014) Angry birds need not apply: a perspective on the flexible form and multifunctionality of avian vocal duets. *Ethology* 120 (1), 1–10.

Dakin, R and Ryder, TB (2018) Dynamic network partnerships and social contagion drive cooperation. *Proceedings of the Royal Society B*, 285(1893) 20181973.

Dalziell, AH and Magrath, RD (2012) Fooling the experts: accurate vocal mimicry in the song of the superb lyrebird, Menura novaehollandiae. *Animal Behaviour* 83 (6), 1401–1410.

Damasio, A (2006) *Descartes' Error. Emotion, Reason and the Human Brain.* (revised edition). Vintage Books, London.

Darwin, C (1890) *The Origin of Species by Means of Natural Selection.* 6th ed. John Murray, London.

Darwin, C (1891) *The Descent of Man, and Selection in Relation to Sex.* Facsimile from the 1871 edition held in the Firestone Library, Princeton University Press, Princeton University, Princeton, NJ.

Darwin, C (1904) *The Expression of the Emotions in Man and Animals.* John Murray, London.

Davidson, GL, Thornton, A and Clayton, NS (2017) Evolution of iris colour in relation to cavity nesting and parental care in passerine birds. *Biology letters* 13 (1), 20160783.

Dawson, BV and Foss, BM (1965) Observational learning in Budgerigars. *Animal Behaviour* 13 (4), 470–474. http://dx.doi.org/10.1016/0003-3472(65)90108-9

Day, LB, Westcott, DA and Olster, DH (2005) Evolution of bower complexity and cerebellum size in bowerbirds. *Brain, Behavior and Evolution* 66 (1), 62–72.

Decety, JE and Ickes, WE (2009) *The Social Neuroscience of Empathy.* MIT Press.

De Coster, L, Verschuere, B, Goubert, L, Tsakiris, M and Brass, M (2013) I suffer more from your pain when you act like me: being imitated enhances affective responses to seeing someone else in pain. *Cognitive, Affective, & Behavioral Neuroscience* 13 (3) 519–532.

De Gelder, B, De Borst, AW and Watson, R (2015) The perception of emotion in body expressions. *Wiley Interdisciplinary Reviews: Cognitive Science* 6 (2), 149–158.

Delhey, K (2015) The colour of an avifauna: A quantitative analysis of the colour of Australian birds. *Nature, Scientific Reports* 5, 18514. DOI: 10.1038/srep18514.

Deng, C, Kaplan, G and Rogers, LJ (2001) Similarity of the song control nuclei of male and female Australian magpies (Gymnorhina tibicen). *Behavioural Brain Research* 123 (1), 89–102.

Derégnaucourt, S and Bovet, D (2016) The perception of self in birds. *Neuroscience and Biobehavioral Review* 69, 1–14.

De Tommaso, M, Kaplan, G, Chiandetti, C and Vallortigara, G (2019) Naïve 3-day-old domestic chicks (Gallus gallus) are attracted to discrete acoustic patterns characterizing natural vocalizations. *Journal of Comparative Psychology*, 133 (1), 118–131. https://psycnet.apa.org/doi/10.1037/com0000132

De Waal, FB (1995) Sex as an alternative to aggression in the bonobo. (pp. 37–56) In: *Sexual Nature/Sexual Culture*, eds PR Abramson and SD Pinkerton, Chicago University Press, Chicago.

di Pellegrino, G, Fadiga, L, Fogassi, L, Gallese, V and Rizzolatti, G (1992) Understanding motor events: A neurophysiological study. *Experimental Brain Research* 91, 176–180.

Diamond, MC, Rosenzweig, MR, Bennett, EL, Lindner, B and Lyon, L (1972). Effects of environmental enrichment and impoverishment on rat cerebral cortex. *Journal of Neurobiology* 3 (1) 47–64.

Dickman, CR, Predavec, M and Downey, FJ (1995) Long-range movements of small mammals in arid Australia: implications for land management. *Journal of Arid Environments* 31, 441–452.

Diekamp, B, Regolin, L, Güntürkün, O and Vallortigara, G (2005) A left-sided visuospatial bias in birds. *Current Biology* 15(10), R372-R373.

Dillard, JR and Westneat, DF (2016) Disentangling the correlated evolution of monogamy and cooperation. *Trends in Ecology and Evolution*31(7), 503–513.

Dingemanse, NJ, Both, C, Drent, PJ and Tinbergen, JM (2004) Fitness consequences of avian personalities in a fluctuating environment. *Proceedings of the Royal Society of London. Series B: Biological Sciences* 271 (1541), 847–852.

Dixit, T, English, S and Lukas, D (2017) The relationship between egg size and helper number in cooperative breeders: a meta-analysis across species. *PeerJ* 5, p.e4028.

Dixson, A (1998) *Primate sexuality.* John Wiley & Sons, Ltd.

Do, KT, McCormick, EM and Telzer, EH (2019) The neural development of prosocial behavior from childhood to adolescence. *Social Cognitive and Affective Neuroscience* 14 (2), 129–139.

Dolby, T and Clarke, R (2014) *Finding Australian Birds.* CSIRO Publishing, Melbourne ISBN 9780643097667.

Doty, A, Stawski, C, Nowack, J, Bondarenco, A and Geiser, F (2015) Increased lyrebird presence in a post-fire landscape. *Australian Journal of Zoology* 63 (1), 9–11.

Double, M and Cockburn, A (2000) Pre-dawn infidelity: females control extra-pair mating in superb fairy-wrens. *Proceedings of the Royal Society of London. Series B: Biological Sciences* 267(1442), 465–470.

Doucet, SM, Mcdonald, DB, Foster, MS and Clay, RP (2007) Plumage development and molt in long-tailed manakins (Chiroxipia linearis) variation according to sex and age. *The Auk* l24, 29–43.

Doucet, SM, Shawkey, MD, Hill, GE and Montgomerie, R (2006) Iridescent plumage in satin bowerbirds: structure, mechanisms and nanostructural predictors of individual variation in colour. *Journal of Experimental Biology* 209 (2), 380–390.

References

Downing, PA, Cornwallis, CK and Griffin, AS (2015) Sex, long life and the evolutionary transition to cooperative breeding in birds. *Proceedings of the Royal Society B: Biological Sciences* 282 (1816), 20151663.

Drent, PJ, Oers, KV and Noordwijk, AJV (2003) Realized heritability of personalities in the great tit (Parus major). *Proceedings of the Royal Society of London. Series B: Biological Sciences* 270 (1510), 45–51.

Dufour, V, Wascher, CAF, Braun, A, Miller, R and Bugnyar, T (2012) Corvids can decide if a future exchange is worth waiting for. *Biology Letters* 8, 201–204. doi:10.1098/rsbl.2011.0726.

Dunbar, RIM (1992) Neocortex size as a constraint on group size in primates. *Journal of Human Evolution*, 22 (6), 469–493.

Dunbar, RIM (1998) The social brain hypothesis. *Evolutionary Anthropology: Issues, News, and Reviews* 6 (5), 178–190.

Dunbar, RIM (2009) The social brain hypothesis and its implications for social evolution. *Annals of Human Biology* 36 (5), 562–572.

Duranton, C and Gaunet, F (2016) Behavioural synchronization from an ethological perspective: overview of its adaptive value. *Adaptive Behavior* 24(3), 181–191.

Durrant, KL and Hughes, JM (2005) Differing rates of extra-group paternity between two populations of the Australian magpie (Gymnorhina tibicen). *Behavioural Ecology and Sociobiology* 57, 536–545. doi: 10.1007/s00265-004-0883-5.

Duval, EH (2007) Cooperative display and lekking behavior of the lance-tailed manakin (Chiroxiphia lanceolata). *The Auk* 124 (4), 1168–1185.

Eaton, MD (2005) Human vision fails to distinguish widespread sexual dichromatism among sexually "monochromatic" birds. *Proceedings of the National Academy of Sciences USA* 102, 10942–10946.

Eaton, MD (2007) Avian visual perspective on plumage coloration confirms rarity of sexually monochromatic North American passerines. *The Auk* 124, 155–161.

Edwards EK, Mitchell NJ, Amanda R, Ridley AR (2015) The impact of high temperatures on foraging behaviour and body condition in the Western Australian Magpie Cracticus tibicen dorsalis. *Ostrich* 86 (1–2), 137–144. doi:10.2989/00306525.2015.1034 219

Edwards, SV and Boles, WE (2002) Out of Gondwana: the origin of passerine birds. *Trends in Ecology and Evolution* 17 (8), 347–349.

Ekman, J (1990) Alliances in winter flocks of willow tits; effects of rank on survival and reproductive success in male-female associations. *Behavioral Ecology and Sociobiology* 26 (4), 239–245.

Ekstrom, JMM, Burke, T, Randrianaina, L and Birkhead, TR (2007) Unusual sex roles in a highly promiscuous parrot: the Greater Vasa Parrot (Caracopsis vasa). *Ibis* 149 (2), 313–320. Wiley Online Library. doi:10.1111/j.1474-919X.2006.00632.x)

Endler, JA, Westcott, DA, Madden, JR and Robson, T (2005) Animal visual systems and the evolution of color patterns: sensory processing illuminates signal evolution. *Evolution* 59 (8), 1795–1818.

Ericson, PG, Irestedt, M and Johansson, US (2003) Evolution, biogeography, and patterns of diversification in passerine birds. *Journal of Avian Biology* 34 (1), 3–15.

Evans, CS (1997) Referential signals. *Perspectives in Ethology* 12, 99–143.

Facchinetti, C, Mahler, B, Di Giacomo, AG and Reboreda, JC (2011) Stages of plumage maturation of the tawny-bellied seedeater: Evidence of delayed plumage maturation and cryptic differentiation between juveniles and females. *The Condor* 113, 907–914. https:// doi.org/10.1525/cond.2011.110010.

Fedorova, N, Evans, CL and Byrne, RW (2017) Living in stable social groups is associated with reduced brain size in woodpeckers (Picidae). *Biology Letters* 13 (3), 20170008.

Feduccia, AA and Duvauchelle, CL (2008) Auditory stimuli enhance MDMA-conditioned reward and MDMA-induced nucleus accumbens dopamine, serotonin and locomotor responses. *Brain Research Bulletin* 77, 189–196. doi:10. 1016/j. brainresbull.2008.07.007

Feenders, G, Liedvogel, M, Rivas, M, Zapka, M, Horita, H, Hara, E, Wada, K, Mouritsen, H and Jarvis, ED (2008) Molecular Mapping of Movement-Associated Areas in the Avian Brain: A Motor Theory for Vocal Learning Origin. *PLoS ONE* 3, e1768. doi:10.1371/ journal.pone.0001768.

Feeney, WE, Medina, I, Somveille, M, Heinsohn, R, Hall, ML, Mulder, RA, Stein, JA, Kilner, RM and Langmore, NE (2013) Brood parasitism and the evolution of cooperative breeding in birds. *Science* 342 (6165), 1506–1508. doi:10.1126/ science.1240039.

Ficken, RW, van Tienhoven, A, Ficken, MS and Sibley, FC (1960) Effect of visual and vocal stimuli on breeding in the Budgerigar (Melopsittacus undulatus). *Animal Behaviour* 8, 104–106.

Field, DJ, Bercovici, A, Berv, JS, Dunn, R, Fastovsky, DE, Lyson, TR, Vajda, V and Gauthier, JA (2018) Early Evolution of Modern Birds Structured by Global Forest Collapse at the End-Cretaceous Mass Extinction. *Current Biology* 28 (11), 1825–1831.e2

Firman, RC, Gasparini, C, Manier, MK and Pizzan, T (2017) Postmating Female Control: 20 Years of Cryptic Female Choice. (Review) *Trends in Ecology & Evolution* 32 (5), 368–382. http://dx.doi.org/10.1016/j.tree.2017.02.010

Fletcher, GJ, Simpson, JA, Campbell, L and Overall, NC (2015) Pair-bonding, romantic love, and evolution: The curious case of Homo sapiens. *Perspectives on Psychological Science* 10 (1), 20–36.

Flood, NJ (1984) Adaptive significance of delayed plumage maturation in male northern orioles. *Evolution* 267–279.

References

Ford, HA (1981) Territorial behaviour in an Australian nectar-feeding bird. *Australian Journal of Ecology* 6(2), 131–134.

Fox, RA and Millam, JR (2010) The use of ratings and direct behavioural observation to measure temperament traits in cockatiels (Nymphicus hollandicus). *Ethology* 116, 59–75.

Franklin, DC, Garnett, S, Luck, G, Gutierrez-Ibanez, C and Iwaniuk, A (2014) Relative brain size in Australian birds. *Emu* 114, 160–170.

Fraser, ON and Bugnyar, T (2010) Do ravens show consolation? Responses to Distressed Others. *PLoS ONE* 5,(5), e10605. doi:10.1371/journal.pone.0010605.

Fraser, ON and Bugnyar, T (2011) Ravens reconcile after aggressive conflicts with valuable partners. *PLoS ONE* 6 (3), e18118. doi:10.1371/journal.pone.0018118.

Friedman, NR and Remeš, V (2015) Rapid evolution of elaborate male coloration is driven by visual system in Australian fairy-wrens (Maluridae). *Journal of Evolutionary Biology* 28, 2125–2135.

Friedman, NR and Remeš, V (2017). Ecogeographical gradients in plumage coloration among Australasian songbird clades. *Global Ecology and Biogeography* 26 (3), 261–274.

Frith, C and Frith, U (2005) Theory of mind. *Current Biology* 15(17), R644-R645.

Frith, CB and Cooper, WT (1996) Courtship display and mating of Victoria's riflebird Ptiloris victoriae, with notes on the courtship displays of congeneric species. *Emu* 96, 102–113.

Frith, HJ (1967) *Waterfowl in Australia*. Angus and Robertson Ltd., Sydney.

Frith, HJ (1982) *Pigeons and Doves of Australia.* Rigby Publishing, Adelaide.

Fry, CH (1980) Survival and longevity among tropical land birds. *Proceedings of the Pan-African Ornithological Congress* 4, 333–343.

Fujioka, M and Yamagishi, S (1981) Extramarital and pair copulations in the cattle egret. *The Auk* 98, 134–144.

Fullagar, PJ and Carbonell, M (1986) The display postures of the Musk Duck. *Wildfowl* 37, 142–150.

Funabiki, Y and Konishi, M (2003) Long memory in song learning by zebra finches. *Journal of Neuroscience* 23 (17), 6928–6935.

Gabriel, PO and Black, JM (2013) Correlates and consequences of the pair bond in Steller's jays. *Ethology* 119 (2), 178–187.

Gagliardo, A, Ioale, P, Odetti, F, Bingman, VP, Siegel, JJ and Vallortigara, G (2001) Hippocampus and homing in pigeons: left and right hemispheric differences in navigational map learning. *The European Journal of Neuroscience* 13, 1617–1624.

Gahr, M (2000). Neural song control system of hummingbirds: Comparison to swifts, vocal learning (songbirds) and nonlearning (suboscines) passerines, and vocal learning (budgerigars) and nonlearning (dove, owl, gull, quail, chicken) non-passerines. *Journal of Comparative Neurology* 426, 182–196.

Gallese, V (2001) The 'Shared Manifold' Hypothesis. From mirror neurons to empathy. *Journal of Consciousness Studies* 8 (5–7), 33–50.

Gallese, V and Goldman, A (1998) Mirror neurons and the simulation theory of mind-reading. *Trends in Cognitive Sciences* 2 (12), 493–501.

Gallese, V (2007) Before and below 'theory of mind': embodied simulation and the neural correlates of social cognition. *Philosophical Transactions of the Royal Society of London B: Biological Sciences* 362 (1480), 659–669.

Galván, I (2008) The importance of white on black: Unmelanized plumage proportion predicts display complexity in birds. *Behavioral Ecology and Sociobiology* 63 (2), 303. doi:10.1007/s00265-008-0662-9.

Galván, I, Naudí, A, Erritzøe, J, Møller, AP, Barja, G and Pamplona, R (2015) Long lifespans have evolved with long and monounsaturated fatty acids in birds. *Evolution* 69 (10), 2776–2784.

Gammie, KK (2013) The evolution of iridescent plumage in the Galliformes: Proximate mechanisms and ultimate functions. *Electronic Theses and Dissertations* 4908.

Garcia-Peña, GE, Sol, D, Iwaniuk, AN and Szekely, T (2013) Sexual selection on brain size in shorebirds (Charadriiformes). *Journal of Evolutionary Biology* 26, 878–888.

Gauthier, JA (2018) Early evolution of modern birds structured by global forest collapse at the End-Cretaceous Mass Extinction. *Current Biology* DOI: 10.1016/j.cub. 2018. 04.062.

Gavin, TA and Bollinger, EK (1985) Multiple paternity in a territorial passerine: the bobolink. *The Auk*, 102(3), 550–555.

Gazzola, V, Aziz-Zadeh, L and Keysers, C (2006) Empathy and the somatotopic auditory mirror system in humans. *Current Biology* 16 (18), 1824–1829.

Gelder, B, de Borst, AW and Watson, R (2015) The perception of emotion in body expressions. *Wiley Interdisciplinary Reviews: Cognitive Science* 6 (2), 149–158.

Glanton, D (2018) Death of Koko, the signing gorilla, reminds us what it means to be an exceptional human being. *Chicago Tribune*, Online 26 June 2018.

Goleman, D (2006) *Emotional intelligence*. Bantam.

Goleman, D, Boyatzis, RE and McKee, A (2013) *Primal leadership: Unleashing the power of emotional intelligence*. Harvard Business Press, Boston.

Gómez, JC (1996) *Ostensive behavior in great apes: The role of eye contact. Reaching into thought: The minds of the great apes*, pp.131-151. New York, NY, US: Cambridge University Press.

Gratto-Trevor, CL, Oring, LW, Fivizzani, AJ, El Halawani, ME and Cooke, F (1990) The role of prolactin in parental care in a monogamous and a polyandrous shorebird. *The Auk* 107, 718-729.

Graves, J (2019) How birds become male or female, and occasionally both. *The Conversation*, March 11, online https://the conversation.com

Griesser, M, Drobniak, SM, Nakagawa, S and Botero, CA (2017) Family living sets the stage for cooperative breeding and ecological resilience in birds. *PLoS Biology* 15 (6), p.e2000483.

Griffioen, PA and Clarke, MF (2002) Large-scale bird-movement patterns evident in eastern Australia. *Emu* 102, (1) 97–125. doi:10.1071/MU01024.

Griffith, SC and Buchanan, KL (2010) The zebra finch: the ultimate Australian supermodel. *Emu* 110 (3), v–xii.

Griffith, SC, Pryke, SR and Buttemer, W (2011) Constrained mate choice in social monogamy and the stress of having an unattractive partner. *Proceedings of the Royal Society B: Biological Sciences* 278, 2798–2805.

Guillette, LM, Reddon, AR, Hoechee, M and Sturdy, CB (2010) Sometimes slower is better: Slow exploring birds are more sensitive to changes in a vocal discrimination task. *Proceedings of the Royal Society B: Biological Sciences* 278, 767–773.

Hagelin, JL and Jones, IL (2007) Bird odors and other chemical substances: a defense mechanism or overlooked mode of intraspecific communication? *The Auk* 124 (3), 741-761.

Hall, ME, Nasir, L, Daunt, F, Gault, EA, Croxall, JP, Wanless, S and Monaghan, P (2004) Telomere loss in relation to age and early environment in long-lived birds. *Proceedings of the Royal Society of London. Series B: Biological Sciences* 271(1548), 1571–1576.

Hall, ML and Langmore, NE (2017) Fitness Costs and Benefits of Female Song. *Frontiers in Ecology and Evolution* 5, 48. doi: 10.3389/fevo.2017.00048

Hall, ML and Magrath, RD (2007) Temporal coordination signals coalition quality. *Current Biology* 17, R406–R407. doi:10.1016/j.cub.2007.04.022

Hall, ML and Peters, A (2008) Coordination between the sexes for territorial defense in a duetting fairy-wren. *Animal Behaviour* 76, 65–73. doi:10.1016/j.anbehav.2008.01.010.

Hamilton, WJ (1967) Social aspects of bird orientation mechanisms. In: Storm RM (ed) *Animal orientation and navigation*. Oregon State University Press, Corvallis, pp 57–71.

Harris CR and Prouvost C (2014) Jealousy in dogs. *PLoS ONE* 9 (7), e94597.

Hatfield, E, Rapson, RL and Le, YCL (2009) Emotional contagion and empathy. In: *The Social Neuroscience of Empathy*. (Eds J. Decety and W. Ickes; pp. 19-30). MIT Press, Mass

Hattori, Y, Kuroshima, H and Fujita, K (2005) Cooperative problem solving by tufted capuchin monkeys (Cebus apella): spontaneous division of labor, communication, and reciprocal altruism. *Journal of Comparative Psychology* 119 (3), 335–342.

Haussmann, MF, Winkler, DW, O'Reilly, KM, Huntington, CE, Nisbet, IC and Vleck, CM (2003) Telomeres shorten more slowly in long-lived birds and mammals than in short–lived ones. *Proceedings of the Royal Society of London. Series B: Biological Sciences* 270 (1522) 1387–1392.

Haussmann, MF, Winkler, DW and Vleck, CM (2005) Longer telomeres associated with higher survival in birds. *Biology Letters* 1 (2), 212–214.

Hawkins, GL, Hill, GE and Mercadante, A (2012) Delayed plumage maturation and delayed reproductive investment in birds. *Biological Reviews* 87 (2), 257–274.

Hazan, C and Zeifman, D (1994) Sex and the psychological tether. In *Advances in Personal Relationships*. Eds K. Bartholomew and D. Perlman, (Vol 5: Attachment processes in adulthood, pp. 151–177). Jessica Kingsley, London.

Heg, D, Bruinzeel, LW and Ens, BJ (2003) Fitness consequences of divorce in the oystercatcher, Haematopus ostralegus. *Animal Behaviour* 66, 175–184.

Heg, D and van Treuren, R (1998) Female–female cooperation in polygynous oystercatchers. *Nature* 391 (6668), 687.

Heidinger, BJ, Blount, JD, Boner, W, Griffiths, K, Metcalfe, NB and Monaghan, P (2012) Telomere length in early life predicts lifespan. *Proceedings of the National Academy of Sciences* 109 (5), 1743-1748.

Heinsohn, R, Legge, S and Barry, S (1997) Extreme bias in sex allocation in eclectus parrots. *Proceedings of the Royal Society B: Biological Sciences* 264, 1325–1329.

Heinsohn, R, Legge, S and Endler, JA (2005) Extreme reversed sexual dichromatism in a bird without sex role reversal. *Science* 309, 617-619.

Heinsohn, RG (1988) Inter-group ovicide and nest destruction in cooperatively breeding white-winged choughs. *Animal Behaviour* 36 (6), 1856-1858.

Heinsohn, RG (1991) Kidnapping and reciprocity in cooperatively breeding white-winged choughs. *Animal Behaviour 41* (6), 1097-1100. http://dx.doi.org/10.1016/S0003-3472 (05)80652-9Ed.

Hemmings, N and Birkhead, T (2017) Differential sperm storage by female zebra finches Taeniopygia guttata. *Proceedings of the Royal Society B: Biological Sciences* 284, 20171032. http://dx.doi.org/10.1098/ rspb. 2017.1032

Herrera, AM, Shuster, SG, Perriton, CL and Cohn, MJ (2013) Developmental basis of phallus reduction during bird evolution. *Current Biology* 23 (12), 1065–1074.

Heyes, C and Saggerson, A (2002) Testing for imitative and nonimitative social learning in the budgerigar using a two-object/two-action test. *Animal Behaviour* 64, 851–859.

Hile, AG, Plummer, TK and Striedter, GF (2000) Male vocal imitation produces call convergence during pair bonding in budgerigars, Melopsittacus undulatus. *Animal Behaviour* 59 (6), 1209–1218.

Hill, GE, Doucet, SM and Buchholz, R (2005) The effect of coccidial infection on iridescent plumage coloration in wild turkeys. *Animal Behaviour* 9 (2), 387-394.

Hillemann, F, Bugnyar, T, Kotrschal, K and Wascher, CA (2014) Waiting for better, not for more: corvids respond to quality in two delay maintenance tasks. *Animal Behaviour* 90, 1-10.

Hindewood, KA (1948) A communal roost of Indian myna. *Emu* 47, 315-317.

Hirschenhauser, K (2012) Testosterone and partner compatibility: evidence and emerging questions. *Ethology* 118 (9), 799-811.

Hobbes, T (1946) *Leviathan, Or, The Matter, Forme and Power of a Commonwealth Ecclesiasticall and Civil*. Yale University Press.

Hockett, CF (1959) Animal «languages» and human language. In *The evolution of man's capacity for culture* (Ed. JN Spuhler, pp. 32-39). Detroit, Wayne State University Press.

Hogg, MA and Turner, JC (1985) Interpersonal attraction, social identification and psychological group formation. *European Journal of Social Psychology* 15 (1), 51-66.

Holland, E (2004) The nature of homosexuality: *Vindication for homosexual activists and the religious right.* New York, iUniverse Publishers.

Hosken, DJ and Stockley, P (2004) Sexual selection and genital evolution. *Trends in Ecology and Evolution* 19, 87–93.

Hostetler, CM, Hinde, K, Maninger, N, Mendoza, SP, Mason,WA, Rowland, DJ, Wang, GB, Kukis, D, Cherry, SR and Bales, KL (2017) Effects of pair bonding on dopamine D1 receptors in monogamous male titi monkeys (Callicebus cupreus). *American Journal of Primatology* 79 (3), 1–9. doi: 10.1002/ajp.22612.

Hu, JC (2014) *What Do Talking Apes Really Tell Us? The Strange, Disturbing World of Koko.* https://slate.com/technology/2014/08/koko-kanzi-and-ape-language-research-criticism-of-working-conditions-and-animal-care.html

Hughes, JM, Mather, PB, Toon, A, Rowley, I and Russell, E (2003) High levels of extra-group paternity in a population of Australian magpies Gymnorhina tibicen: evidence from microsatellites. *Molecular Ecology* 12, 3441–3450. doi:10.1046/j.1365-294X.2003.01997.x.

Hunt, S, Bennett, AT, Cuthill, IC and Griffiths, R (1998) Blue tits are ultraviolet tits. *Proceedings of the Royal Society of London B: Biological Sciences* 265 (1395), 451-455.

Hutchison, W, Davis, K, Lozano, A, Tasker, R and Dostrovsky, J (1999) Pain related neurons in the human cingulate cortex. *Nature Neuroscience* 2, 403–405.

Huxley, JS (1914) The courtship-habits of the Great Crested Grebe (Podiceps cristatus); with an addition to the Theory of Sexual Selection. *Proceedings of the Zoological Society of London* 84, (3), 491-562.

Hyder, F, Rothman, DL, and Bennett, MR (2013) Cortical energy demands of signaling and nonsignaling components in brain are conserved across mammalian species and activity levels. *Proceedings of the National Academy of Science U.S.A.* 110, 3549–3554. doi: 10.1073/pnas.1214912110

Iacoboni, M (2009) Imitation, empathy and mirror neurons. *Annual Review of Psychology* 60, 653–70. 10.1146/annurev.psych.60.110707.163604

Iacoboni, M, Molnar-Szakacs, I, Gallese, V, Buccino, G, Mazziotta, JC, and Rizzolatti, G (2005) Grasping the intentions of others with one's own mirror neuron system. *PLoS Biolog* 3 (3), p.e79.

Ihle, M, Kempenaers, B and Forstmeier, W (2015) Fitness benefits of mate choice for compatibility in a socially monogamous species. *PLoS Biology* 13 (9), p.e1002248.

Iwaniuk, AN and Nelson, JE (2003) Developmental differences are correlated with relative brain size in birds: a comparative analysis. *Canadian Journal of Zoology* 81, 1913–1928. doi:10.1139/z03-190.

Iwaniuk, AN and Wylie, DR (2006) The evolution of stereopsis and the Wulst in caprimulgiform birds: a comparative analysis. *Journal of Comparative Physiology A* 192 (12), 1313-1326

Järvilehto, T (2009) The Theory of the Organism-Environment System as a Basis of Experimental Work in Psychology. *Ecological Psychology* 21, 112-120.

Jarvis ED, Güntürkün O, Bruce L, Csillag, A, Karten, H, Kuenzel, W, Medina, L, Paxinos, G, Perkel, DJ, Shimizu, T and Striedter, G (2005) Avian brains and the new understanding of vertebrate brain evolution. *Nature Neuroscience* 6, 151–159. doi:10.1038/ nrn1606.

Jennions, MD and Petrie, M (1997) Variation in mate choice and mating preferences: a review of causes and consequences. *Biological Reviews* 21 (2), 283-327.

Johnsgard, PA (1983) Cranes of the World: Australian Crane (Grus rubicundus). http://digitalcommons.unl.edu/bioscicranes/2

Johnson, G (2003) Vocalizations in the grey butcherbird Cracticus torquatus with emphasis on structure in male breeding song: implications for the function and evolution of song from a study of a Southern Hemisphere species. *PhD thesis.* Griffith University, Brisbane.

Jones, AE, Ten Cate, C and Slater, PJB (1996) Early experience and plasticity of song in adult male Zebra Finches (Taeniopygia guttata). *Journal of Comparative Psychology* 110(4), 354–369.

Jones SS (2007) Imitation in infancy: the development of mimicry. *Psychological Science* 18, 593–599. doi:10.1111/j.1467-9280.2007.01945.x

Jønsson, KA, Fabre, PH, Ricklefs, RE and Fjeldså, J (2011) Major global radiation of corvoid birds originated in the proto-Papuan archipelago. *Proceedings of the National Academy of Sciences* 108 (6), 2328–2333

Joseph, L, Wilke, T, Ten Have, J and Chesser, RT (2006) Implications of mitochondrial DNA polyphyly in two ecologically undifferentiated but morphologically distinct migratory birds, the masked and white-browed woodswallows Artamus spp. of inland Australia. *Journal of Avian Biology* 37 (6), 625-636.

Jouventin, P, Charmantier, A, Dubois, MP, Jarne, P and Bried, J (2007) Extra-pair paternity in the strongly monogamous Wandering Albatross Diomedea exulans has no apparent benefits for females. *Ibis* 149 (1), 67-78.

Juola, FA (2018) The rate of telomere loss is related to maximum lifespan in birds. *Philosophical Transactions of the Royal Society of London B: Biological Sciences* 373 (1741), 20160445.

Kaplan, G (2009) Animals and Music: Between cultural definitions and sensory evidence. *Sign System Studies* 37 (3/4): 75–101.

Kaplan, G (2011) Pointing gesture in a bird- merely instrumental or a cognitively complex behavior? Online http://www.currentzoology.org/ Special Issue 'Animal Cognition' *Current Zoology* 57 (4), 453-467.

Kaplan, G (2015a) Animal Communication. Invited Advanced Review. *WIREs Cog Science* 5(6), 661-677. doi: 10.1002/wcs.1321, 17pp.

Kaplan, G (2015b) *Bird Minds. Cognition and Behaviour of Australian native species.* CSIRO Publishing, Melbourne. (pp. 286).

Kaplan, G (2016) Don Quixote's Windmills. Ch.12 in *Thinking about Animals in the Age of the Anthropocene.* (ed. by M. Tonnessen, K Armstrong Oma and S Rattasepp) pp.284–305. Lexington Books (imprint of Rowman & Littlefield).

Kaplan, G (2017a) Babbling in a bird shows same stages as in human infants: The importance of the 'Social' in vocal development. *Trends in Developmental Biology* 10, 97-123.

Kaplan, G (2017b) Audition and hemispheric specialization in songbirds and new evidence from Australian magpies. *Symmetry* 9 (99), 27. doi:10.3390/sym9070099.

Kaplan, G (2018a) Development of meaningful vocal signals in a juvenile territorial songbird (*Gymnorhina tibicen*) and the dilemma of vocal taboos concerning neighbours and strangers. *Animals* 8, 228. doi:10.3390/ani8120228.

Kaplan, G (2018b) *Tawny Frogmouth.* CSIRO Publishing. Melbourne

Kaplan, G (2018c) Passerine Cognition. In: *Encyclopedia of Animal Cognition and Behavior*. Eds. J.Vonk, T.K. Shackelford, Springer International Publishing AG/ Nature, Cham, Switzerland.

Kaplan, G (2019a) *Australian Magpie: Biology and Behaviour of an Unusual Songbird.* 2nd edition, CSIRO Publishing, Melbourne.

Kaplan, G (2019b) Holding up the mirror: mirror neurons and humanity's dark side. *Animal Sentience* 23 (24), 186–190.

Kaplan, G and Rogers, LJ (1990) Scientific construction, cultural productions: scientific narratives of sexual attraction. In *Feminine, Masculine and Representation.* (Eds T. Threadgold and A.Cranny-Francis; Ch.12, pp.211-230). Allen & Unwin, Sydney.

Kaplan, G and Rogers, LJ (2000) *The orang-utans. their evolution, behavior, and future.* Perseus Publishing, Cambridge, Mass., ISBN 0 7382 0290 8.

Kaplan, G and Rogers, LJ (2001) *Birds. Their Habits and Skills.* Allen & Unwin, Sydney, ISBN 1 86508 376 3.

Kaplan, G and Rogers, LJ (2004) Charles Darwin and Animal Behavior. In *Encyclopedia of Animal Behavior.* (Eds M. Beckoff and J. Goodall, vol.2, pp. 471-479, introductory essay to vol.2). Greenwood Publishing, Westport, CT, ISBN 0-313-32745-9.

Kaplan, G, and Rogers, LJ (2004) *Gene Worship. Moving Beyond the Nature/Nurture Debate over Genes, Brain and Gender.* Other Press LLC, New York and London, ISBN: 1590510348.

Kaplan, G, Johnson, G, Koboroff, A and Rogers, LJ (2009) Alarm Calls of The Australian Magpie (Gymnorhina tibicen): I. Predators Elicit Complex Vocal Responses and Mobbing Behaviour. *The Open Ornithology Journal* 2, 7-16.

Kaplan, G, Pines, M and Rogers, LJ (2012). Stress and stress reduction in common marmosets. *Journal of Applied Animal Welfare Science* 137: 175-182: DOI 10.1016/j.applanim.2011.04.011

Karubian, J (2013) Female ornamentation in Malurus fairy-wrens: a hidden evolutionary gem for understanding female perspectives on social and sexual selection. *Emu* 113, 248–258.

Karubian, J, Sillett, TS and Webster, MS (2008) The effects of delayed plumage maturation on aggression and survival in male red-backed fairy-wrens. *Behavioral Ecology* 19(3), 508-516.

Kayabayi, C, Taylor, AC, von Bayern, AMP and Osvath, M (2016) Ravens, New Caledonian crows and jackdaws parallel great apes in motor self-regulation despite smaller brains. *Royal Society Open Science* 3 (4), 160104. doi.org/10.1098/rsos.160104.

Keagy, J, Lettieri, L, Janette, W and Boughman, JW (2016) Male competition fitness landscapes predict both forward and reverse speciation. *Ecology Letters* 19 (1), 71. doi: 10.1111/ele.12544.

Keagy, J, Savard, JF and Borgia, G (2009) Male satin bowerbird problem-solving ability predicts mating success. *Animal Behaviour* 78 (4), 809-817.

Keagy, J, Savard, JF and Borgia, G (2011) Complex relationship between multiple measures of cognitive ability and male mating success in satin bowerbirds, Ptilonorhynchus violaceus. *Animal Behaviour* 81(5), 1063-1070.

Keast, A (1968) Moult in birds of the Australian dry country relative to rainfall and breeding. *Journal of Zoology, Zoological Society London* 155, 185-200.

Keehn, RJJ, Iversen, JR, Schulz, I and Patel, AD (2019) Spontaneity and diversity of movement to music are not uniquely human. *Current Biology* 29, R1–R3.

Kelley, LA, Coe, RL, Madden, JR and Healy, SD (2008) Vocal mimicry in songbirds. *Animal Behaviour* 76 (3), 521-528.

Kelley, LA and Endler, JA (2012) Male great bowerbirds create forced perspective illusions with consistently different individual quality. *Proceedings of the National Academy of Sciences* 109, 20980–20985.

Kenny, E, Birkhead, TR, and Green, JP (2017) Allopreening in birds is associated with parental cooperation over offspring care and stable pair bonds across years. *Behavioral Ecology* 28 (4), 1142–1148.

Kervinen, M, Alatalo, RV, Lebigre, C, Siitari, H and Soulsbury, CD (2012) Determinants of yearling male lekking effort and mating success in black grouse (Tetrao tetrix). *Behavioral Ecology* 23, 1209–1217.

Kervinen, M, Lebigre, C, Alatalo, RV, Siitari, H and Soulsbury, CD (2014) Life-history differences in age-dependent expressions of multiple ornaments and behaviors in a lekking bird. *The American Naturalist* 185 (1), 13-27. doi: 10.1086/679012.

Keysers, C and Gazzola, V (2010) Social neuroscience: mirror neurons recorded in humans. *Current Biology* 20 (8), R353-4. doi: 10.1016/j.cub.2010.03.013.

Kluyver, HN and Tinbergen, L (1953) Territory and the regulation of density in titmice. *Netherlands Journal of Zoology* 10, 265-287.

Koboroff, A, Kaplan, G and Rogers, LJ (2008) Hemispheric specialization in Australian magpies (Gymnorhina tibicen) shown as eye preferences during response to a predator. *Brain Research Bulletin* 76 (3), 304–306.

Koenig, WD, and Dickson, JL, eds. (2016) *Cooperative breeding in vertebrates: studies of ecology, evolution, and behaviour.* Cambridge: Cambridge University Press.

Koenig, WD (2017) What drives cooperative breeding? *PLoS Biology* 15 (6), p.e2002965.

Kohda, M, Hotta, T, Takeyama, T, Awata, S, Tanaka, H, Asa,i J-y. and Jordan, AL (2019) If a fish can pass the mark test, what are the implications for consciousness and self-awareness testing in animals? *PLoS Biol* 17(2): e3000021. https://doi.org/10.1371/ journal. pbio. 3000021.

Kraaijeveld, K, Kraaijeveld-Smit, FJL and Komdeur, J (2007) The evolution of mutual ornamentation. *Animal Behaviour* 74, 657e677. doi:10.1016/j.anbehav.2006.12.027.

Kramer, KL and Russell, AF (2015) Was monogamy a key step on the Hominin road? Reevaluating the monogamy hypothesis in the evolution of cooperative breeding. *Evolutionary Anthropology: Issues, News, and Reviews,* 24 (2), 73-83.

Krech, D, Rosenzweig, MR and Bennett, EL (1962) Relations between brain chemistry and problem-solving among rats raised in enriched and impoverished environments. *Journal of Comparative and Physiological Psychology* 55(5), p.801.

Kriegsfeld, LJ, Ubuka, T, Bentley, GE, and Tsutsui, K (2015) Seasonal control of gonadotropin-inhibitory hormone (GnIH) in birds and mammals. *Frontiers in Neuroendocrinology* 37, 65-75.

Lakin, JL, Jefferis, VE, Cheng, CM and Chartrand, TL (2003) The chameleon effect as social glue: Evidence for the evolutionary significance of nonconscious mimicry. *Journal of Nonverbal Behavior* 27(3), 145-162.

Langmore, NE (1998) Functions of duet and solo songs of female birds. *Trends in Ecology & Evolution* 13 (4), 136-140.

Langmore, NE, Stevens, M, Maurer, G, Heinsohn, R, Hall, MA, Peters, A and Kilner, RM (2011) Visual mimicry of host nestlings by cuckoos. *Proceedings of the Royal Society B: Biological Sciences* 278 (1717). DOI: https://doi.org/10.1098/rspb.2010.2391.

Lauay, C, Gerlach, NM, Adkins-Regan, E and DeVoogd, TJ (2004) Female zebra finches require early song exposure to prefer high-quality song as adults. *Animal Behaviour* 68 (6), 1249-1255.

Laurita, AC, Hazan, C and Spreng, RN (2019) An Attachment Theoretical Perspective for the Neural Representation of Close Others. *Social Cognitive and Affective Neuroscience*, nsz010, https://doi.org/10.1093/scan/nsz010.

Lazarus, R (1982) Thoughts on the relations between emotions and cognition. *American Psychologist* 37 (9), 1019-1024.

Leal, M and Fleshman, LJ (2002) Evidence for habitat partitioning based on adaptation to environmental light in a pair of sympatric lizard species. *Proceedings of the Royal Society of London B: Biological Sciences* 269, 351-359.

Lee, WY, Lee, S, Choe, JC and Jablonski, PG (2011) Wild birds recognize individual humans: experiments on magpies, Pica pica. *Animal Cognition* 14, 817–825. doi:10.1007/s10071-011-0415-4.

Lee, J, Sarre, SD, Joseph, L and Robertson, J (2015) Microscopic characteristics of the plumulaceous feathers of Australian birds: a preliminary analysis of taxonomic discrimination for forensic purposes. *Australian Journal of Forensic Sciences* DOI: 10.1080/00450618.2015.1076034.

Legge, S, Heinsohn, R, Double, MC, Griffiths, R and Cockburn, A (2001) Complex sex allocation in the laughing kookaburra. *Behavioral Ecology* 12 (5), 524-533.

Leitner, S and Catchpole, CK (2002) Female canaries that respond and discriminate more between male songs of different quality have a larger song control nucleus (HVC) in the brain. *Journal of Neurobiology* 52, 294–301. doi:10.1002/neu.10085.

Lenz, N (1994) Mating behaviour and sexual competition in the regent bowerbird, Serculus chrysocephalus. *Emu* 94:263–272.

Leonard, ML and Picman, J (1988) Mate choice by marsh wrens: the influence of male and territory quality. *Animal Behaviour* 36 (2), 517-528.

Levey, DJ, Londoño, GA, Ungvari-Martin, J, Hiersoux, MR, Jankowski, JE, Poulsen, JR, Stracey, CM and Robinson, SK (2009) Urban mockingbirds quickly learn to identify individual humans. *Proceedings of the National Academy Science USA* 106:8959–8962. doi:10.1073/pnas. 0811422106.

Lifjeld, JT, Dunn, PO and Westneat, DF (1994) Sexual Selection by Sperm Competition in Birds: Male-Male Competition or Female Choice? *Journal of Avian Biology* 25 (3), 244-250.

Liker, A, Freckleton, RP and Székely, T (2013). The evolution of sex roles in birds is related to adult sex ratio. *Nature Communications* 4, 1587. DOI: 10.1038/ncomms2600 |www.nature.com/naturecommunications.

Liker, A, Freckleton, RP and Székely, T (2014) Divorce and Infidelity Are Associated with Skewed Adult Sex Ratios in Birds. *Current Biology* 24, 880–884. http://dx.doi.org/10.1016/j.cub.2014.02.059.

Lill, A (1979) An assessment of male parental investment and pair bonding in the polygamous superb lyrebird. *The Auk* 96, 489–498.

Lill, A (1986) Time-energy budgets during reproduction and the evolution of single parenting in the superb lyrebird. *Australian Journal of Zoology* 34 (3), 351-371.

Lima, HH and Pike, TW (2016) Dietary carotenoid availability affects avian color discrimination. *Behavioral Ecology* 27 (6), 1579–1584. doi:10.1093/beheco/arw116.

Lind, O and Kelbe, A (2009) The intensity threshold of colour vision in two species of parrot. *The Journal of Experimental Biology* 212, 3693-3699. doi:10.1242/jeb.035477.

Lindstedt, SL and Calder, WA (1976) Body size and longevity in birds. *The Condor* 78 (1), 91-94.

Lindstedt, SL and Calder, WA (1981) Body size, physiological time, and longevity of homeothermic animals. *Quarterly Review of Biology* 1, 91-181.

Lippolis, G, Westman, W, McAllan, B and Rogers, LJ (2005) Lateralisation of escape responses in the stripe-faced dunnart, Sminthopsis macroura (Dasyuridae: Marsupialia). *Laterality: Asymmetries of Body, Brain, and Cognition* 10 (5) 457–470.

Little, AC, Jones, BC, Waitt, C, Tiddeman, BP, Feinberg, DR, Perrett, DI, Apicella, CL and Marlowe, FW (2008) Symmetry is related to sexual dimorphism in faces: data across culture and species. *PloS ONE* 3 (5), p.e2106.

Lize, A, Price, TAR, Heys, C, Lewis, Z and Hurst, GDD (2014) Extreme cost of rivalry in a monandrous species: male-male interactions result in failure to acquire mates and reduced longevity. *Proceedings of the Royal Society B: Biological Sciences* 281 (1786), 20140631 DOI: 10.1098/rspb.2014.0631.

Logue, DM and Hall, ML (2014) Migration and the evolution of duetting in songbirds. *Proceedings of the Royal Society of London B: Biological Sciences* 281,20140103. doi: 10.1098/rspb.2014.0103.

Lorenz, K (1952) *King Solomon's Ring: New Light on Animal Ways.* Illustrated by the Author and with a Foreword by Julian Huxley. [Translated from German by Marjorie Kerr Wilson, 1st German ed.1949]. Methuen.

Lorenz, K (1964) Ritualized Fighting. In *The Natural History of Aggression.* Eds JD Carthy and F.Ebling (pp. 39-50). Academic Press, London and New York.

Lowman, MD (1992) Leaf growth dynamics and herbivory in five Australian rainforest canopy trees. *Journal of Ecology* 80, 433-447.

Lu, S and Li, L (2008) Carotenoid metabolism: biosynthesis, regulation, and beyond. *Journal of Integrative Plant Biology* 50 (7), 778-785.

Luef, EM, Ter Maat, A and Pika, S (2017) Vocal similarity in long-distance and short-distance vocalizatios in raven pairs (Corvus corax) in captivity. *Behavioural Processes* 142, 1-7.

MacFarlane, GR, Blomberg, SP, Kaplan, G and Rogers, LJ (2006) Same-sex sexual behavior in birds: expression is related to social mating system and state of development at hatching. *Behavioral Ecology* doi:10.1093/beheco/arl065.

MacLean, EL, Hare, B, Nunn, CL, Addessi, E, Amici, F, Anderson, RC, Aureli, F, Baker, JM, Bania, AE, Barnard, AM and Boogert, NJ (2014) The evolution of self-control. *Proceedings of the National Academy of Sciences* 111(20), E2140-E2148.

Madden, RJ and Tanner, K (2003) Preferences for coloured bower decorations can be explained in a nonsexual context. *Animal Behaviour* 65, 1077–1083. doi:10.1006/anbe.2003.2126.

Magrath, RD, Leedman, AW, Gardner, JL, Giannasca, A, Nathan, AC, Yezerinac, SM and Nicholls, JA (2000) Life in the slow lane: reproductive life history of the white-browed scrubwren, an Australian endemic. *The Auk* 117 (2), 479-489.

Maguire, EA, Gadian, DG, Johnsrude, IS, Good, CD, Ashburner, J, Frackowiak, RS and Frith, CD (2000) Navigation-related structural change in the hippocampi of taxi drivers. *Proceedings of the National Academy of Sciences* 97 (8), 4398-4403.

Maguire, EA, Woollett, K and Spiers, HJ (2006) London taxi drivers and bus drivers: a structural MRI and neuropsychological analysis. *Hippocampus* 16 (12), 1091-1101.

Maher, WJ (1996) Nestling food and feeding frequencies of the Brown-backed Honeyeater Ramsayornis modestus and the Yellow-bellied Sunbird Nectarinia jugularis in northern Queensland. *Emu* 96 (1), 17–22.

Mahr, K, Seifert, CL and Hoi, H (2016) Female and male blue tits (Cyanistes caeruleus) sing in response to experimental predator exposition. *Journal of Ornithology* 157 (3), 907. DOI:10.1007/s10336-016-1345-3.

Maninger, N, Mendoza, SP, Williams, DR, Mason, WA, Cherry, SR, Rowland, DJ, Schaefer, T and Bales, KL (2017) Imaging, behavior and endocrine analysis of "Jealousy" in a monogamous primate. *Frontiers in Ecology and Evolution* 5, 119.

Manson, JH, Perry, S and Parish, AR (1997) Nonconceptive sexual behavior in bonobos and capuchins. *International Journal of Primatology* 18(5), 767-786.

Margoliash, D (2002) Evaluating theories of bird song learning: implications for future directions. *Journal of Comparative Physiology* 188, 851-866.

Mariette, MM and Griffith, SC (2012) Nest visit synchrony is high and correlates with reproductive success in the wild zebra finch Taeniopygia guttata. *Journal of Avian Biology*, 43 (2), 131-140.

Marino, L, Connor, RC, Fordyce, RE, Herman, LM, Hof, PR, Lefebvre, L, Lusseau, D, McCowan, B, Nimchinsky, EA, Pack, AA and Rendell, L (2007) Cetaceans have complex brains for complex cognition. *PLoS Biology*, 5(5), p.e139.

Marki, PZ, Jønsson, KA, Irestedt, M, Nguyen, JMT, Rahbek, C and Fjeldså, Jon (2017) Supermatrix phylogeny and biogeography of the Australasian Meliphagides radiation (Aves: Passeriformes). *Molecular Phylogenetics and Evolution* 107, 516–529.

Martin, AJ, Vickers-Rich, P, Rich, TH and Hall, M (2014) Oldest known avian foot-prints from Australia: Eumeralla Formation (Albian), Dinosaur Cove, Victoria. *Palaeontology* 57 (1), 7–19. doi:10.1111/pala.12082.

References

Martin, GR (2012) Through birds' eyes: insights into avian sensory ecology. *Journal of Ornithology* 153 (1), 23–48.

Martin, GR (2017) The sensory ecology of collisions and entrapment. (Ch. 9) In: *The Sensory Ecology of Birds* by G.R. Martin. Oxford Avian Biology Series. Oxford University Press, Oxford, UK.

Martinho, III A, Biro, D, Guilford, T, Gagliardo, A and Kacelnik, A (2015) Asymmetric visual input and route recapitulation in homing pigeons. *Proceedings of the Royal Society of London B: Biological Sciences* 282 (9), 20151957. http://dx.doi.org/10.1098/rspb.2015.1957

Marzluff, JM, Miyaoka, R, Minoshima, S and Cross, D (2012) Brain imaging reveals neuronal circuitry underlying the crow's perception of human faces. *Proceedings of the National Academy of Sciences* 109 (39), 15912–15917. doi:10.1073/pnas.1206109109

Marzluff, JM, Walls, J, Cornell, HN, Withey, JC and Craig, DP (2010) Lasting recognition of threatening people by wild American crows. *Animal Behaviour* 79, 699–707. doi:10.1016/j.anbehav.2009. 12.022.

Maslow, AH (1943) A theory of human motivation. *Psychological Review* 50 (4), 370–396. CiteSeerX10.1.1.334.7586. doi:10.1037/h0054346

Maslow, AH (1954) *Motivation and Personality. A general theory of human motivation based upon a synthesis primarily of holistic and dynamic principles.* Harper, New York, NY.

Matheson, SM, Asher, L and Bateson, M (2008) Larger, enriched cages are associated with 'optimistic' response biases in captive European starlings (Sturnus vulgaris). *Applied Animal Behaviour Science* 109, 374–383. doi:10.1016/j.applanim.2007.03.007.

Maurer, G (2006) Ecology and evolution of sex-roles in the pheasant coucal, centropus phasianinus. PhD thesis. Australian National University, Canberra.

Maurer, G (2008) Who cares? Males provide most parental care in a monogamous nesting cuckoo. *Ethology* 114 (6), 540-547.

Maurer, G, Double, MC, Milenkaya, O, Süsser, M and Magrath, RD (2011) Breaking the rules: sex roles and genetic mating system of the pheasant coucal. *Oecologia* 167 (2), 413.

Maynard-Smith, J and Price, GR (1973) The Logic of Animal Conflict. *Nature* 246 (5427), 15–18.

Maynard Smith, J *(1982) Evolution and the Theory of Games.* Cambridge University Press, Cambridge, UK.

Mayr, E (1963) Animal Species and Evolution. Cambridge: Harvard University Press

Mays NA, Vleck CM, Dawson J (1991) Plasma luteinizing hormone, steroid hormones, behavioral role, and nest stage in cooperatively breeding Harris' hawks (Parabuteo unicinctus). *The Auk* 108 (3), 619–37.

Mazur, A (2015) A biosocial model of status in face-to-face groups. In *Evolutionary Perspectives on Social Psychology* (pp. 303-315). Eds. V.Zeigler-Hill, LLM Welling, TK Shackelford, Springer International Publishing, Switzerland.

McCaig, T, Brown, M and Jones, DN (2015) Exploring possible functions of vocalisations in the Torresian Crow 'Corvus orru'. Australian Field Ornithology 32 (4), 201.

McCracken, K (1999) Systematics, ecology, and social biology of the musk duck (Biziura lobata) of Australia. LSU Historical Dissertations and Theses. 6896. https:// digitalcommons.lsu.edu/gradschool_disstheses/6896P.

McFarland, DC (1986) Determinants of feeding territory size in the New Holland Honeyeater Phylidonyris novaehollandiae. *Emu* 86 (3), 180-185.

McGlothlin, JW, Neudorf, DLH, Casto, JM, Nolan, V and Ketterson, ED (2004) Elevated testosterone reduces choosiness in female dark-eyed juncos (Junco hyemalis): evidence for a hormonal constraint on sexual selection? *Proceedings of the Royal Society of London B: Biological Sciences* 271 (1546), 1377-1384.

McGraw, KJ and Nogare, MC (2005) Distribution of unique red feather pigments in parrots. *Biology Letters* 1 (1), 38–43.

McGraw, KJ, Massaro, M, Rivers, TJ and Mattern, T (2009) Annual, sexual, size-and condition-related variation in the colour and fluorescent pigment content of yellow crest-feathers in Snares Penguins (Eudyptes robustus). *Emu-Austral Ornithology* 109 (2), 93-99.

McGraw, KJ, Wakamatsu, K, Ito, S, Nolan, PM, Jouventin, P, Dobson, FS, Austic, RE, Safran, RJ, Siefferman, LM, Hill, GE and Parker, RS (2004) You can't judge a pigment by its color: carotenoid and melanin content of yellow and brown feathers in swallows, bluebirds, penguins, and domestic chickens.*The Condor* 106 (2), 390-395.

McQueen, A, Naimo, AC, Teunissen, N, Magrath, RD, Delhey, K and Peters, A (2017) Bright birds are cautious: seasonally conspicuous plumage prompts risk avoidance by male superb fairy-wrens. *Proceedings of the Royal Society of London B: Biological Sciences* 284, 20170446.

Medina, I, Delhey, K, Peters, A, Cain, KE, Hall, ML, Mulder, RA and Langmore, NE (2017) Habitat structure is linked to the evolution of plumage colour in female, but not male, fairy-wrens. *BMC Evolutionary Biology* 17 (1), 35.

Mehlhorn, J, Haastert, B and Rehkamper, G (2010) Asymmetry of different brain structures in homing pigeons with and without navigational experience. *The Journal of Experimental Biology* 213, 2219-2224.

Meissner, TW, Friedrich, P, Ocklenburg, S, Genç, E and Weigelt, S (2017) Tracking the Functional Development of the Corpus Callosum in Children Using Behavioral and Evoked Potential Interhemispheric Transfer Times. *Developmental Neuropsychology* 42 (3), 172–186.

Mennill, DJ and Rogers, AC (2006) Whip it good! Geographic consistency in male songs and variability in female songs of the duetting eastern whipbird Psophodes Olivaceus. *Journal of Avian Biology* 37, 93–100. doi:10.1111/j.0908-8857.2006.03548.x.

Menyhart, O, Kolodny, O, Goldstein, MH, DeVoogd, TJ and Edelman, S (2015) Juvenile zebra finches learn the underlying structural regularities of their fathers' song. *Frontiers in Psychology* 6, 571.

Miles, FA (1998) The neural processing of 3-D visual information: evidence from eye movements. *European Journal of Neuroscience* 10, 811-822.

Miller, DB (1979) Long-term recognition of father's song by female zebra finches. *Nature* 280 (5721), 389.

Mittermeier, RA (2000) *2000 IUCN red list of threatened species.* IUCN.

Miyata, H, Gajdon, GK, Huber, L and Fujita, K (2011) How do keas (Nestor notabilis) solve artificial-fruit problems with multiple locks? *Animal Cognition* 14 (1), 45-58.

Møller, AP (1987) Mate guarding in the swallow Hirundo rustica. *Behavioral Ecology and Sociobiology* 21(2), 119-123.

Moore, BR (1992) Avian movement imitation and a new form of mimicry: tracing the evolution of a complex form of learning. *Behavior* 122, 231–263. doi:10.1163/1568539 92X00525.

Moore, BR (1996) The evolution of imitative learning. In *Social Learning in Animals. The Roots of Culture.* (Eds CM Heyes and BG Galef Jr) pp. 245–265. Academic Press, San Diego, CA.

Moore, IT, Wingfield, JC and Brenowitz, EA (2004c) Plasticity of the avian song control system in response to localized environmental cues in an equatorial songbird. *Journal of Neuroscience* 24, 10182-10185.

Moreno-Rueda, G (2017) Preen oil and bird fitness: A critical review of the evidence. *Biological Reviews* 92 (4), 2131-2143.

Morrison, ES and Badyaev, AV (2018) Structure versus time in the evolutionary diversification of avian carotenoid metabolic networks. *Journal of Evolutionary Biology* 31 (5), 633-779.

Moser-Purdy, C and Mennill, DJ (2016) Large vocal repertoires do not constrain the dear enemy effect: a playback experiment and comparative study of songbirds. *Animal Behaviour* 118, 55-64.

Moyle, RG, Oliveros, CH, Andersen, MJ, Hosner, PA, Benz, BW, Manthey, JD, Travers, SL, Brown, RM and Faircloth, BC (2016) Tectonic collision and uplift of Wallacea triggered the global songbird radiation. *Nature Communications* 7, 12709.

Mulder, RA and Magrath, MJ (1994) Timing of prenuptial molt as a sexually selected indicator of male quality in superb fairy-wrens (Malurus cyaneus). *Behavioral Ecology* 5 (4), 393-400.

Mulder, RA (1997) Extra-group courtship displays and other reproductive tactics of superb fairy-wrens. *Australian Journal of Zoology* 45 (2), 131-143.

Muñoz, AP, Kéry, M, Martins, PV, and Ferraz, G (2018) Age effects on survival of Amazon forest birds and the latitudinal gradient in bird survival. *The Auk, Ornithological Advances* 135, 299–313. doi: 10.1642/AUK-17-91.

Murphy, S, Legge, S and Heinsohn, R (2003) The breeding biology of palm cockatoos (Probosciger aterrimus): a case of a slow life history. *Journal of Zoology* 261 (4),327-339.

Mynott, J (2018) *Birds in the Ancient World*. Oxford University Press, Oxford. ISBN: 9780198713654.

Newton, J (2018) Evolutionary Game Theory: A Renaissance. *Games* 9 (2). doi:10.3390/g9020031.

Ngugi, MR, Doley, D, Cant, M, and Botkin, DB (2015) Growth rates of Eucalyptus and other Australian native tree species derived from seven decades of growth monitoring. *Journal of Forestry Research* 26 (4).

Nimchinsky, EA, Gilissen, E, Allman, JM, Perl, DP, Erwin, JM and Hof, PR (1999) A neuronal morphologic type unique to humans and great apes. *Proceedings of the National Academy of Sciences* 96 (9), 5268-5273.

Noguera, Jc, Sin-Yeon, K and Velando, A (2017) Family-transmitted stress in a wild bird. *Proceedings of the National Academy of Science*, USA 114 (26), 6794–6799.

Nowicki, S, Peters, S, Searcy, WA, and Clayton, C (1998) The development of within-song type variation in song sparrows. *Animal Behaviour* 57 (6), 1257-1264.

Nowicki, S and Searcy, WA (2014) The evolution of vocal learning. *Current Opinion in Neurobiology* 28, 48–53.

Nugent, DT, Leonard, SWJ, and Clarke, MF (2014) Interactions between the superb lyrebird (Menura novaehollandiae) and fire in southeastern Australia. *Australian Wildlife Research* 41, 203–211.

Numan, M, and Young, LJ (2016) Neural mechanisms of mother-infant bonding and pair bonding: Similarities, differences, and broader implications. *Hormones and Behaviour* 77, 98–112. doi:10.1016/j.yhbeh.2015.05.015.

Ocklenburg, S, and Güntürkün, O (2017) *The Lateralised Brain: The Neuroscience And Evolution Of Hemispheric Asymmetries*. Academic Press, London.

Ödeen, A and Håstad, O (2003) Complex distribution of avian color vision systems revealed by sequencing the SWS1 opsin from total DNA. *Molecular Biology and Evolution* 20 (6), 855-861.

Odom, KJ, Hall, ML, Riebel, K, Omland, KE and Langmore, NE (2014) Female song is widespread and ancestral in songbirds. *Nature Communications* 5, 3379. DOI: 10.1038/ncomms4379 |www.nature.com/naturecommunications

Oetting, S, Pröve, E and Bischof, H-J (1995) Sexual imprinting as a two-stage process: mechanisms of information storage and stabilization. *Animal Behaviour* 50 (2), 393-403.

Olkowicz, S, Kocourek M, Lučan, RK, Porteš, M, Fitch WT, Herculano-Houzel S and Němec P (2016) Birds have primate-like numbers of neurons in the forebrain. *Proceedings of the National Academy of Sciences* 113 (26), 7255–7260. www.pnas.org/ cgi/ doi/10.1073/pnas.1517131113.

Olssen, P, Lind, O, and Kelber, A (2018) Chromatic and achromatic vision: parameter choice and limitations for reliable model predictions. *Behavioural Ecology* 29 (2), 273-282. Doi:10.1093/beheco/arx133.

Opie, C, Atkinson, QD, Dunbar, RIM and Shultz, S (2013) Male infanticide leads to social monogamy in primates. *Proceedings of the National Academy of Science, USA* 110, 13328–13332. doi:10.1073/pnas.1307903110.

Osorio, DM and Vorobyev, M (2008) A review of the evolution of animal colour vision and visual communication signals. *Vision Research* 48, 2042–2051.

Osvath, M and Sima, M (2014) Sub-adult ravens synchronize their play: a case of emotional contagion. *Animal Behavior and Cognition* 1 (2) 97-205.

Ota, N, Gahr, M and Soma, M (2018) Couples showing off: Audience promotes both male and female multimodal courtship display in a songbird. *Science Advances* 4 (10), p.eaat4779.

Ouyang, JQ, van Oers, K, Quetting, M and Hau, M (2014) Becoming more like your mate: hormonal similarity reduces divorce rates in a wild songbird. *Animal Behaviour* 98, 87-93.

Overington, SE, Morand-Ferron, J, Boogert, NJ and Lefebvre, L (2009) Technical innovations drive the relationship between innovativeness and residual brain size in birds. *Behaviour* 78, 1001–1010. doi:10.1016/j.anbehav.2009.06.033.

Palagi, E, Leone, A, Mancini, G and Ferrari, PF (2009) Contagious yawning in gelada baboons as a possible expression of empathy. *Proceedings of the National Academy of Sciences* 106(46) 19262-19267.

Parker, AR (2000) 515 million years of structural colour. *Journal of Optics A: Pure and Applied Optics* 6, R15-R28.

Partan, SR and Marler, P (2005) Issues in the classification of multimodal communication signals. *The American Naturalist*, 166 (2), 231–245.

Patel, AD, Iversen, JR, Bregman, MR and Schulz, I (2009a) Experimental evidence for synchronization to a musical beat in a nonhuman animal. *Current Biology* 9 (10), 827-830.

Patel, AD, Iversen, JR, Bregman, MR and Schulz, I (2009b) Studying synchronization to a musical beat in nonhuman animals. *Annals of the New York Academy of Sciences* 1169 (1), 459-469.

Patel, AD, Iversen, JR, Bregman, MR, Schulz, I and Schulz, C (2008) Investigating the human-specificity of synchronization to music. In *Proceedings of the 10th International Conference on Music and Cognition* (pp. 100-104). Sapporo, Japan.

Patterson, F and Cohn, RH (1985) *Koko's Kitten*. Scholastic Publishing, New York.

Pell, AS and Tidemann, CR (1997a) The ecology of the common myna in urban nature reserves in the Australian Capital Territory. *Emu* 97 (2), 141-149.

Pell, AS and Tidemann, CR (1997b) The impact of two exotic hollow-nesting birds on two native parrots in savannah and woodland in eastern Australia. *Biological Conservation* 79 (2-3), 145-153.

Pepperberg, IM (2009) *The Alex Studies: cognitive and communicative abilities of grey parrots.* Harvard University Press, Boston.

Pettigrew, JD, Wallman, J and Wildsoet, CF (1990) Saccadic oscillations facilitate ocular perfusion from the avian pecten. *Nature* 343 (6256), 362.

Plutchik, R (2001) The Nature of Emotions. *American Scientist* 89 (4), 344-350.

Poiani, A and Pagel, M (1997) Evolution of avian cooperative breeding: comparative tests of the nest predation hypothesis. *Evolution* 51: 226–40.

Poldmaa, T, Montgomerie, R and Boag, P (1995) Mating system of the cooperatively breeding noisy miner Manorina melanocephala, as revealed by DNA profiling. *Behavioral Ecology and Sociobiology* 37, 137-143.

Poole, J (1997) *Elephants.* Voyageur Press. Stillwater, MN-USA.

Pozner, T, Vistoropsky, Y, Moaraf, S, Heiblum, R and Barnea, A (2018) Questioning Seasonality of Neuronal Plasticity in the Adult Avian Brain. *Scientific Reports*, 8 (1), 11289. DOI:10.1038/s41598-018-29532-1

Prather JF, Peters S, Nowicki S and Mooney R (2008) Precise auditory–vocal mirroring in neurons for learned vocal communication. *Nature* 451, 305–310. doi:10.1038/nature06492

Price, JJ (2015) Rethinking our assumptions about the evolution of bird song and other sexually dimorphic signals. *Frontiers in Ecology and Evolution* 3, 40. doi: 10.3389/fevo.2015.00040.

Price, JJ, Lanyon, SM and Omland, KE (2009) Losses of female song with changes from tropical to temperate breeding in the New World blackbirds. *Proceedings of the Royal Society of London B: Biological Sciences* 276, 1971-1980. doi:10.1098/rspb.2008.1626.

Price, JJ and Eaton, MD (2014) Reconstructing the evolution of sexual dichromatism: current color diversity does not reflect past rates of male and female change. *Evolution* 68,2026-2037. doi:10.1111/evo.12417.

Price, JR, Iwaniuk, AN, Gutiérrez-Ibáñez, C, Birkhead, T and Wylie, DR (2015) Diversity in olfactory bulb size in birds reflects allometry, ecology, and phylogeny. *Frontiers in Neuroanatomy* 9, 102.

Prior, H, Schwarz, A and Güntürkün, O (2008) Mirror-induced behavior in the magpie (Pica pica): evidence of self-recognition. *PLoS Biology* 6, e202. doi:10.1371/journal. pbio.0060202.

Procter, DS, Cottrell, JE, Watts, K, A'Hara, SW, Hofreiter, M and Robinson, EJH (2016) Does cooperation mean kinship between spatially discrete ant nests? *Ecology and Evolution* 6 (24), 8846-8856.

Pujol, J, Vendrell, P, Junqué, C, Martí-Vilalta, JL and Capdevila, A (1993) When does human brain development end? Evidence of corpus callosum growth up to adulthood. *Annals of Neurology: Official Journal of the American Neurological Association and the Child Neurology Society*, 34 (1), 71-75.

Ramos-Fernández, Gabriel, Morales, Juan M (2014) Unraveling fission-fusion dynamics: how subgroup properties and dyadic interactions influence individual decisions. *Behavioral Ecology and Sociobiology* 68 (8), 1225–1235. doi:10.1007/s00265-014-1733-8.

Rehkämper, G, Frahm, HD and Zilles, K (1991) Quantitative development of brain and brain structures in birds (galliformes and passeriformes) compared to that in mammals (insectivores and primates) (Part 1 of 2). *Brain, Behavior and Evolution* 37(3), 125-134.

Reichert, MS, and Quinn, JL (2017) Cognition in contests: mechanisms, ecology, and evolution. *Trends in Ecology and Evolution* 32 (10), 773-785.

Ręk, P and Magrath, R, (2016) Multimodal duetting in magpie-larks: how do vocal and visual components contribute to a cooperative signal's function? *Animal Behaviour* 117, 35-42.

Ręk, P and Magrath, RD (2017) Deceptive vocal duets and multimodal display in a songbird. *Proceedings of the Royal Society of London B: Biological Sciences* 284 (1864), 20171774.

Reneerkens, J, Morrison, RG, Ramenofsky, M, Piersma, T and Wingfield, JC (2002) Baseline and stress-induced levels of corticosterone during different life cycle substages in a shorebird on the high arctic breeding grounds. *Physiological and Biochemical Zoology* 75 (2), 200–208.

Requena, GS and Alonzo, SH (2017) Sperm competition games when males invest in paternal care. *Proceedings of the Royal Society of London B: Biological Sciences* 284, 20171266. http://dx.doi.org/10.1098/rspb.2017.1266.

Ricklefs, RE (2004) The cognitive face of avian life histories. *The Wilson Bulletin* 116 (2), 119–133. doi:10.1676/04-054.

Riebel, K (2003) The" mute" sex revisited: vocal production and perception learning in female songbirds. *Advances in the Study of Behavior* 33 (4), 49-86.

Riehl, C and Stern, CA (2015) How cooperatively breeding birds identify relatives and avoid incest: new insights into dispersal and kin recognition. *BioEssays* 37 (12), 1303-1308.

Rizzolatti, G, Fadiga, L, Gallese, V and Fogassi, L (1996) Premotor cortex and the recognition of motor actions. *Cognitive Brain Research* 3, 131–141.

Roberts, G (1998) Competitive altruism: from reciprocity to the handicap principle. *Proceedings of the Royal Society of London. Series B: Biological Sciences* 265(1394) 427–431.

Robinson, EJ, and Barker, JL (2017) Inter-group cooperation in humans and other animals. *Biology Letters* 13 (3), 20160793.

Robinson, FN and Curtis, HS (1996) The vocal displays of the lyrebirds (Menuridae). *Emu, 96* (4), 258-275.

Rogers, AC (2005) Male and female song structure and singing behaviour in the duetting eastern whipbird, Psophodes olivaceus. *Australian Journal of Zoology* 53, 157–166. doi:10.1071/ZO04083.

Rogers AC, Mulder RA and Langmore NE (2006) Duet duels: sex differences in song matching in duetting eastern whipbirds. *Animal Behaviour* 72, 53–61. doi:10.1016/j. anbehav.2005.08.019.

Rogers AC, Langmore NE and Mulder RA (2007) Function of pair duets in the eastern whipbird: cooperative defense or sexual conflict? *Behavioral Ecology* 18 (1), 182–188.

Rogers, LJ (2012) The two hemispheres of the *avian brain: their differing roles in perceptual processing and the expression of behavior. Journal of Ornithology* 153 (Suppl 1), S61–S74. DOI 10.1007/s10336-011-0769-z.

Rogers, LJ and Kaplan, G (2003) *Spirit of the Wild Dog.* Allen & Unwin, Sydney, ISBN 186508 673 8

Rogers, LJ and Kaplan, G (2004) *Comparative Vertebrate Cognition: Are Primates Superior to Nonprimates?* Kluwer, New York. (ISBN 0-306-47727-0).

Rogers, LJ, Koboroff, A and Kaplan, G (2018) Lateral Asymmetry of Brain and Behaviour in the Zebra Finch, Taeniopygia guttata. *Symmetry* 9 (99), 27. doi:10.3390/sym9070099.

Rogers, LJ and McCulloch, H (1981) Pair-bonding in the galah, Cacatua roseicapilla. *Bird Behaviour* 3 (3), 80-92.

Rogers, LJ, Vallortigara, F and Andrew, R (2013) *The Divided Brain.* Cambridge University Press, Cambridge, UK.

Romero, T, Konno, A and Hasegawa, T (2013) Familiarity bias and physiological responses in contagious yawning by dogs support link to empathy. *PloS One* 8 (8), p.e71365.

Roper, A and Zann, R (2006) The onset of song learning and song tutor selection in fledgling zebra finches. *Ethology* 112 (5), 458-470.

Roper, TJ (1999) Olfaction in birds. *Advances in the Study of Behavior* 28, 247–247.

Rosen, LB (2012) Avian reproductive disorders. *Journal of Exotic Pet Medicine* 21 (2), 124–131.

Roughgarden J, Oishi M, Akcay E (2006) Reproductive social behavior: cooperative games to replace sexual selection. *Science* 311, 965–969.

Rowley, I (1991) Petal-carrying by Fairy-wrens of the Genus Malarus. *Australian Field Ornithology* 14 (3), 75-81.

Russell, EM, Yom-Tov, Y, and Geffen, E (2004) Extended parental care and delayed dispersal: northern, tropical, and southern passerines compared. *Behavioral Ecology* 15 (5), 831-838.

Ryan MJ, Cummings ME (2013) Perceptual biases and mate-choice. *Annual Review of Ecology, Evolution and Systematics* 44, 437-459. Doi:10.1146/annurev-ecolsys-110512- 135901.

Sæther, BE (1989) Survival rates in relation to body weight in European birds. *Ornis Scandinavica* 20 (1), 13-21.

Saino, N, Romano, M, Rubolini, D, Teplitsky, C, Ambrosini, R, Caprioli, M, Canova, L and Wakamatsu, K (2013) Sexual dimorphism in melanin pigmentation, feather coloration and its heritability in the barn swallow (Hirundo rustica). *PLoS ONE* 8 (2), e58024. https://doi.org/10.1371/journal. pone.0058024.

Sakai, M, Morisaka, T, Kogi, K, Hishii, T and Kohshima, S, 2010. Fine-scale analysis of synchronous breathing in wild Indo-Pacific bottlenose dolphins (Tursiops aduncus). *Behavioural Processes* 83 (1), 48-53.

Salovey, P and Mayer, JD (1990) Emotional intelligence. *Imagination, cognition and personality* 9 (3), 185–211.

Salva, OR, Regolin, L and Vallortigara, G (2007) Chicks discriminate human gaze with their right hemisphere. *Behavioural Brain Research* 177 (1), 15–21.

Sasaki, A, Sotnikova, TD, Gainetdinov, RR and Jarvis, ED (2006) Social context-dependent singing-regulated dopamine. *The Journal of Neuroscience* 26, 9010–9014. Doi:10.1523/ JNEUROSCI. 1335-06.2006.

Savage, J, Browning, L, Manica, A, Russell, AF, and Johnstone, RA (2017) Turn-taking irule? *Behavioral Ecology and Sociobiology* 71 (11), 162.

Sayol, F, Maspons, J, Lapiedra, O, Iwaniuk, AN, Szekely, T, and Sol, D (2016) Environmental variation and the evolution of large brains in birds. *Nature Communications* 7, 13971. doi:10.1038/ncomms13971.

Scharff, C, and Nottebohm, F (1991) A comparative study of the behavioural deficits following lesions of the various parts of the zebra finch song system: implications for vocal learning. *Journal of Neuroscience* 11, 2896-2913.

Schassburger, R (1993) *Vocal Communication in the Timber Wolf, Canis lupus, Linnaeus. Structure, Motivation, and Ontogeny*. Paul Parey Scientific Publishers, Berlin.

Schodde, R (1982) *The Fairy-wrens: a monograph of the Maluridae.* Lansdowne Editions.

Schoech, SJ, Mumme, RL, and Wingfield, JC, (1996) Prolactin and helping behaviour in the cooperatively breeding Florida scrub-jay, Aphelocoma c. coerulescens. *Animal Behaviour* 52 (3), 445-456.

Schoech, SJ, Rensel, MA, Heiss, RS (2011) Short- and long-term effects of developmental exposure on avian physiology, behavioral phenotype, cognition and fitness. *Current Zoology* 57 (4), 514-530.

Schuett, W, Godin, JG and Dall, SRX (2011a) Do female zebra finches, Taeniopygia guttata, choose their mates based on their 'personality'? *Ethology* 117, 908-917.

Schuett, W, Dall SRX, Royle, NJ (2011b) Pairs of zebra finches with similar 'personalities' make better parents. *Animal Behaviour* 81, 609–618.

Schuett W, Tregenza T and Dall, SRX (2010) Sexual selection and animal personality. *Biological Reviews* 85, 217–246.

Schutte, NS, Malouff, JM, Bobik, C, Coston, TD, Greeson, C, Jedlicka, C, Rhodes, E, and Wendorf, G (2001) Emotional intelligence and interpersonal relations. *The Journal of Social Psychology* 141(4), 523-536.

Schweiger, D, Stemmler, G, Burgdorf, C and Wacker, J (2013) Opioid receptor blockade and warmth-liking: effects on interpersonal trust and frontal asymmetry. *Social, Cognitive and Affective Neuroscience* 9(10), 1608-1615.

Schwing, R, Nelson, XJ, Wein, A and Parsons, S (2017) Positive emotional contagion in a New Zealand parrot. *Current Biology* 27 (6) R213-R214.

Searcy, WA, Akçay, C, Nowicki, S and Beecher, MD (2014) Aggressive signaling in song sparrows and other songbirds. In *Advances in the Study of Behavior* 46, 89-125. Academic Press.

Seybold, U and Rahmann, H (1985) Brain gangliosides in birds with different types of postnatal development (nidifugous and nidicolous type). *Developmental Brain Research* 17(1-2), 201-208.

Seyfarth, RM, Cheney, DL, and Marler, P (1980) Monkey responses to three different alarm calls: evidence of predator classification and semantic communication. *Science* 210 (4471), 801-803.

Shamay-Tsoory, SG and Abu-Akel, A (2016) The social salience hypothesis of oxytocin. *Biological Psychiatry* 79 (3), 194–202.

Sharrock, R, Day, A, Qazi, F, and Brewin, CR (1990) Explanations by professional care staff, optimism and helping behaviour: An application of attribution theory. *Psychological Medicine* 20 (4), 849-855.

Shaughnessy, DW, Hyson, RL, Bertram, R, Wu, W and Johnson, F (2019) Female zebra finches do not sing yet share neural pathways necessary for singing in males. *Journal of Comparative Neurology* 527 (4), 843-855.

Shawkey, MD and Hill, GE (2005) Carotenoids need structural colours to shine. *Biology Letters* 1 (2), 121-124.

Shultz, S and Dunbar, RI (2007) The evolution of the social brain: anthropoid primates contrast with other vertebrates. *Proceedings of the Royal Society of London B: Biological Sciences* 274 (1624), 2429–2436.

Shultz, S and Dunbar, RI (2010) Social bonds in birds are associated with brain size and contingent on the correlated evolution of life-history and increased parental investment. *Biological Journal of the Linnean Society*100 (1), 111-123.

Shute, E, Prideaux, GJ, and Worthy, TH, (2016) Three terrestrial Pleistocene coucals (Centropus: Cuculidae) from southern Australia: biogeographical and ecological significance. *Zoological Journal of the Linnean Society* 177, 964-1002.

Sibley, CG, Ahlquist, JE (1990) *Phylogeny and Classification of Birds: a Study in Molecular Evolution.* Yale University Press, New Haven, CT.

Sih, A, and Bell, AM (2008) Insights for behavioral ecology from behavioral syndromes. *Advances in the Study of Behavior* 38, 227-281.

Silk, JB, Alberts, SC and Altmann, J (2004) Patterns of coalition formation by adult female baboons in Amboseli, Kenya. *Animal Behaviour* 67 (3), 573-582.

Sillett, TS, and Holmes, RT (2002) Variation in survivorship of a migratory songbird throughout its annual cycle. *Journal of Animal Ecology* 71 (2), 296-308.

Simons, MJ, and Verhulst, S (2011) Zebra finch females prefer males with redder bills independent of song rate—a meta-analysis. *Behavioral Ecology* 22 (4), 755-762. (doi:10.1093/beheco/arr043).

Singer T, Seymour J, O'Doherty J, Kaube H, Dolan RJ and Frith CD (2004) Empathy for pain involves the affective but not the sensory components of pain. *Science* 303, 1157–1162. doi:10.1126/science.1093535.

Slater, PJB, Eales, LA and Clayton, NS (1988) Song learning in zebra finches (Taeniopygia guttata): progress and prospects. In *Advances in the Study of Behavior* 18, 1–34.

Smith, M (1941) Similarities of marriage partners in intelligence. *American Sociological Review* 697-701.

Smith, MA, Gesell, T, Stadler, PF and Mattick, JS (2013) Widespread purifying selection on RNA structure in mammals. *Nucleic Acids Research* 41 (17), 8220-36. DOI: 10.1093/nar/gkt596.

Smith, PM, Paterson, JR, Brock, GA (2016) Trilobites and agnostids from the Goyder Formation (Cambrian Series 3, Guzhangian; Mindyallan), Amadeus Basin, central Australia. *Zootaxa* 4396 (1), 1-67.

Sol, D, Garcia, N, Iwaniuk, A, Davis, K, Meade, A, Boyle, WA and Szekely, T (2010) Evolutionary divergence in brain size between migratory and resident birds. *PLoS One* 5 (3), e9617. DOI:10.1371/ journal.pone.0009617.

Soma, M, and Garamszegi, LZ (2015) Evolution of courtship display in Estrildid finches: dance in relation to female song and plumage ornamentation. *Frontiers in Ecology and Evolution* 3, p.4.

Sonnemann, P, and Sjölander, S (1977) Effects of cross-fostering on the sexual imprinting of the female zebra finch Taeniopygia guttata. *Zeitschrift für Tierpsychologie* 45 (4), 337-348.

Spence, CE, Osman, M, and McElligott, AG (2017) Theory of animal mind: Human nature or experimental artefact? *Trends in Cognitive Sciences* 21 (5), 333-343.

Stel, M, Van Baaren, RB and Vonk, R (2008) Effects of mimicking: Acting prosocially by being emotionally moved. *European Journal of Social Psychology* 38 (6), 965–976. https://doi.org/10.1002/ejsp.472.

Stern, JA and Cassidy, J (2017) Empathy from infancy to adolescence: An attachment perspective on the development of individual differences. *Developmental Review* 47, 1–22. https://doi.org/10.1016/j.dr.2017.09.002

Stoddard, MC, and Prum, RO (2011) How colorful are birds? Evolution of the avian plumage color gamut. *Behavioral Ecology* 22 (5), 1042-1052.

Strier, KB, Dib, LT, and Figueira, JE (2002) Social dynamics of male muriquis (Brachyteles arachnoides hypoxanthus). *Behaviour* 139 (2-3), 315-342.

Sutter, E (1951) *Growth and Differentiation of the Brain in Nidifugous and Nidicolous Birds.* Almqvist & Wiksell, Uppsala.

Szentirmai, I, Komdeur, J and Székely, T (2005) What makes a nest-building male successful? Male behavior and female care in penduline tits. *Behavioral Ecology* 16, 994-1000. doi:10.1093/beheco/ari080.

Takeda, KF and Kutsukake, N (2018) Complexity of mutual communication in animals exemplified by pair dances in the red-crowned crane. *Japanese Journal of Animal. Psychology* 68, 25–37.

Tamm, S (1980) Bird orientation. Single homing pigeons compared with small flocks. *Behavioral Ecology and Sociobiology* 7, 319-322.

Tarr, HE (1947) Courtship Display of the Little Wattle-bird. *Emu* 47 (4), 318–318.

Tarvin, KA and Murphy, TG (2012) It isn't always sexy when both are bright and shiny: considering alternatives to sexual selection in elaborate monomorphic species. *Ibis* 154 (3), 439-443.

Taylor, EL, Blache, D, Groth, D, Wetherall, JD, and Martin, GB (2000) Genetic evidence for mixed parentage in nests of the emu (Dromaius novaehollandiae). *Behavioral Ecology and Sociobiology* 47 (5), 359-364.

Taylor, H (2008) Decoding the song of the pied butcherbird: An initial survey. *Trans. Revista Transcultural de Música* 12.

Taysom, AJ, Stuart-Fox, D and Cardoso, GC (2011) The contribution of structural-psittacofulvin- and melanin-based colouration to sexual dichromatism in Australasian parrots. *Journal of Evolutionary Biology* 24, 303–313.

Teitelbaum, CS, Converse, SJ and Mueller, T (2017) Birds choose long-term partners years before breeding. *Animal Behaviour* 134, 147–154.

Templeton, CN, Philp, K, Guillette, LM, Laland, KN, and Benson-Amram, S (2017) Sex and pairing status impact how zebra finches use social information in foraging. *Behavioural Processes* 139, 38-42.

Terrill, RS (2018) Feather growth rate increases with latitude in four species of widespread resident Neotropical birds. *The Auk* 135 (4), 1055-1063. https://doi.org/10.1642/AUK-17-176.1.

The Green Eye (2013) Sulphur-crested Cockatoo (mating) (Cacatua galerita) (Cacatuidae:) (Canberra: Australia), video clip uploaded Tuesday, September 10, 2013 at 6:54 AM EST via CyberLink.

Theimer, TC, Sogge, MK, Cardinal, SN, Durst, SLEH and Paxton, EH (2018) Extreme drought alters frequency and reproductive success of floaters in Willow Flycatchers. *The Auk* 135 (3), 647. DOI: 10.1642/AUK-17-206.1.

Tidemann, C (2005) Indian mynas–can the problems be controlled. In *Proceedings of the 15th National Urban Animal Management Conference.* (Ed. M. Hayward.) (pp. 55-57).

Tinbergen, N (1953) *Social Behaviour in Animals.* Methuen, London.

Tinbergen, N (1957) The functions of territory. *Bird Study* 4, 14-27.

Tobias, JA, Gamarra-Toledo,V, Garcia-Olaechea, D, Pulgarin, PC, and Seddon, N (2011) Year-round resource defence and the evolution of male and Female song in suboscine birds:social armaments are mutual ornaments. *Journal of Evolutionary Biology* 24, 2118–2138. doi:10.1111/j. 1420-9101.2011.02345.x

Tobias, JA, Montgomerie, R, and Lyon, BE (2012) The evolution of female ornaments and weaponry: social selection, sexual selection and ecological competition. *Philosophical Transactions of the Royal Society of London B*, 367(1600), 2274-2293.

Tommasi, L and Vallortigara, G (2004) Hemispheric processing of landmark and geometric information in male and female domestic chicks (*Gallus gallus*). *Behavioural Brain Research* 155 (1), 85–96.

Toomey, MB, Collins, AM, Frederiksen, R, Cornwall, MC, Timlin, JA and Corbo, JC (2015) A complex carotenoid palette tunes avian colour vision. *Journal of the Royal Society Interface* 12 (111), 20150563.

Tops, M, Koole, SL, Ijzerman, H, Buisman-Pijlman, FTA (2014) Why social attachment and oxytocin protect against addiction and stress: insights from the dynamics between ventral and dorsal corticostriatal systems. *Pharmacology, Biochemistry and Behavior* 119, 39–48.

Trail, PW (1990) Why should lek-breeders be monomorphic? *Evolution* 33 (7), 1837-1852.

Trefry, SA, and Diamond, AW (2017) Exploring hypotheses for sexual size dimorphism in frigatebirds. *Evolutionary Ecology Research* 18 (3), 225-252.

Tricola, GM, Simons, MJ, Atema, E, Boughton, RK, Brown, JL, Dearborn, DC, Divoky, G, Eimes, JA, Huntington, CE, Kitaysky, AS and Juola, FA (2018) The rate of telomere loss is related to maximum lifespan in birds. *Proceedings of the Royal Society of London B: Biological Sciences* 373 (1741), 20160445.

Tsutsui, K (2009) A new key neurohormone controlling reproduction, gonadotropin-inhibitory hormone (GnIH): Biosynthesis, mode of action and functional significance. *Progress in Neurobiology* 88, 76–88.

Tucker, MW and O'Grady, KE (1991) Effects of Physical Attractiveness, Intelligence, Age at Marriage, and Cohabitation on the Perception of Marital Satisfaction. *The Journal of Social Psychology* 131 (2), 253-269.doi:10.1080/00224545.1991.97138 48.

Turner, PS (2016) *Crow smarts: Inside the brain of the world's brightest bird*. Houghton Mifflin Harcourt.

Vaillant, GE (2011) The Neuroendocrine System and Stress, Emotions, Thoughts and Feelings. *Mens Sana Monographs* 9(1), 113–128.

Vallortigara, G (1992) Right hemisphere advantage for social recognition in the chick. *Neuropsychologia* 30 (9), 761-768.

Vallortigara, G and Andrew, RJ (1994) Differential involvement of right and left hemisphere in individual recognition in the domestic chick. *Behavioural Processes* 33 (1–2), 41–57.

Vallortigara, G, Chiandetti, C, Rugani, R, Sovrano, VA and Regolin, L (2010) Animal cognition. *Wiley Interdisciplinary Reviews: Cognitive Science* 1, 882-893, doi:10.1002/wcs.75.

van Buuren, M, Auersperg, A, Gajdon, G, Tebbich, S and von Bayern, A (2018) No evidence of mirror self-recognition in keas and Goffin's cockatoos. *Behaviour* 1(aop), 1-24.

Van den Bos, W, van Dijk, E, Westenberg, M, Rombouts, SA and Crone, EA (2010) Changing Brains, Changing Perspectives: The Neurocognitive Development of Reciprocity. *Psychological Science* 22 (1), 60-70.

Van Ruijssevelt, L, Chen, Y, von Eugen, K, Hamaide, J, De Groof, G, Verhoye, M, Güntürkün, O, Woolley, SC, and Van der Linden, A (2018) fMRI reveals a novel region for evaluating acoustic information for mate-choice in a female songbird. *Current Biology* 28 (5), 711-721.

Van Schaik, CP and Kappeler, PM (1997) Infanticide risk and the evolution of male–female association in primates. *Proceedings of the Royal Society of London B: Biological Sciences* 264 (1388), 1687–1694.

Vancouver, George (1757–1798) *A Voyage of Discovery to the North Pacific Ocean: and round the world; in which the coast of north-west America has been carefully examined and accurately surveyed.* London, Printed for GG and J Robinson etc (1798).

Van de Pitte, MM (1998) 'The Female is Somewhat Duller': The Construction of the Sexes in Ornithological Literature. *Environmental Ethics* 20 (1) 23–39.

Van der Willigen, RF, Frost, BJ and Wagner, H (1998) Stereoscopic depth perception in the owl. *Neuroreport* 9, 1233-1237.

Varela, FJ, Palacios, AG, and Goldsmith, TH (1993) Color vision of birds. In *Vision, Brain, and Behavior in Birds.* H. P. Zeigler & H.-J. Bischof, Eds. (pp. 77-98). The MIT Press, Cambridge, MA, US.

Veltman, CJ and Carrick, R (1990) Male-biased dispersal in Australian magpies. Animal *Behaviour* 40, 190–192. doi:10.1016/S0003-3472(05)80682-7

Veltman, CJ and Hickson, RE (1989) Predation by Australian magpies (Gymnorhina tibicen) on pasture invertebrates: are non-territorial birds less successful? *Australian Journal of Ecology* 14 (3), 319-26.

Venz, S (2016) Pretty with a purpose: the anatomy of a feather. Posted on http://www.wideopenpets.com/pretty-with-a-purpose-the-anatomy-of-a-feather

Vincze, O, Vágási, CI, Kovács, I, Galván, I, Péter, L and Pap, PL (2013) Sources of variation in uropygial gland size in European birds. *Biological Journal of the Linnean Society* 110, 543–563.

Voigt, C, Leitner, S and Gahr, M (2007) Socially induced brain differentiation in a cooperatively breeding songbird. *Proceedings of the Royal Society B: Biological Sciences* 274 (1626), 2645–2652.

Vos, DR (1995) The role of sexual imprinting for sexual recognition in zebra finches: a difference between males and females. *Animal Behaviour* 50, 645–653.

Wagner, RH (1996) Male-male mountings by a sexually monomorphic bird: mistaken identity or fighting tactic? *Journal of Avian Biology* 27, 209–214.

Wallace, AR (1877) The colour of animals and plants. The American Naturalist 11 (11), 641-662.

Wang, Z, Yu, G, Cascio, C, Lui, Y, Gingrich, B and Insel, TR (1999) Dopamine D2 receptor-mediated regulation of partner preferences in female prairie voles (Microtus ochrogaster): a mechanism for pair bonding? *Behavioural Neuroscience* 113, 602–611.

Watts, ME, Pocock, R and Claudianus, C (2018) Brain Energy and Oxygen Metabolism: Emerging Role in Normal Function and Disease. *Frontiers Molecular Neuroscience* https://doi.org/10.3389/fnmol.2018.00216

Weathers, WW and Schoenbaechler, DC (1976) Regulation of Temperature in the Budgerygah, Melopsittacus undulates. *Australian Journal of Zoology* 24, 39-47.

Weimerskirch, H, Lallemand, J and Martin, J (2005) Population sex ratio variation in a monogamous long-lived bird, the wandering albatross. *Journal of Animal Ecology* 74 (2), 285-291.

Wein, A, Schwing, R, Hausberger, M, Rodriguez, R, and Huber, L (2018) Vocal conditioning in kea parrots (Nestor notabilis). *Journal of Comparative Psychology*, 132(1), 97–105.

West-Eberhard, MJ (2014) Darwin's forgotten idea: the social essence of sexual selection. *Neuroscience and Biobehavioral Reviews* 46, 501-508.

White, P (1957) *Voss*. Eyre & Spottiswoode, London.

White, P (2012) *The cockatoos: shorter novels and stories*. Random House.

Whiten, A, Custance, DM, Gomez, JC, Teixidor, P, and Bard KA (1996) Imitative learning of artificial fruit processing in children (Homo sapiens) and chimpanzees (Pan troglodytes). *Journal of Comparative Psychology* 110 (1), 3.

Whitfield, MC, Smit, B, McKechnie, AE and Wolf, BO (2015) Avian thermoregulation in the heat: scaling of heat tolerance and evaporative cooling capacity in three southern African arid-zone passerines. *The Journal of Experimental Biology* 218 (11), 1705-1714. doi:10. 1242/jeb.121749.

Whittaker, DJ, Gerlach, NM, Soini, HA, Novotny, MV and Ketterson, ED (2013) Bird odour predicts reproductive success. *Animal Behaviour* 86 (4), 697–703.

Wikelski, M, Spinney, L, Schelsky, W, Scheuerlein, A, and Gwinner, E (2003) Slow pace of life in tropical sedentary birds: a common-garden experiment on four stonechat populations from different latitudes. *Proceedings of the Royal Society of London B: Biological Sciences* 270 (1531), 2383-2388.

Wiltschko, W, Traudt, J, Gunturkun, O, Prior, H and Wiltschko, R (2002) Lateralization of magnetic compass orientation in a migratory bird. *Nature* 419, 467-470.

Wingfield, JC (1993) Control of testicular cycles in the song sparrow, Melospiza melodia melodia: interaction of photoperiod and an endogenous program? *General and Comparative Endocrinology* 92, 388–401.

Wingfield JC (2008) Organization of vertebrate annual cycles: implications for control mechanisms. *Philosophical Transactions of the Royal Society of London. Series B, Biological Sciences*; 363:425–41.

Wingfield, JC, Robert, E, Hegner, Dufty, AM and Ball, GF (1990) The Challenge Hypothesis: Theoretical Implications for Patterns of Testosterone Secretion, Mating Systems, and Breeding Strategies. *The American Naturalist* 136 (6), 829-846.

Woinarski, JCZ, Legge, SM and Dickman, CR (2019) *Cats in Australia.* CSIRO Publishing. Melbourne.

Wolf, LL and Stiles, FG (1970) Evolution of pair cooperation in a tropical hummingbird. *Evolution* 24 (4), 759-773.

Wormington, K and Lamb, D (1999) Tree hollow development in wet and dry sclerophyll eucalypt forest in south-east Queensland, Australia. *Australian Forestry* 62 (4), 336-345. DOI: 10.1080/00049158.1999.10674801

Wrangham, RW and Peterson, D (1996) *Demonic males: Apes and the origins of human violence.* Houghton Mifflin Harcourt.

Wright, TF, Schirtzinger, EE, Matsumoto, T, Eberhard, JR, Graves, GR, Sanchez, JJ, Capelli, S, Müller, H, Scharpegge, J, Chambers, GK and Fleischer, RC (2008) A multilocus molecular phylogeny of the parrots (Psittaciformes): Support for a Gondwanan origin during the Cretaceous. *Molecular Biology and Evolution* 25 (10), 2141–2156. doi:10. 1093/ molbev/msn160.

Yamamoto, JT, Shields, KM, Millam, JR, Roudybush, TE and Grau, CR (1989) Reproductive activity of force-paired cockatiels (Nymphicus hollandicus). *The Auk* 106, 86-93.

Yanagihara, S and Yazaki-Sugiyama, Y (2016). Auditory experience-dependent cortical circuit shaping for memory formation in bird song learning. *Nature Communications* 7, 11946. doi: 10.1038/ncomms11946.

Young, LC, Zaun, BJ, and VanderWerf, EA (2008) Successful same-sex pairing in Laysan albatross. *Biology Letters* 4 (4), 323-325.

Yu, Y, Karbowski, J, Sachdev, RNS and Feng, J (2014) Effect of temperature and glia in brain size enlargement and origin of allometric body-brain size scaling in vertebrates. *BMC Evolutionary Biology* 14 (1), 178-192. doi.org/10.1186/s12862-014-0178-z.

Zahavi, A and Zahavi, A (1997) *The Handicap Principle.* Oxford University Press, Oxford.

Zann, RA (1996) *The Zebra Finch: a Synthesis of Field and Laboratory Studies.* Oxford University Press, Oxford, UK.

Ze, O, Thoma, P, and Suchan, B, (2014) Cognitive and affective empathy in younger and older individuals. *Aging and Mental Health* 18 (7), 929-935.

Zeng, SJ, Szekely, T, Zhang, XW, Lu, K, Liu, L and Zuo, MX (2007) Comparative analyses of song complexity and song-control nuclei in fourteen oscine species. *Zoological Sciences* 24, 1–9.

Zhang, G, Li, C, Li, Q, Li, B, Larkin, DM, Lee, C, Storz, JF, Antunes, A, Greenwold, MJ, Meredith, RW, Ödeen, A et al. (2014) Comparative genomics reveals insights into avian genome evolution and adaptation. *Science* 346 (6215), 1311–1320.

Index

Figures and tables in the text are indicated using bold page numbers. Image inserts are indicated using 'Ins1' for the first set and 'Ins2' for the second set.

Index

Index

Index

Index

Index

Index

Acknowledgements

Writing books is an arduous task that never gets any easier. However, there is also a certain degree of compulsion involved which makes one believe, erroneously or not, that one must put pen to paper and express what cannot be said in any other form. Ironically, writing is such a lonely and private activity and it is one of the greatest surprises or even a source of embarrassment to find later that a book, once out, is a very public affair, and entirely out of the hands of the author. I had once been told by various publishers that writing about birds, let alone a single species, was a ludicrous idea and would not have much of an audience. This turned out to be entirely incorrect and not a week has gone by in the last fifteen years without emails about birds or readers debating what I had written or sending me extensive letters filled with interesting and detailed observations. I have appreciated all of these and enjoyed reading them and have learned a great deal in the process. I wish to thank all the correspondents, commentators, scientists and interested parties partial to our bird life that have made their time and thoughts available. And, of course, the publishing team at Pan Macmillan was a hundred per cent behind the project and displayed the kind of enthusiasm that was of great assistance generally in helping me over rough patches. I thank my friends and partner for their forbearance because writing makes this writer socially rather inept, perhaps more so during the writing of this book with its more radical interpretations of long-lasting bird bonds. For all these signs of friendship, intellectual engagements and shared interests I am very grateful.